Seen, Written

GREGORY R. MILLER & CO. **M**

Gregory R. Miller & Co.
62 Cooper Square
New York, New York 10003
www.grmandco.com

Available through D.A.P./Distributed Art Publishers, Inc.
155 Avenue of the Americas, Second Floor
New York, New York 10013
www.artbook.com

Design: Lily Probst for Daydream Library

Printed and bound in the United States

Library of Congress Cataloging-in-Publication Data

Kertess, Klaus.
  Seen, written : selected essays / Klaus Kertess.
    p. cm.
  ISBN 978-09800242-9-6 (alk. paper)
  1. Art, American—20th century. 2. Art, American—21st century. I. Title.
  N6512.K47 2010
  709.73'0904—dc22
                        2010036486

Klaus Kertess

Seen, Written

Selected Essays

Gregory R. Miller & Co.

I would like to dedicate this book to the memory of my partner in the Bykert Gallery, Jeff Byers, whose generous support of and belief in me was crucial to my development, and to my partner in life and love, Billy Sullivan.

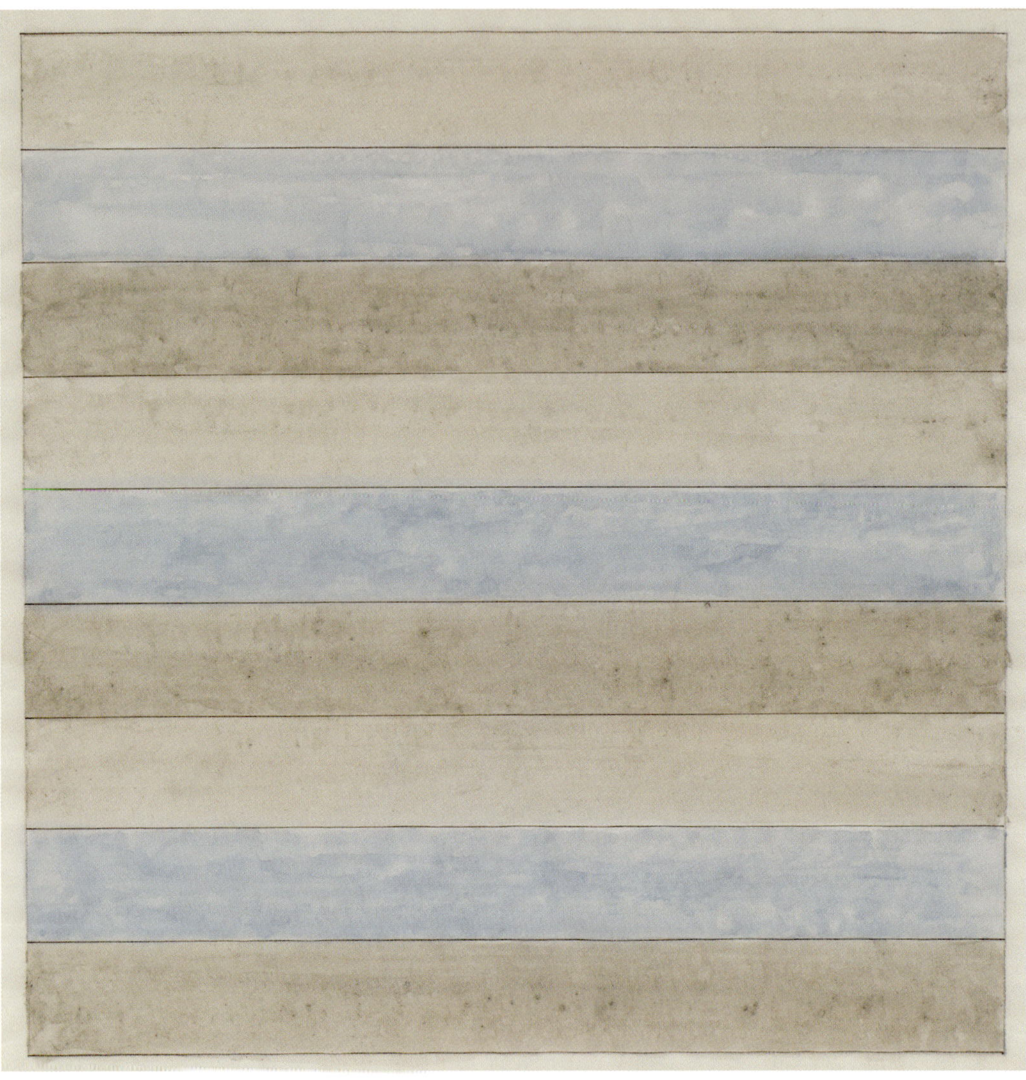

Agnes Martin, *Untitled*, 1975

Introduction

When I was invited to publish this book of essays, I wanted to give it a loose narrative structure at least partially related to the development of whatever visual intelligence I have been able to acquire. And so I decided to gather monographic essays in groups, the first of which includes artists I represented and/or was strongly influenced by in the course of cofounding and directing the Bykert Gallery. The second and third sections include monographic essays on artists included in two group exhibitions I curated. The book concludes with the catalogue essay for the inaugural exhibition I curated for the Museum of Contemporary Art Detroit.

In college I already knew I would spend my career in art and, at first, was convinced I would have been happier living in fifteenth-century Florence making occasional side trips to Arezzo to watch Piero della Francesca at work on his frescoes in the Church of San Francesco. However, reading books like Robert Rosenblum's *Cubism and Twentieth-Century Art*, studying with George Heard Hamilton, and, most of all, spending time in the Yale University Art Gallery drifting and/or shocked into works like Vincent Van Gogh's *Night Café* (1888) began to propel me five centuries forward. After completing my first year in graduate school, including a too-hastily written masters thesis, I informed the head of Yale's art history department Egbert Haverkamp-Begemann that I didn't want to go for my doctorate and had decided I wanted to open a contemporary art gallery in Manhattan. "Whore, whore, you will become a whore," he repeated and repeated in ever-higher decibels, as I walked out of his office. And so began my life in the contemporary art world, in the spring of 1964.

Of course, I knew almost nothing about contemporary art when I moved to New York. I was extremely fortunate to have a job that paid reasonably well and required almost no work on my part. In 1964, the art world's gallery spaces existed largely on 57th Street and Madison Avenue up to 86th Street; one could see most of them in the course of one week. I spent my days going to galleries and to the Museum of Modern Art, gradually edging into the present—not exactly leaving Picasso behind but more and more letting Jackson Pollock and Willem de Kooning perform their liquid magic, seeing Robert Ryman's paintings for the first time and Frank Stella's and works by artists my own age like Robert Mangold as well as amazing performances/happenings by Robert Rauschenberg and Bob Whitman and dance by choreographers like Yvonne Rainer and Trisha Brown—all making visceral theatrical magic out of everyday objects and movement. I was beginning to learn anew.

After a year or so, the unproductive nature of my job began to weigh me down. Then, one night, having one of my frequent dinners with Jeff Byers, a friend from my undergraduate days, and his wife Hilary, I once more bemoaned my inability to find a backer for a gallery. Hilary turned to Jeff and said, "Why don't you do it?" And so the Bykert Gallery was born.

More than just a backer, Jeff was generous with his spirit and became a vital part of the gallery's life. I was amazingly fortunate because, at the time, few dealers (the word *gallerists* had yet to be minted) were going to studios, and that combined with the tribal nature and relatively small size of the contemporary art scene compared to today quickly made me known and welcomed.

One of the most exciting galleries I had visited was the Green Gallery run by the legendary and tantalizingly inscrutable Dick Bellamy. There I might see Lucas Samaras emerge from a boxlike structure in the middle of the gallery to pad around in his underwear, or struggle to come to grips with Dan Flavin's fluorescent light fixtures-cum-altarpieces. One of the last exhibitions held at the Green Gallery before it closed, in 1965, was of paintings by Ralph Humphrey—most of them about five feet high by seven feet wide, each with a wide border of a distressed shade of dusty pink or green or blue, framing an interior of thinly brushed gray nothingness. Abrasive, dismaying, nonsensical—why would anyone paint such emptiness? I was pissed off. The next day I returned, why I didn't know. Fuming, I left, only somehow to be drawn back again the following day. I stood and I looked, and I looked, and I looked. Suddenly, out of nowhere I realized the paintings were framing my space, framing me, creating a context in which I could regard my being, if I so chose.

Ralph Humphrey became the foundation of the Bykert Gallery. An essay on Ralph's work begins this book in the section titled "New Vision." "New Vision" refers to the new lenses I had to acquire to begin to be able to see the work I would exhibit. Brice Marden, Alan Saret, and Barry Le Va are among those discussed in this section; the Bykert Gallery represented the works of all three. At the opening of the seminal exhibition *Primary Structures*, at the Jewish Museum in 1966, Carlos Villa introduced me to Brice Marden, then a guard at the Jewish Museum, after I told him of my love for Humphrey's work. I visited Brice's studio the next day. There I was almost instantly enveloped by his enigmatic monochrome paintings, each in an ambiguous shade of gray slowly shifting from foreboding wall to misty, sensuous slab of the buried strokes of its making. Almost as strong an impact was made on my seeing by the older Agnes Martin's grids of lyric silence; she became a friend and a kind of oracle of beauty. The short text on her work was one of a series of pieces I did for *Elle Decor*—partially to see if I could write for a mass-market magazine without compromising my subject and myself.

The gallery opened on September 20, 1966, in what previously had been the Green Gallery space. At the time, the sculptors who would become known as Process artists were just beginning to come to the fore. Alan Saret and Barry Le Va were at the forefront of this group, as was Keith Sonnier. Barry had already completely atomized sculpture's objecthood into dispersals of felt, ball bearings, glass, etc. that transformed the once stable floor into a shifting plane of material processes (cutting, throwing, shattering). With the movements of his body, Alan choreographed chicken wire into buoyant, transparent vessels of spirit. Keith drew magically with light on glass, set walls aflutter with gauzy fabric, and in countless other ways made mysteriously sensual mundane materials. Although older and seldom given the credit, John Chamberlain, with his crushed car-part sculptures visibly confabulated out of combinative play, is surely the godfather of this group; his sculptures' precarious construction, lush blossoming, and color conspire in some of the sexiest process-reflective works I have experienced. And, finally, a photographer is included in this section—Peter Hujar, master of shadows, explorer of souls and many a body, celebrating and bemoaning the fragility of our flesh. Peter taught me that one could draw with a camera and much more. These were my new teachers.

In 1975, I left the Bykert Gallery. The gallery had become a critical success and was poised to become a financial success, but I preferred trying to clear a path for emerging artists to managing the careers of now-successful gallery artists like Brice Marden and Chuck Close. And I had begun to write and needed to test my commitment to that undertaking. Since leaving the gallery, I have worked as a freelance curator and writer and occasionally as an art advisor, with the exception of my two-year full-time stint curating the 1995 Whitney Biennial.

I built a house in East Hampton in 1973, so I could be near the ocean, and ended up being a part-time curator at the Parrish Art Museum in Southampton from 1983 to 1989. I continue to be involved with the museum and curated several shows after leaving my post. The museum celebrated its centennial in 1998, and Director Trudy Kramer invited me to curate one of the exhibitions. I chose to celebrate the ocean's impact on American modernism and was quick to discover that seeing long-familiar artists in the context of my subject led me to new thoughts on a number of those artists, including Pollock. Curating and writing have fed each other. *Sea Change* moved out of the nineteenth century with Winslow Homer, Albert Pinkham Ryder, and others into the first round of American modernists (Marsden Hartley, John Marin), on to the second (de Kooning, Adolph Gottlieb, Pollock, Mark Rothko), and ended with a twenty-five-foot wall drawing of a surfer in the curl of a giant wave by Raymond Pettibon.

The Parrish's collection boasts over one hundred paintings by Fairfield Porter. In addition to his painted clarities, Porter, in his many essays, sought to reestablish a painterly tradition that, he maintained, had been interrupted by the linearity of Cubism and Constructivism. He favored Pierre Bonnard and Edouard Vuillard, deeply admired Marin's painterly "Oriental Cubism," as Porter called it, and admired as well de Kooning and Franz

Kline (not Pollock). Porter's writing introduced me to the singular work of Albert York and inspired me to study Marin. I curated the first exhibition devoted solely to Marin's oil paintings (his major promoter Alfred Stieglitz had built Marin's reputation on his mastery of the medium of watercolor); and he was included in *Sea Change* with one of his countless wondrous seascapes. De Kooning's move to the East End of Long Island in 1963 led to an involvement with the ocean (he regularly compared his paintings to reflections on water), just as Pollock's earlier move had immersed him in the sea and surely helped catalyze his flung and dripped paintings with their gestures often reminiscent of the drawing left on the sand by incoming waves. I have curated four de Kooning exhibitions with accompanying catalogues, always surprised that I have a long long way to go before I arrive anywhere near exhausting his beauty. Painterly gesture readily translates into oceanicity as it did for de Kooning and later for Joan Mitchell and Malcolm Morley; and it led my prose into *Sea Change*.

While *Sea Change* grew out of a personal love of the ocean, *Fabulism* grew out of my desire to explore the work of a number of the artists who grew out of the final collapse of modernism's hegemony, in the early 1990s, now making possible the exploration of the wilder shores of the imagination, the reinvention of narrative, metaphor, myth, and more. The exhibition included Carroll Dunham, whose work I have had the pleasure of observing since its beginnings. He has, over the years, urged paintings of landscape mounds to morph slowly into mutant figures somewhere between blind moles and Mayan glyphs—polluted figures polluting the territory they battle for, and who more recently have given way to multi-sexed monsters, first more male and most recently more female. All the while Dunham has galvanized his canvas with astoundingly adept and varied mark making. As with de Kooning and Chamberlain, I have written on Dunham's work a number of times and still have not fully plumbed its depths. Matthew Ritchie has managed to give his astoundingly wide-ranging intelligence visual form, creating history paintings and installations that move forward from the Big Bang through the creation and destruction of the universe as he draws from advanced scientific knowledge, noir detective novels, the Old Testament prophecies of Ezekiel, William Blake, the exhaustible energy of our planet, and his own inexhaustible energy and ambition. Chris Ofili's sensuous and sometimes savagely bling beauties always leave a celebratory glow in my memory. His has been and continues to be a brave and gorgeous attempt to restore physicality and some much needed credibility to Christian iconography and to create a beauty as vivid as medieval bejeweled reliquaries and the Technicolor transparencies of stained glass—with a hip-hop vitality.

I had not written on any of the artists I included in *Meditations in an Emergency*, and previously worked with only one of them—Nari Ward, whom I included in the 1995

Whitney Biennial. I spent a year in which I traveled to Detroit almost once a month, almost never without being simultaneously stunned by its devastation and its still-positive spirit (as though Motown was in the air). This is the first exhibition I have curated in which the host city and institution's building impacted my choices; several of the artists (Ward, Barry McGee, Jon Pylypchuk) were similarly affected—the inclusion of the virtuoso local musician/composer/sculptor Christopher Fachini, Roxy Paine (with his high-tech computer-driven sculpture-fabricating machine seemingly riffing on Detroit assembly lines), and Ward (basing one of his installations on an obscure Detroit monument to the 1968 Black uprising) being the most specific examples.

No formal ending concludes this collection. While gathering these texts, I often thought of what and whom I had not written about. The paintings and drawings of Pollock and Cy Twombly have often been reference points but never the full-blown subject—something I really regret. The work gathered here is clearly New York–centric as, of course, are most of my experiences. Ofili is the only European here chronicled, although I have written recently on Albert Oehlen, whom I believe to be one of the most vital and influential practitioners of painting alive, Georg Baselitz, Gerhard Richter, and Nasreen Mohamedi, whose sublime drawings created in the 1970s resonate with the essence of grace. More travel is now on my calendar. Still so much more to see.

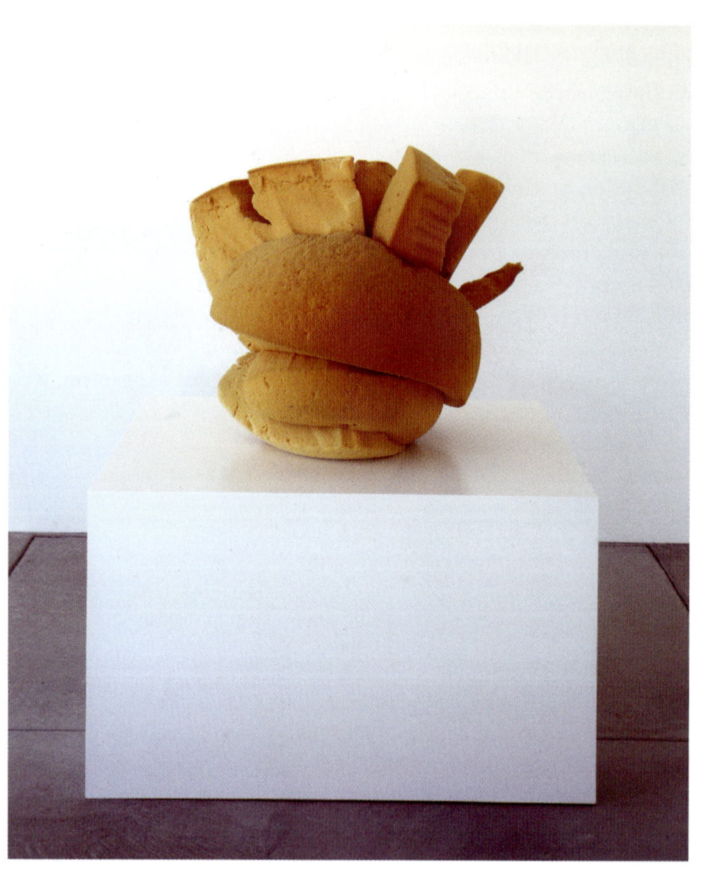

I. NEW VISION

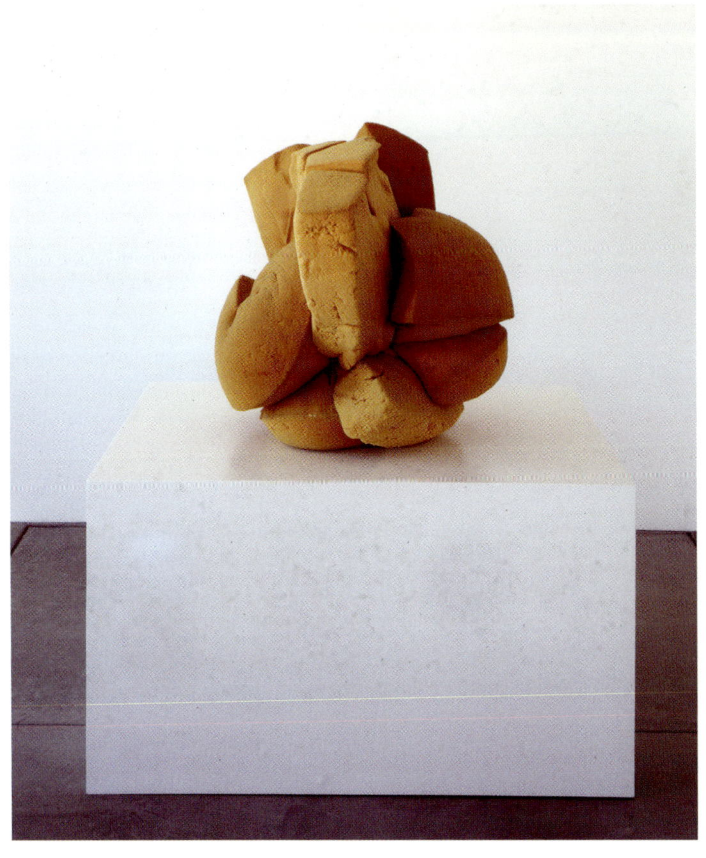

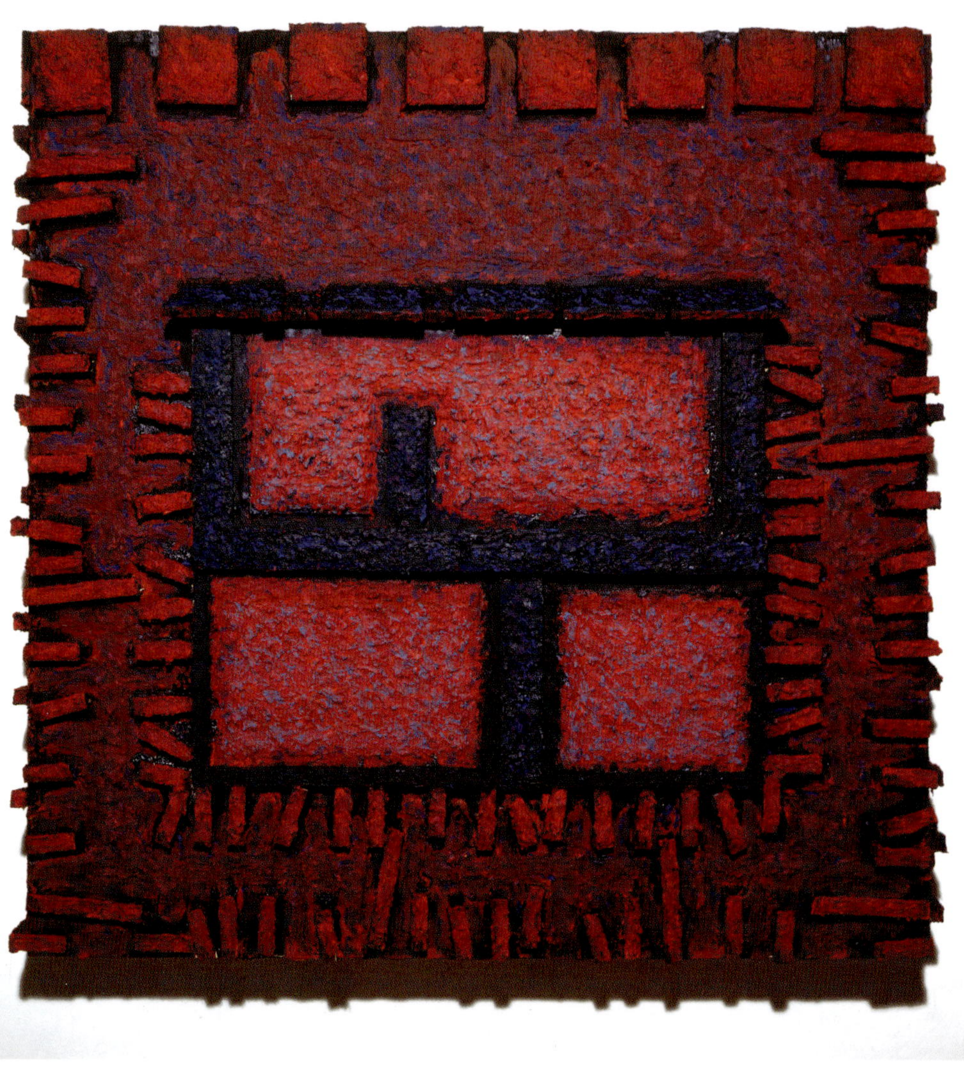

On the Edge

The Paintings of Ralph Humphrey

At first confrontational and emblematic, then slowly rumbling, gliding, sliding, and turning into the enigmatic, Ralph Humphrey's paintings retrieve lapsed pictorial illusionism only to convert it back into the implacable materiality of its planarity and pointedness. Imagined space is made viscous and viscerally immediate. Humphrey's constructed and painted geometries become impure, still-life objects of paint, radically tilted forward and momentarily mesmerized by gravity as they hover on and in the shallow relief of their planar containment. Their bristling physicality of edge and surface calls these objects back from the possibility of illusion into the disillusion of their thereness. The contingencies of time, not transcendence, shape and color Humphrey's geometries and draw them reluctantly into beauty. His is an architecture of mortality.

Real illusion, not the illusion of the real, has been a continuing concern of Humphrey's endeavor since the mid-1960s. While his paintings have undergone frequent shifts of means and configuration, they have continuously relied on his acute awareness of edge. Always directly painted, occasionally somewhat ruthlessly made, his edges have an incisiveness that gives breath to color and space; they are the exposed nerves of the body of his painting. It is on the edge that the real and the imagined are conflated. Humphrey's painting is literally and figuratively on the edge.

Humphrey's early work was informed by his experience of Abstract Expressionism, especially by the paintings of Clyfford Still and Mark Rothko. He drew breath from, rather than neutralizing and purging, the intuitive acts of making and the emotional resonance of color so crucial to Abstract Expressionism. But the solace of a redemptive sublime was simply alien to him, as it was to so many of his peers. While the dry, pulled, and flaky surfaces of Humphrey's paintings of the late 1950s take cues from the seething thin cragginess of Still's paint, they reject his mythic portentousness in favor of the more ambiguous and secular immediacy of monochromatic alloverness. More distressed than elevated, an impure color and surface arrive at a physical shape vibrating with an inscrutable but eloquent bleakness. The edges of the plane of the support define and limit the moody resonance of the single, scruffy color (a murky blue, a smudged, time-worn white, a rusty red)—the logic of the support embroils the emotionality of the color and vice versa.

In a subsequent group of paintings, culminating in eleven Frame paintings, done in 1964 and 1965, Humphrey focused and made more trenchant the role of the rectangular support. A broad band of a muted single color (such as a grayish salmon, a dusty ocher, or a chalky green-blue) was brushed and sponged around the interior border of the planar canvas support and encloses a more thinly painted interior field of gray. The frame that formerly heightened the illusion of the interior view and separated the painting's space from the viewer's space is now drawn into the painting itself. The exterior edge of the frame merges with the physical edge of the support; the interior edge of the frame is purely painted (imagined) but more physically insistent than the gray it borders. The acutely and tremulously painted interior edge of the frame drains the residual vapors of the illusion of the framed gray and pushes them out into the physicality of the canvas support. The frame frames the viewer's space; the viewer becomes the view and the viewed. The view is exasperatingly empty, alternately wishing to attract (be filled and fulfilled) and to repel. As color and illusion are subdued, so too is surface execution—the strokes are active and visible but willed into a merging blandness. Color, paint, and painting are not so much neutralized as they are anesthetized. They might, at any moment, be aroused into elemental pain. Here emptiness confronts and confounds with rare and rigorous eloquence.

The Frame paintings are partially beholden to the simply structured but complex emotional atmospherics of Rothko, but they convert his elusive ecclesiastical pulsations into strenuous and profaned physicality. Their restrained, radical reductiveness and support proclaiming structure led many to assume that Humphrey was an early enlistee in the growing ranks of Minimalism. However, like the younger Brice Marden, upon whom the Frame paintings made such a strong impression, Humphrey opted for a wider range of painterly and emotional solutions than was prevalent amongst the more objectively systematic and neutrally phenomenological conclusions arrived at by Minimalist painters and sculptors. His work has never been easy to classify. Indeed, Humphrey has frequently reacted against what he has perceived as the troublesome rules and polemics imposed upon abstraction. Idiosyncratic but never blindly eccentric, his independence and willingness to take risks are as formally sophisticated as they often are surprising.

The exploration of the space between the viewer and the painting grew visually more complex as events of relationship began to impinge upon the emptiness of the field of the canvas and project themselves outward. Made between 1965 and 1967, the Three Line paintings deploy three equal and equidistant bars of color/light on the pale wash of the rectangular field. The powdery dryness of the bars, each a different variegated hue and value, literally and figuratively lifts off the more thinly painted ground. The weightier grays of the Frame paintings are whited and lighted out into pastel mutations. The more intense light of the flickering lines has been heightened with Day-Glo paint. Reductive and plane-dependent structure dissolves in a sweet and sour dance of light projected out into the viewer's space. Matter and stable structure become light. The startling gaseous chemistry of Humphrey's palette quietly destabilizes the viewer's space and place. The relatively thick stretchers reinforce the forwardness of the paint and turn the canvases into taut pneumatic volumes of space and light. Infinities of atmosphere are materialized. The subversion is slow and subtle; virtual space becomes an equivocation.

As thin and restrained as the paint in these paintings is, it has still been put down with a directness and modulated visibility that discreetly insists upon its pointedness. In spite of the softness of palette, the painting retains a kind of raw edginess that is far removed from the more seamless purity of execution employed in Robert Irwin's similarly structured and intended paintings that were begun, in California, slightly earlier than Humphrey's group. Physicality of paint and optical elusiveness were simultaneously intensified in Humphrey's succeeding paintings, and the implications of their outward-projecting airborneness were made more specific. The edges of the stretchers were softly rounded and beveled out from the wall. A more thickly painted multiplicity of lines (now of the same color) was made to end in points rather than in vertical edges. Their intense light pierces the paler-toned skin of the ground, while their tapering pointedness creates an illusion of convexity that mimes and heightens the actual umbel plushness of the canvas's enclosed volume. The lines seem to have been stretched and distended as the canvas was inflated. This is painting precariously hovering between inflation and deflation of materiality, between the possibility and the impossibility of illusion. Painting grappling with the devaluation of painting into an analytically verifiable objectness.

The neutralization and demystification of art that attended so much of the abstraction of the 1960s and early 1970s was inevitably accompanied by a suppression (often denial) of color and its vagrant inclination to emotion and referentiality outside the dictates of the analytically irrefutable. Humphrey's color, on the other hand, was traversing the realm of the uncensored. The alienated paleness of the Three Line paintings was subsequently heated up into awkwardly vulgar tones of cosmetic fleshiness capable of liaisons with acid yellows and electric blues that denatured the pristine rigor of the structure. Abstraction's inclination to decorative dignity took on a kind of manic comicness. This derangement of abstraction became more marked in the late 1960s as Humphrey's shaped canvases became more distended or turned into tondos, and the lines of color were broadened into more erratic, serpentine trails of fluorescence. A sort of delirious abstraction in extremis—painting pushed to the edge to mock and retrieve its forbidden feelings.

In what at first seemed like another radical change, in 1972 Humphrey retrieved (and thickened) the materiality of paint, the somber color, and the frame structure of his 1965 paintings. But the change was more of means than intentions. He was seeking to make more concrete the painting's (the painter's and the viewer's) ambivalent materiality. The heightened objectness was accompanied by an exponential increase in illusion. This is the path that has logically (but unprogrammatically) led to the current group of paintings with their hyper-specific duality. Humphrey retained the beveled stretchers and rounded corners of his previous paintings but made the angling out more acute so that the interior edge of the stretcher embossed itself on the canvas and became a virtual interior edge of the frame. The frame was painted with a dark-toned, gravelly textured color; the interior was painted more thinly in a lighter hue. A lozenge-shaped piece of canvas, as thickly painted and as deeply toned as the frame, was glued down slightly above the center of the interior. This concretized shape of paint, with its rawly frayed and painted, bristling edges, clings to its host with all the awkward and anxious tenacity of a handmade prosthetic device—vulnerable simultaneously to the concavity imposed by the stretcher and the concavity implied by the paler interior field. It is the physically and spatially vulnerable protagonist of paint that the viewer is challenged to identify with.

As this group progressed, the lozenge-shaped patches were multiplied and overlapped in shifting spatial complexities, and more rectangular strips of canvas were affixed to the beveled frame. Color and surface became denser and weightier (modeling paste was mixed with the casein paint). A palpable thickness of deep, lunar blue or charred brown rumbles with smooth but heavy mottling that has the friction-glazed cast of the obsessive wear and tear of its making. Here and there, pebbled flashes of a more radiant hue shine through. The rippling buildup of paint and the physical edges of the added patches literally absorb light and cast shadows. The paintings are like night-fragrant envelopes of disturbed and disturbing space. Their melancholy beauty is firmly grounded in a more formal awareness that looks back not only to the geometric dynamics of Piet Mondrian but also to the atomization of light and personal touch into a flickering skein of opticality that was first ventured by the Impressionists and later brought to more private conclusions by Pierre Bonnard. Humphrey achieved a synthesis at once physically implacable, deeply emotional, and coolly constructed—an architecture of space and consciousness.

The insistent physicality of Humphrey's rematerialization of painting made a strong impression on younger artists seeking to move abstraction beyond its reductive constraints. He himself was beginning to push painting toward the material finality of sculpture. The outward thrusting motivated by the beveled edges of his stretchers implied a kind of reverse perspectival foreshortening, like that in Byzantine mosaics

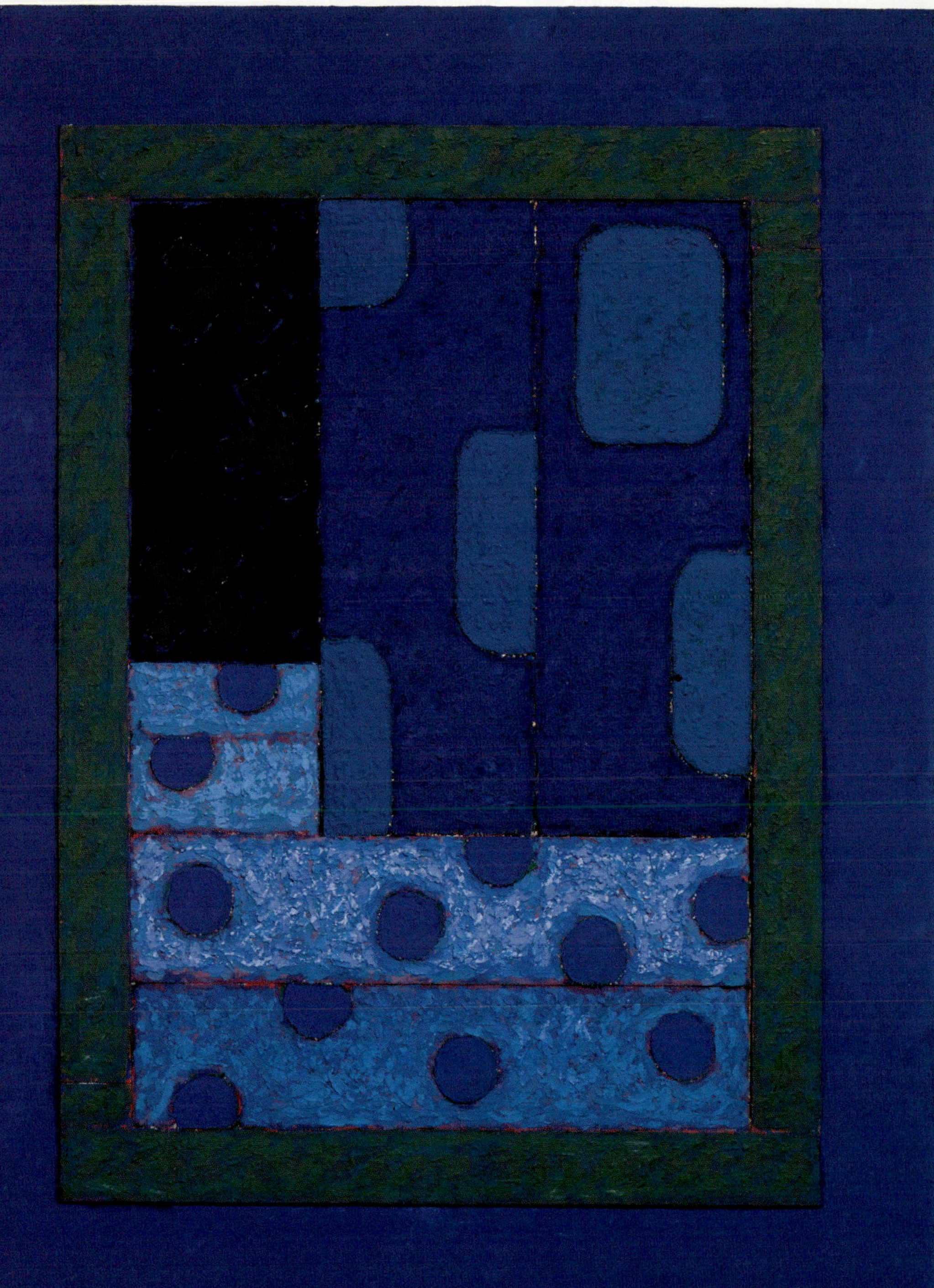

and much medieval painting, that projected its vanishing point into the viewer's space rather than into an imagined beyond. And it was precisely this reversal that Humphrey set about making material in 1974. With a depth of some six inches, his wood stretchers became boxlike; the angled sides became virtually foreshortened planes. The painting on the angled stretcher was made to erratically echo its actual and imagined objectness. The painting was propelled ever more emphatically into the viewer's space to become a verifiable dimensional object in that space and time and a meditation on that object's distended spatiality. Objecthood in space and the imagining of objecthood in space become one.

Humphrey's materialization of illusion permitted him to approach the sculptural without puncturing or fully denying painting's uniform skin. Frank Stella's concurrent efforts to physically extend painting and to restore the rich drama of spatiality, so long purged from abstraction, sacrificed painting's pneumatic membrane to fuller, more in-the-round sculptural relief. Humphrey achieved a more perplexing ambiguity, but one whose weightiness he started to reduce before it grew too cumbersome. While retaining his thick stretchers and wood surface, he gradually, in the late 1970s, returned to a flat rectangular plane that incorporated gradations of relief whose illusionistic potential replaced that of the radically angled sides. The brooding, monotonic, percolating surface was cooled to a thinner simmer activated with more complex underlying layers of subtly lustrous shimmering. The palette and surface lightened with the structure, and wry, sometimes raucous, vernacular humor began to mock melancholy with the ridiculous.

Why I Don't Paint Like Mark Rothko (1977–78) externalizes and makes concrete the dense light and atmosphere, as well as the reductive structure, of Rothko's lushly somber, vaporous rectangles of mystic breath. Like Rothko, Humphrey opted for a palette of blues, lavenders, and oranges as weighty in implications of volume and space as they are in mood. However, his mottled deep rose and light-inflated purple are grounded in sheerest physicality. The cut-out, constructed, rectangular appendages of his planar configuration resemble nothing so much as a deliriously patched-up side of a shanty with a window in the middle. This painting recalls the idiosyncratic obsessiveness of the "Tramp art" made during the Depression as much as it does Rothko and early modernist geometries.

In his more three-dimensional paintings, Humphrey collaged appendages that erratically reinforce (reforeshorten) the boxlike structure of the support. As he turned to flatter relief, his appendages began to take on a freer, more intuitive pictorial logic, circular cutouts of painted canvas began to populate his space (as in *Rainbow Grill* of 1978–80), and the window likeness of his architectural structures became more specifically figurative and more manically animated. In *Storm Field* (1981–82), one of a group of related window paintings, the cutout additions make physically perspectival (in very shallow relief) an open window with windblown star-spangled yellow curtains on a bluish purple ground (wall) that pulsates with thick gray disks. Perspective blows the curtains out into the viewer's space. The bright red of both the window shade and the space below it pushes the view out further. The window views the viewer literally and figuratively. The carefully constructed geometric equilibrium animates looney tunes, whose stylized melodies make mock pictorializations of abstraction's inscrutable viewlessness. The coarse but sardonically subtle humor of these paintings of windows risked the ire of many a peer but opened up new possibilities for Humphrey's figures of paint. They permitted a new visual complexity and freedom without requiring the sacrifice of geometric clarity and rigor. In the next group of paintings, Humphrey suppressed the wonderfully gaudy depictiveness but retained a windowlike structure that now filled the plane with destabilizing shifts of pane-and-mullion–like assemblages; they turn the pictorial inside out.

In his most recent group of paintings, Humphrey has urged the conflation of the pictorially and the materially constructed into concrete poems that become tonally exquisite and intimate metaphors of the transience of their very materiality. A thin balsa wood frame is glued down on the interior of the flat plane of the wood support (in one painting, the two vertical sides of the frame extend to the exterior edges of the support). The framed interior is then filled with adjoining but dissimilar rectangles of canvas which in turn have circular or rectangular or elliptical or cross shapes of canvas glued on them (one class of shape per rectangular area). Humphrey starts with a rough sketch, which is modified in the course of the actual making. The shapes are first pinned down and often rearranged, then finally glued into position. Humphrey's geometrically dynamic equilibrium is intuited, as was that of Mondrian, who, in his last paintings, glued down strips of colored paper to determine his configuration. Whereas Mondrian removed his paper and replaced it with pure paint that sought a utopian smoothness and seamlessness of surface, Humphrey retains his material shapes and gives each plane and planar shape its own virtual and separate space and surface. Color and paint conspire with the variegation of the shifting low relief of canvas and balsa-wood edges that lift away from each other. Not pure color but flickering modulations of impure, atmospheric greens, blues, mauves, and purples inflate and deflate the physical spatiality. The cut-out shapes now are flat in their rectangular field, now are truncated and sit on the actual edge of their field and seem to slip behind it. The granular viscosity of paint, brushed or put down with a palette knife, is alternately dragged and stippled in diagonal, circular, or randomly overlapping constellations of strokes that often parallel the implied movement or stasis of the shapes they paint and surround. The green circles sitting on a blue ground in one of the paintings have their greenness shot through here and there with lavender; their edges are pushed forward by shocks of electric red, while their blue ground charges the implied revolutions of their roundness with its whirling paths of short strokes. Like the shallow relief construction, the paint materializes the dematerialization of illusion. Acutely and subtly differentiated, color surface, edge, and structure are in a densely muted flux.

Humphrey's recent paintings are like stilled lifes of geometry that make virtual the earlier American tradition of a radically frontal trompe l'oeil (as in the paintings of William Harnett and John Frederick Peto). And he has reconstituted the linear, more sculptural chiaroscuro of analytical cubism's shallow, shifting planes and embodied it with a rich painterliness beholden to late Pierre Bonnard, Giorgio Morandi, and Rothko. His color and surface resonate with intuitive intimacy and invention. The mauves and dense slowness of his paint are suffused with pangs of mortal reverie, but their fin de siècle vapors are firmly grounded and resigned to the vacillating transience of their physicality and the geometric clarity of their construction. The harmonics of Humphrey's physical and physically vulnerable edges do not just embody illusion but enrapture the ambivalence of consciousness. The object is painting.

Brice Marden

Drawing

Drawing has always been crucial to Brice Marden's art. For many artists in the 1960s, the acts of the hand had become anathema, and any notion of drawing that remained was largely subsumed into painting. Marden, however, insisted on the primal importance of mark making, not only in his paintings but in a wholly separate body of drawings as well. Throughout the late 1960s and early 70s, his drawings directly paralleled his paintings, but by 1972 his marks began to seek a more explicitly active role in space and image, which differed from the paintings' intentions. These drawing pursuits would, in 1986, lead into Marden's new paintings, and the two would once again become like-minded in look and meaning. How to draw has been a question Marden daily poses and explores. He has made drawings that, together with those of his immediate elders Jasper Johns and Cy Twombly, are some of the most remarkable since Jackson Pollock's and Willem de Kooning's reinventions of the power of the line.

In his drawings, as in his paintings, Marden at first sought to make marks that claimed and became the ineluctable modality of the plane. The greater directness and intimacy inherent in drawing brought his intentions to the surface with a firm ease more readily accessible than in the less compliant matter of his paint medium. The grace available to his touch was already apparent in an untitled pencil drawing done in 1964 that employed the grid so ubiquitous in the art of the 1960s. If, for Sol LeWitt, the equal modules of the grid assured the virtual neutralization and overall sameness of space and form, then for Marden, the grid reflected not only the virtual measure and shape of the plane, but also the more evasive space and image born out of the intuitive movements of the hand. The implied sameness of the grid of equal vertical rectangles is warped by lines whose rule wavers, thickens, and thins to reflect the more subjective volitions of the maker. The grid is still more emphatically warped by the varying direction and weight of the tonal vapors that animate its interior.

As appealing as the casual virtuosity of this and other early Marden drawings is, its self-proclaiming finesse compromises the wholeness of image that he sought. Personal drawing needed to become meta-personal; hand, mind, and plane needed to become one. In a small monochrome drawing begun in 1964 (the year before his first fully monochrome oil painting), Marden switched to the denser medium of graphite, floated a rectangle on the top two-thirds of the paper support, and flayed it with layers of left-leaning, linear strokes—literally excavating the surface of the paper and covering it with a glistening, jet skin that becomes what it has displaced. Simultaneously facing, defacing, and self-effacing, the near homogeneity of the congealing layers of line reflects the maker, the making, and the made (plane). The repetitive accumulation of similar marks causes the individual marks to dissolve their identity in that of the plane. The plane becomes a euphoria of itself as Marden's spartan compulsion seeks to claim its emptiness and transform it into a specific space.

This metaphysics of the obvious, wrought by Marden's obsessive repetitiveness, closely parallels his painting intentions; but, in the drawings, the mark making accumulates with a greater immediacy and a frequently more visible urgency. The more homogenizing actions of the painting knife are clearly absent. Since the shape of the drawn plane is carefully adjusted to the shape of the paper support but almost never envelops the entire sheet, the drawing tools' interaction with and physical transformation of the surface are more readily apparent than they are in the paintings. Also more apparent, and more delicate, are the rigorously tuned differences between a drawn edge and an edge that is physically given.

In *Teddy's Drawing* (1964–65) and in a 1966 group of identically shaped drawings (all twenty-six by twenty-six inches, marking the rare appearance of an isolated square), Marden employed the wax he had already introduced into his painting/medium. He emblazoned the strokes to create a daunting mirror out of graphite's darkness. The drawn plane's more complete occupation of the shape of the paper (only a narrow border is left unmarked) and the heightened physicality imbued by the wax to the skin of strokes bring these drawings closer to the monolithic aspect of the paintings. The wax solidifies drawn space and shape and renders more visible the differences between the surface of the drawn shape and that of its support. In one of these 1966 drawings, the transformation of absence into presence courts invisibility. A very fine outline and the graphite band at the bottom of the drawn plane are all that tenuously separates its shape from that of its paper host. The surface of the interior has been "removed" and modified with sandpaper. The resulting evanescence turns erasure into an atmosphere.

Within the narrow parameters he set for himself, Marden continually searched for new ways to make the absence of the plane fertile and momentous. Using a variety of tools and mediums (wax, graphite, pencil, razor, sandpaper), he explored and excavated the plane. The drawn shape is always carefully calibrated to and in tension with the shape of the paper; the boundaries of the drawn expand and contract with and against the boundaries of the physical support. Sometimes a single shape hovers on the paper, sometimes two identical shapes merge and diverge in ambiguous attraction. Sometimes the intuitive mark making expands into a dense mass of light and space; sometimes it is counterpointed by the rational measure of the grid. The objectivity of the grid itself is impinged upon by the subjective will of the hand's changing pressure. Now the lines of the grid only score the top layer of marks, now they press down to the paper's bare whiteness to create a flickering that pushes geometry toward a tremulous illusion of itself. Whatever the tool employed, the pressure and directionality exerted on it are always light-and-space responsive. No mark or series of marks is permitted to become self-proclaiming; each is infused with duty to the plasticity of the plane. The identity of the marks and the identity of the plane become an organic unity. As gesture becomes rectangular plane, so does rectangular plane become gesture. Marden freed the hand by subordinating it to the plane, and vice versa.

The coagulation of line into shape and edge, the almost exclusive reliance on pencil's and graphite's tonal variations drawn in concert with the given light of the paper, and the regimentation of the irregularities of the hand into planar order all relate Marden's marks to those found in Georges Seurat's extraordinary conté drawings. But more immediately important were Johns and de Kooning. All three are artists whose works regularly incorporate an extra-abundance of marks deployed in self-erasing layers. Like Johns and, to some degree, because of him, Marden sought partially to neutralize and more completely objectify de Kooning's agitated spontaneity of gesture in an effort to make space more physically frontal and virtual. Johns fractured and all but totally depersonalized de Kooning's marks; he broke them down into coolly cerebral units of the structure of making. Marden, however, sought to retain de Kooning's emotionality but to moderate it with and contain it within the geometric dictates of the plane. The ghostlike residues of the marks in Marden's drawings (and paintings) are freer and more subjectively charged than Johns's marks, but less volatile and more measured than de Kooning's. The lessons of Johns and de Kooning are integrated with the lessons of Paul Cézanne and Piet Mondrian.

The evasive mirroring of the plane in Marden's drawings continued into the late 1970s, keeping in step with his paintings. After 1975, the drawings, like the paintings, began to come to more obdurate conclusions; the linear gestures were made to parallel more persistently the measure and shape of the plane they defined. In *Mosaic Study #2* (1978), the shiny graphite is very tightly packed and ruled by a grid whose linear measure becomes a dominant shape. The grid's lines are rectangular shapes; the vertical members are thicker than the horizontals and are equal in width to the interstices they enclose—more martial rhythms are imposed on the flickering light. The increasing tightness and literalness of the drawings done in the last half of the 1970s are at a far remove from the completely separate and different groups of drawings Marden had already started in 1972—drawings that opened up the plane to the possibility of more intuited images. Gestures were now liberated in configurations that were no longer buried in the imagination of planar matter but became a matter of imagining the plane.

It seems only natural that, being as compelled by drawing as he is, Marden would sooner or later react against the spartan limits he himself had imposed on the movements of his hand. Like Pollock before him, Marden had subjugated the line's urge to figuration to the more pressing desire for seamless and implacable physicality. In his drip paintings, started in the winter of 1946–47, Pollock had so totally reinvented drawing and then subsumed it into painting that drawing as a separate enterprise was deemed, at best, peripheral by many of the artists in the generations that followed. Pollock himself returned to drawing on paper (in

1948), and by 1951 he had begun to exhort his line into ink- or paint-dependent, gestural figuration. He looked back to the mythic subjects of his pre-drip paintings and dissolved their descriptiveness in the flatter space and openness of his liquid automatism. Pollock's ability to make line both referential and abstract and to destabilize the plane with more complex spatial vacillations, which were still drawn out of and into the plane's flatness, became revelatory for Marden. In addition, Marden's new drawing was informed by a reconsideration of Franz Kline's often geometricized gestures, by the stark directness of the organic geometries and figures painted on the Mimbres pots Marden had begun to collect, and by the late-Pollock–related, casually sybaritic graffiti of Twombly. Of Marden's immediate predecessors, Twombly was one of the few abstract painters to have risked disassembling and reconfiguring the overallness that had for so long purged painting of almost all interior incident.

In one of the first of his redirected drawings—*Bavaria* (1972)—two sets of scratchy diagonals lean toward each other in a hairpin configuration; the lack of closure at the bottom and the irresolution at the top frustrates the conclusion of a discrete form and keeps the configuration open and visibly dependent upon the plane. Now the diagonal bundles of lines aspire to become an upward-pointing cleft in the plane, now the volume of an organic, cone-like form. The image's awkward tentativeness bristles with a freshness that invokes wonder at the simple magic of line's ability to become an illusion. And to become illusionary (not illusionistic) is what Marden's new drawings had in mind.

The primal directness of *Bavaria* was achieved with a conventional pen, but in other drawings Marden began to employ a more basic tool that literally forced him to learn to draw all over again. Perhaps in response to his recent forays into printmaking, he chose a tool (in 1972) with some of the trenchant directness and delicate incisiveness of etching tools: ailanthus twigs of various length and thickness that he picked from a tree near his house on Bond Street and dipped in ink. The unrefined points of the twigs and their extenuated length and thinness, relative to conventional drawing tools, imposed a greater distance between his hand and the support. Here was an elemental tool that generated elemental drawing—a kind of primary directness that often decreased the distance between the memory of the observed and the drawn. Pollock, too, had used sticks, but in his paintings. While Pollock flung paint in an ecstatic dance, partnering paint as line and gravity, Marden explored the plane frontally (vertically) with a slower deliberateness.

The lugubriously titled notebook *Suicide Notes* (1972–73) became an experimental laboratory for Marden's new lines. More a beginning than the end implied by the title, the notebook charts Marden's attempts to give greater independence to subjective gestures as they search for a new integration with the objectivities of the plane. The warping of the plane is now more disoriented but still controlled and in control. The drawings are almost

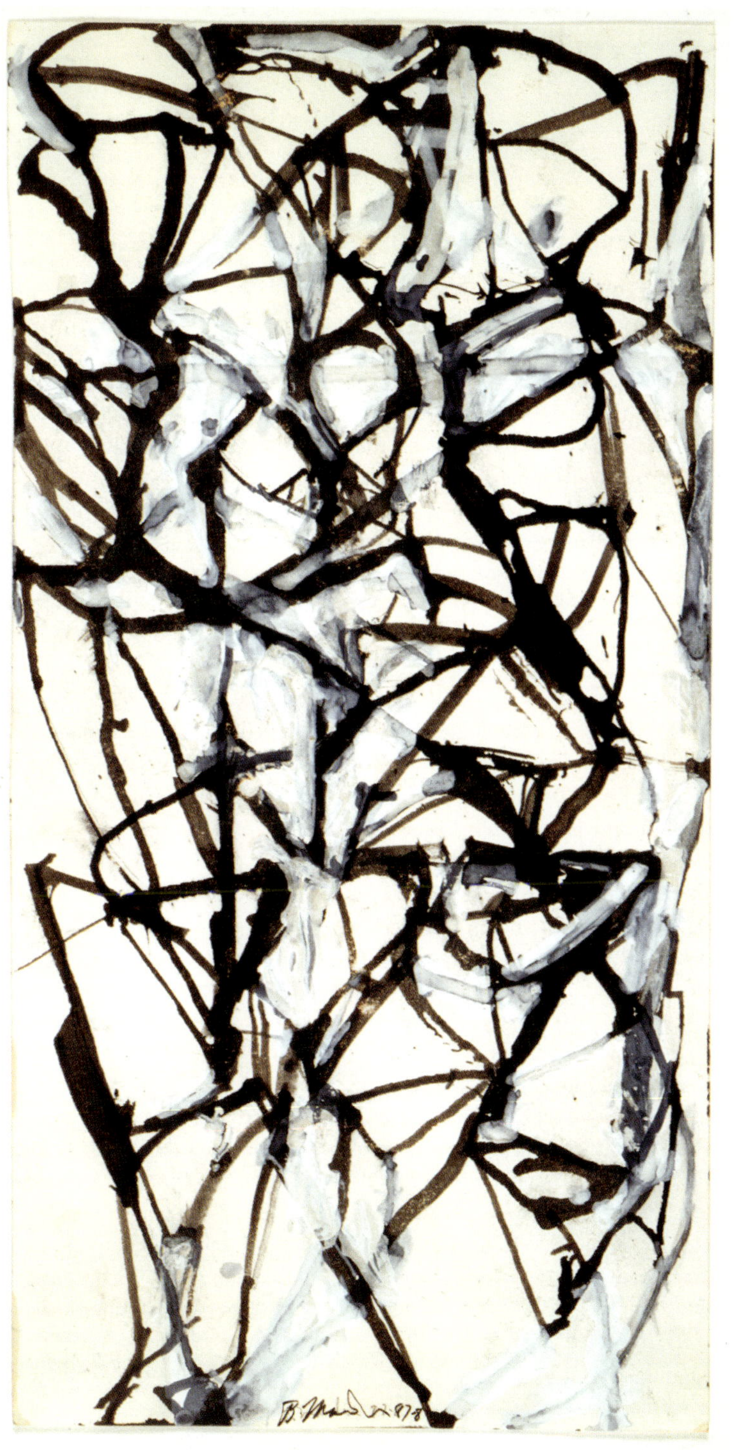

all of rectangles, completely and tenuously figured by the irregular measure of the hand; they are in varying stages of closure and completion. Changing weights and shapes of the lines are now deployed with more irregular moves and rules; webs, veils, and shadows figure the plane rather than an homogenous skin. The near-glyphic interior configuration of one of these drawings (*China Problem*), with its diagonals opening and closing into triangular figures, presages the helical structures and the influence of Oriental calligraphy that would dominate Marden's work some thirteen years later.

Much to the consternation of some of his more doctrinaire, abstractionist peers, Marden in 1973 began a group of drawings that combine postcards of artworks with his signature graphite masses. Unlike the deconstructing ironies and willed clichés of later "appropriation-ists" like Sherrie Levine, Marden's Homage to Art drawings are just that. They wear their heart on and in the plane. They incorporate postcards of art that had entranced him (classical Greek sculpture, works by Zurbáran, Goya, Mondrian, et al.) into "little lectures on my attitudes about the plane and about images." In these drawings, Marden scraped away some of the surface of the support so that the postcard was set into the paper on the same plane and in the same space as the graphite image. Photo-reproductive memory mirrors drawn memory.

Throughout the 1970s and into the beginning of the 80s, Marden continued to refine his linear mutations of the plane. On occasion, the networks of marks approach the more specifi-cally referential, as in the bark- and branch-like rhythmic coruscations of *Ghost Tree* (1976). But more often than not, his marks still incline to the vertical and horizontal straightness of their hosting rectangle: post-and-lintel structures, window- or door-like structures, and grids. Frequently the grid was still ruled by rational measure, but one that opened up the plane in panoplied transparency. Irregular grids, sometimes like fine meshes, sometimes like tartan plaids, spread out in shimmering asymmetries that trigger changes of light and space within the unity of the same plane. The unity of the playfully precarious shifts—nowhere more so than in the *Card Drawings* (1982), where Marden reworked cards that reproduced one of his unrealized projects for an art magazine. To the printed cards, he added still more verticals and horizontals and introduced diagonals to multiply the instabilities. The rich and complex tonal harmonics of these drawings, like the other grid drawings done after 1972, relate to the open asymmetries of Mondrian's late work, but Marden's asymmetries court greater spatial discord.

Complex irregularities also marked Marden's more purely intuited mark making, as an increasing variety of configurations made their claim on the plane. In the six groups (each of five drawings) done for his first daughter (*Mirabelle Drawings*, 1978–79), the inked stick acquires a delicate (often serene) and masterful versatility, whether in fine, threadlike lines vibrating with the deviations of the paper's surface as they are woven on their rectangular loom, or in the wetter, more spontaneous rivulets of ink that warp the bottom of their shape with landscape referentiality. This liquid pulse quickened its meter and its weight with the addition of gouache marks to those in ink when Marden undertook a group of drawings for his second daughter (*Melia Group*, 1980–81). Color was incorporated, but color inherent to the paper; three of the drawings are on a smoky pink paper, three on a dusty gray, three on an off-white.

In 1977, Marden was asked to submit a proposal for the creation of stained-glass windows for the late-Gothic chevet of the cathedral in Basel, Switzerland (to replace an earlier set that had been removed in 1950). For much of the first half of the 1980s, Marden focused on drawing and window proposals. The drawings frequently approached the aerated transparency and light of stained glass more readily than the related oil paintings. Employing colored inks, he scattered lines loosely based on the windows' tracery into delicate crystalline webs. The distortions of the grid now took on still more spontaneous finesse. The polyphonies of the grid's potential transparency were made more windowlike in the open configurations of Marden's drawings created in 1984. Here, chance and liquid solutions claimed greater visibility on and in the plane. The more spontaneous gestures of his painting procedures now infiltrated the measure of the grid, instead of vice versa. In these drawings, the weight and color of the paint literally and figuratively mask the geometric regularity of the grid. The act of painting soaks into the surface of the paper and binds the translucent grid to the plane of its making. Drawing and painting were coming closer together.

The Mardens had spent most summers since 1971 on the Greek island of Hydra, where they had acquired several small houses, high up on a rocky hill, overlooking the limpid blueness of the Aegean. Marden's arrival in Hydra coincided with the beginning of his search for a range of new color, structure, and space. Now Marden's geometricized restraints became ever looser and started to dissolve under the pressure of more organic and subjective restraints. He was making more concerted attempts to align the structures of his intuition with those of nature. His deepening involvement with Hydra's landscape (the irregular contours of the steep hills, the coruscation of the rocks, the clear Aegean light) took root in his marks. In two groups of drawings created in 1983 in Hydra, the transparency of his more imagined spaces was constructed with more imagined line. In *Thirteen Drawings–Hydra #11*, straightness of line gives way to the erratic fluidity of spinning layers of webs hung from the edge of the plane. In *Fourteen Drawings–Hydra #6*, a meandering line changes internal weight and shape to unravel into a graceful glyph drawn out of the mottled markings of the paper's surface. Marden was seeking a

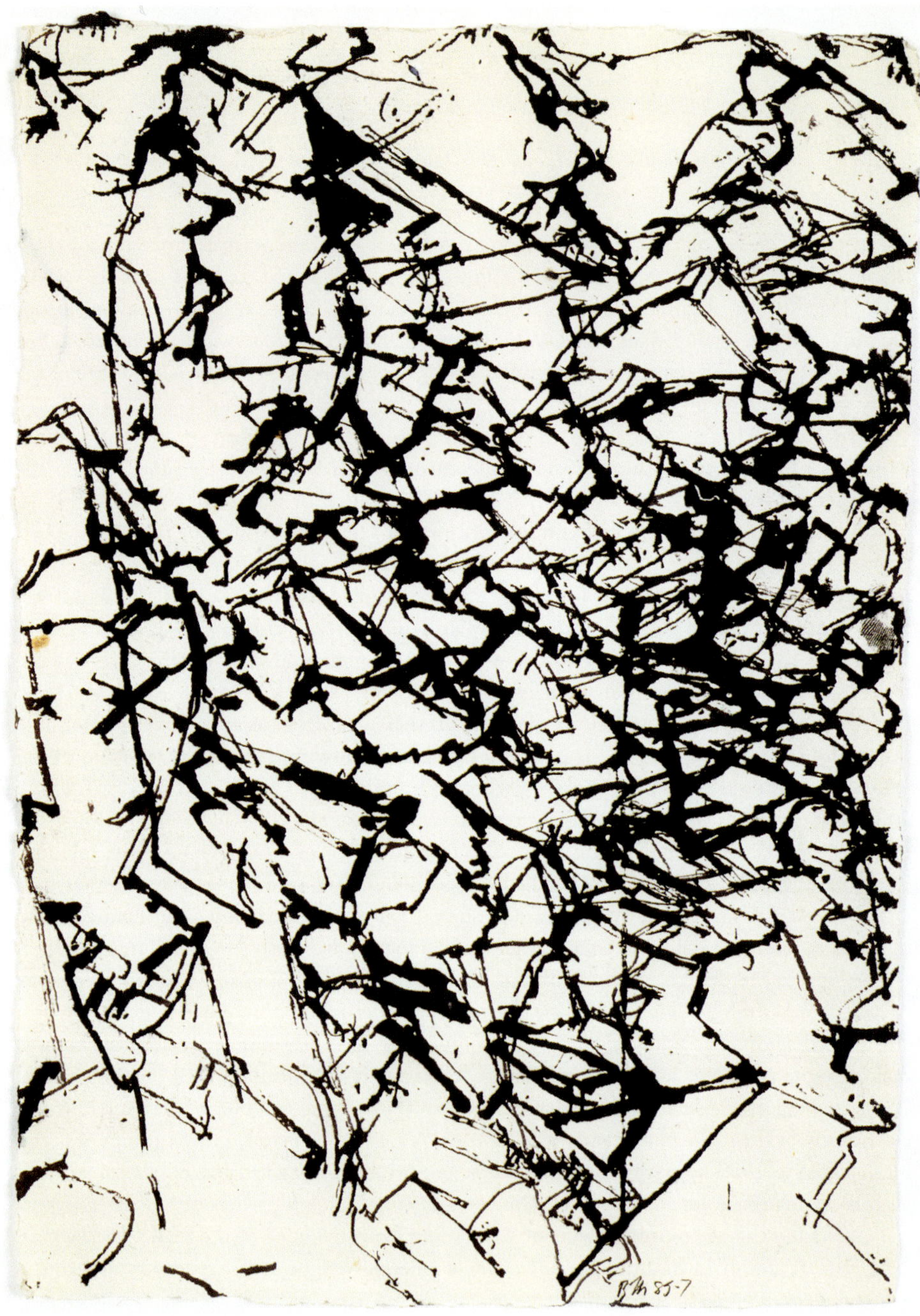

Brice Marden, *Shell Drawing #5*, 1985–87

new unity of gesture with the plane—one that gave more freedom and visibility to mark making and brought line and nature closer to the surface.

Marden's increasing urge to liberate organic mark making ran parallel to the imagined transparencies of the asymmetrical geometries employed in his drawn and painted grids. In 1984, he began more deliberately to unite these two realms. He sought a new synthesis that took him back to his formative attraction to the intuitive, gestural spontaneity of de Kooning and Kline; then he recombined it with the protocols of the discipline that had so deeply immersed him in the traditions of geometric structuring. He needed to join the painterly opticality reintroduced and reinvented by the Abstract Expressionists with the measure of the grid. This meant making the grid that was implicit under de Kooning's strokes more dynamically and integrally visible on the surface. Now, instead of mark making striving for obeisance to the rectilinearity of the grid, the grid's rectilinearity would have to strive for obeisance to the will of mark making. The reign of plane as image, which first had been so physically actual and then had become more imagined, was not to be overthrown but reconfigured.

In his quest for new structure, Marden turned to both art historical models and natural ones whose resolutions were visibly both systemic and organic—most notably, Japanese and Chinese calligraphy and seashells. In addition, Marden now entered a more impassioned dialogue with Pollock's painting and drawing. The "China Problem" tentatively proposed in his 1972 drawing would now slowly become a clear and elegant solution.

Felicitously timed, the 1984 exhibition *Masters of Japanese Calligraphy, 8th–19th Century* in New York provided Marden with firsthand exposure to forms of writerly drawing and painting that he had already begun to explore. The subject of calligraphy had been rarely presented in the West, and this exhibition marked its first comprehensive treatment in the United States. From Japanese calligraphy, Marden moved to its source, Chinese calligraphy. According to myth, early rulers of China (in the third millennium B.C.) based their first efforts at writing on the patterns of natural phenomena—for example, "grain ear" script and "cloud" script. Such a process is most complementary with Marden's intentions. Even as calligraphy went on to gather sophisticated aesthetic and pictographic complexity and refinement, it retained the mesh of the traces of the kinesthetic movements of the hand with the patterns of the forces of nature. The unification of writing, painting, and structure that Chinese calligraphy achieved is, of course, a solution not available to our culture; but it had a major impact on Marden's new work.

The importance of Chinese and Japanese art to American modernism, so frequently line dependent, is undeniable but often only vaguely verifiable. The teachings of the premier Orientalist Ernest Fenollosa, especially as passed on by his disciple Arthur Dow, were crucial to the early strivings of Georgia O'Keeffe and Max Weber, among others. Some of John Marin's watercolors, done around 1910, are related to the Sung paintings he is known to have admired, though the closeness of his more writerly mode of the late 1940s and early 50s to Oriental calligraphy cannot be documented. The Orientalization of Cubism and Paul Klee seen in the mystic intimacies of Mark Tobey's "white writing" of the 1940s grew out of his studies in a Zen monastery in Japan in 1934. Bradley Walker Tomlin's retreat, in 1949, from his gentle automatism toward greater control and regularity bears a strong enough resemblance to Chinese calligraphy to permit us to assume his familiarity with it. (Tomlin, like Tobey and occasionally Marin, often referred to his paintings as "written.") The monumentality and spontaneity of Kline's configurations seem mostly to justify his denial of direct Oriental influence, and the writerliness of Pollock's late drawing is probably more closely allied to nature than to calligraphy. However, given their (and their peers') investigations of non-European models, as well as their quest for fluid openness and non-hierarchical structure, both of these artists must surely have been aware of Japanese and Chinese art.

Simultaneously with his study of calligraphy, Marden intensified and made more marked his involvement with the patterns of nature that were calligraphy's source. Helen Marden's longtime enthusiasm for Asia and its cultures had already resulted in several trips to the East taken alone, but in 1984 she convinced her husband to join her and their two daughters on another journey to the East. While in the south of Thailand, they went to a seashell museum that turned out to be simply a large slab of petrified shell dotted with huts in which shells were sold. Marden was strongly attracted to the shells and has continued to acquire them ever since, whether on the beach in places like Madras or from dealers. The family of volutes is what he has been most taken with. Like all shelled animals, volutes carry their skeletons on their exteriors. The simplicity and seemingly indeterminate silhouette of the volute's spiraling shape makes elegantly concrete the hardened sequences of the secretions of its forming: a fossil of a process that continues to take place. Surface marks record both random disturbances and predetermined, linear patterns of growth. The generation of the shell's structure provided an excellent analog to the structural seeking of Marden's new intentions. While he was still in Thailand, he began drawings that were influenced by the patterning of shells and the bark of trees.

Marden's striving for a more gesturally responsive and organic drawing brought him closer to Pollock's similarly inclined spontaneous opticality. The lessons of Pollock's intuitive, gestural painterliness were gradually integrated with the cooler reasoning and rectilinearity of Chinese calligraphy and the slow spiraling that so transparently reveals the volute shell's sequences of growth. Marden was now able to loosen the rule of the plane's grid and make it kinesthetically responsive. He could claim a fuller set of options that included more visible and varied permutations of gestural forming and pressures, as well as a more complex deployment of spatial energies.

Agnes Martin

Geometry of Joy

Agnes Martin's gray-blue eyes sparkle with a riveting, steadfast clarity that seems to reflect the bliss of solitude she sees with her Wordsworthian inward eye. Her lyrically austere abstract paintings make visible her awareness of beauty, a wordless awareness unattached to any external object or event. As she puts it, "Beauty illustrates happiness." Her paintings, like her presence, radiate and articulate the sense of wonder that makes her like a very wise child. She greets visitors to her studio, not far from Santa Fe, with a sturdy handshake, and wonders aloud why anyone would come all the way to New Mexico to photograph her, now that she's turned eighty.

In New York, the Whitney Museum of American Art is currently celebrating Martin's achievement with a thirty-year retrospective [the exhibition opened at the Whitney in 1992 and subsequently traveled to museums in Milwaukee, Miami, Houston, and Madrid]. Much honored but seldom seen in public, Martin is that rarity, a contemporary art world legend who has eschewed the trappings of celebrity, and in times fraught with apocalyptic foreboding she manages unequivocally to declare "My paintings are positive."

Descended from Scottish pioneers who settled in Saskatchewan, Canada, where she was born, Agnes Martin has always been attuned to landscape. She came to the United States in 1930, where except for the formative decade 1957 to 1967, spent on Coenties Slip in Lower Manhattan, she's always lived close to nature. But landscape itself has never directly inspired Martin. There are no straight lines in nature, and it is straight lines that rule her work.

She came to prominence in the 1960s. Like the work of the younger Minimalists, with whom she was often grouped, her painting relied on simple, self-contained geometry, on the suppression of the personal in her touch, and on a generally very muted palette. While most of the reductive abstractionists of the 1960s employed a coolly calculated rigor that sought near-industrial neutrality, she planned her grids as a measure of joy. Her hand-drawn straight lines, with their infinitely subtle changes of pressure, transmit the vibrations of her emotional intent, as do the pale, transparent washes of color that spread their shifting suffusion of light across her canvases. Her geometry is not exclusively conceptual but intuitive, plainly comprehensible and at the same time mysterious.

While Martin's revelatory grids were heralded as hallmarks of the 1960s, she herself felt very much more in tune with many of the aims of the Abstract Expressionists (she was born in 1912, the same year as Jackson Pollock). Their paintings' dissolution of form, space, and composition—in favor of a diffused and formless all-overness that

Agnes Martin, *Untitled #4*, 1987

heroically sought to visualize the ethers of the sublime—remain crucial to Martin. So, too, does the amorphous grace of Chinese landscape painting. Martin, who did not have her first solo exhibition until 1958, two years after Pollock died, bestirred but did not reject the agitated emotion of much Abstract Expressionism. Her own sublimities are more plainspoken, and the beauty of her painting, like that of much Chinese art, resides in its contemplativeness.

In 1967, the dislocation brought on by the threatened demolition of her quiet studio overlooking the East River spurred Martin to leave New York. She wandered the States for a year and a half, towing a trailer, before she finally decided to buy land on a desolate mesa in Cuba, New Mexico. On her own, she built a simple adobe structure and, with only deer as neighbors, gave herself up to "being with beauty" instead of painting it. "Selective solitude," not isolation, is Martin's wont, so when she was ready to make art again, six years later, she left the stark drama of her mesa to move to sparsely populated Galisteo, a drive of twenty minutes or so south of Santa Fe. There she built a pair of spare and completely utilitarian structures: a fifteen-by-sixty-foot living space and a twenty-by-forty-foot studio. If her stuccoing of the trailer with red earth is any indication, her wandering days are over. As you might expect, given her penchant for construction, Martin's hands are solid, strong, and well shaped. It is precisely Martin's resoluteness of hand that gives a discreet firmness and strength to her otherwise evanescent art.

Almost all of Martin's work since 1974 has been marked by horizontal bands. These horizontals both stretch toward infinity and remain contained within the human-scale seventy-two-inch square canvases that the artist has chosen as her format since the early 1960s. The fact that seventy-two is divisible by almost every digit—two, three, four, six, eight, nine—permits Martin to set an endless variety of regular rhythms resonating across her planes. She never violates the cadence of her horizontal bands, but now she paints more freely. She works with the canvas hung on the wall and turned so that the bands are vertical. This way, gravity encourages the paint to flow as she works, reinforcing (once the finished painting is righted) her bands' horizontal reach. She has made her surfaces physically more substantial by adding an even layer of gesso into which she sinks thinly brushed acrylic and India ink, or India ink alone, occasionally including her humming pencil line. She orchestrates her linear rhythms with two or more variants of cool and warm—suave grays, or the more startling play of muted yellow, pink, and blue. The gesso's chalky white absorbs color and light, spreading an inner glow across the canvas. The grace of Martin's touch and intent propels her measure and materials into lightness and light—into a kind of profound usefulness.

So focused is Martin's vision that she "sees" her paintings before she paints. She makes no preliminary studies; once she starts, she introduces no changes of color or configuration. She measures off the horizontals and begins. She freely admits to mistakes (usually errors in scale). But year in, year out, Agnes Martin succeeds on a score of occasions annually in transforming her awareness into visual music. She wants us to see very clearly, she says, that "perception is joy."

Barry Le Va's Sculpture

Ellipsis and Ellipse

The murder novel has also a depressing way of minding its own business,
solving its own problems and answering its own questions.
— Raymond Chandler,
The Simple Art of Murder (1950)

Like most mystery novels, Barry Le Va's sculpture presents a superimposition of two interdependent sequences of time—an action performed in the past, and an investigation of that action gradually unfolding in the present to explain the past: a real event (a "crime," a configuration in space) for which the motivation is not initially self-evident, and an analysis of that event, deducing and discovering its missing links. Le Va's work is about more than meets the eye—about an absence. "Clue" is a very important word in Le Va's vocabulary.

The reader of a mystery novel passively observes the narrator retracing the steps of the plot. The narrator is a surrogate for the writer, explaining the writer's construction. The viewer of a Le Va sculpture is invited to become the narrator and to retrace the artist's actions from the work's material back to the motivation for it. The conditions that facilitate the viewer's participation are remarkably similar to the dictates of most mystery novels: a general structure simultaneously ambiguous and transparent, suppression of superfluous detail, plainness and clarity—any strong image or significant form hinders the progress of the investigation.

While Le Va has occasionally incorporated violence into his work and has once or twice indulged in sexy material (red iron oxide, mineral oil), nothing even as mildly picturesque as an excess of whiskey or a flashy convertible intrudes upon his work. His continuous use of materials with a minimum of art references (felt, flour, wooden dowels, particle board) achieves the same elegant deadpan so crucial to the pared-down prose of such writers as Dashiell Hammett and Raymond Chandler.

The comparison to a narrative genre is made to emphasize Le Va's persistent pursuit of the temporal dimension. His configurations do not congeal into static constructions, but present residues of activities that overlap and shift in time. Le Va creates diagrams of the unfolding dialogue between mind and matter; he ritualizes the act of making a choice, bringing rhythm and ration to the space between decision and action.

Since 1967, the activities that generate Le Va's sculpture have shifted from simple physical interactions (e.g., throwing, placing, rolling) with one or more materials (e.g., felt, ball bearings) to more complex mental interactions employing the materials as markers involved in systems of logical measure. Le Va's most recent work engages purely visual decision making and moves from logic to experience; the more conscious visual focus engenders a more pronounced physicality and an urge to objectness. However, this urge is cantankerous, self-doubting, and precarious, giving volume to flux rather than to form.

Transience, or homelessness, has been the plight of sculpture (and almost all art) in modernist/bourgeois times; sculpture needs more place than painting, and has received less. Le Va is part of the generation of sculptors that came to the fore in the late 1960s, radically questioning the klatch and clutter of cocktail table art and sculpture garden. This generation made transience a trenchant partner in the making of the work and replaced product with process. Objects dissolved into residues of activity and intent, which reclaimed sculpture's architectural dependence while renouncing its permanence as object (a work's material life often being limited to the duration of the exhibition it was made for). Once-pristine exhibition spaces now appeared to be occupied by mattress manufacturers or active volcanoes. Perhaps for the first time, sculptors, not painters, were pulling the stuffing out of art to see what was inside—sculptors like Le Va, Eva Hesse, Bruce Nauman, and Richard Serra.

Le Va's rejection and dissection of the object was arrived at quite early (1966 to 1967) and independently in Los Angeles (he moved to New York in 1970). The aspects of his dispersed felt pieces from 1967 and 1968 that most readily connected him to artists in New York were their configurations—derived from simple activities that punctuated process—and their restriction to the horizontal plane of the floor. Le Va was less interested in phenomenology, process, and an active partnership with gravity, however, than such artists as Serra and Robert Morris. Serra's splashed-lead sculpture and Morris's work in hung and draped felt, both from the late 1960s, present rhythmical, continuous sequences of activities that are visually coherent materializations of the interaction between artist, material, and gravity. Although clearly generated by simple activities (cutting, tearing, placing, throwing), Le Va's layers of felt are not sequentially coherent; they reflect the zigzagging vagaries of mental process as much as the clearer dictates of material process. The disparity of clusters of tiny shreds of felt overlapping large rectangles of felt breaks up visual continuity and calls attention to the juncture of two discontinuous but related layers of time. How are they related? What is the logic of the placement of the felt? What is the role (roll) of the ball bearings, included in most of the felt works? The viewer is given clues but no certainty of an answer—certainty and finality are not part of Le Va's vocabulary.

The felt pieces, like most of Le Va's works, take up the entire space they are situated in—the viewer is almost always within the piece and must (re)perform its construction to move through it. No overall view or distance is possible, no configuration is dominant; the almost intolerable profusion of units creates a field of constant shifts, junctures, and overlaps that frustrates any attempt at a unified reading. Intent is not clearly apparent; the viewer must deduce and intuit Le Va's actions as he turned material into the nonsequential transitions in space and time that reflected his mental processes of deduction and intuition.

Formless, shapeless, structureless—clues, no conclusions. Can sculpture be purely about relations and transitions? How much responsibility should be given to the viewer? At what point does the material risk turning from being "sculpture" into becoming the vestige or trace of "performance"? Where is intent located? Le Va's work continuously asks these questions. You must think harder than you see.

By 1970, the procedural residues of simple physical interactions with a variety of materials (glass, bricks, flour, felt, etc.) were replaced by residues of systems of measurement and sections of geometric figures. The material (wooden rods, dowels, Masonite, etc.) no longer denotes itself; it becomes more and more connotative of a set of purely mental activities. An example from this period is the *Circle Series* (1970–71), which employs stone markers for the centers of circles, points of tangency, or overlapping of circles. While these works appear to have more order than the earlier pieces, they are just as resistant to any sequentially unified viewing. The units of material are fragments of figures and systems overlapping in time and space, frequently interrupting and partially erasing each other. They are not visually "logical" the way a Sol LeWitt wall drawing is.

The walls that act as passive boundaries for the felt pieces are now incorporated into the work. A 1973 work titled *An Attempt to Fit: 16 in 4: Centerpoints Outwards (walked end-over end; ends touch, ends cut)* is divided into four overlapping rectangles determined by and including the layout of the floor and walls. Wood sticks have been walked separately, end over end, through the space, their ends cut each time they touch the ground, leaving paths of dowels separated by ever-diminishing spaces; ultimately each stick (measure) either exhausts itself or hits a wall where it then remains. The space becomes a map of itself and the viewer is left with overlapping traces of the cartographer's measuring instruments.

As Le Va's work develops, paths of measure turn into segments of lines of perspective and the space turns into a projection (illusion) of itself, first from a single vantage point, then, in the group of works titled *Accumulated Vision* (1975–79), from multiple vantage points. The material now becomes a sign for a system of measurement rather than itself being the measure, as were the walked sticks. The wood is now dispersed in open angles and diagonals which represent sections of perspective lines projected from a vantage point outside the space. The viewer is inside the space; the point of view is outside. Reconstruction of the projection(s) becomes more and more difficult as the number of points of view increases. The distance between what is seen and what is (was) conceived is pushed to an extreme. The materials become a set of complex signifiers that resist visual decoding—perhaps more hieroglyphic than "sculptural." Le Va's language is now almost impossible for the viewer to penetrate without a dictionary.

At the same time, titles become necessary rather than merely helpful adjuncts to the work. Le Va's titles are always descriptive of the operations that compose a specific work, providing verbal clues and context without fully describing the content—providing a common denominator but not a solution. The need for titles varies with the degree to which the visual procedures that constitute a work are self-evident, and with the viewer's knowledge. If knowledge of the operations that comprise a work is necessary to the understanding of that work, then the titles of the Accumulated Vision pieces begin to weigh more than the materials—e.g., *Accumulated Vision: Boundaries Designated (configurations indicated) corner sections (of 2 four-sided boundaries that cut through corners of this space where designated) separately projected. From eight positions of viewing, each position (not necessarily stationary) is located at a specific height above floor level and outside the boundaries of corner sections* (1977 installation at Sonnabend Gallery, New York).

How visually self-evident must a "sculpture" be? How much responsibility should the viewer be given? Is the content of a work of art the sum of its operations? Mystery novels require a solution—does a sculpture? What is a sculpture?

The Accumulated Vision pieces ask more questions than they answer, while seeming to turn Cubism inside out. Instead of an object being analyzed and layered in planes of multiple points of view, the observer is split into multiple points of view. The viewer moves from vanishing point to vanishing point inside a series of illusions, and must attempt to project himself or herself backwards to the outside; artist and viewer unite on the other side of first one, then many, lenses. The illusion is almost totally conceptual, and the degree of (re)creation required of the viewer is extreme.

While the distance between material and intent here is greater and more perplexing than before, the Accumulated Vision pieces have a visuality and physicality common to most of Le Va's work: radical horizontal compression, denial of unified form or gestalt, and material dispersed in a large field in configurations implying movement in one or more planes and resisting any visually sequential reading. Surfaces are totally eventless—generally matte, flat, and ungiving. Because of the multiplicity of units and their refusal to congeal, the floor appears to shift constantly. The viewer is in the piece but seems to view it from above—the generally small size of the units makes them seem to float far below eye level. Le Va turns space into a rather disconcerting nowhere place, both matter of fact and alien, simultaneously immense and measurable. The work's openness and seeming incompleteness encourage investigation and completion.

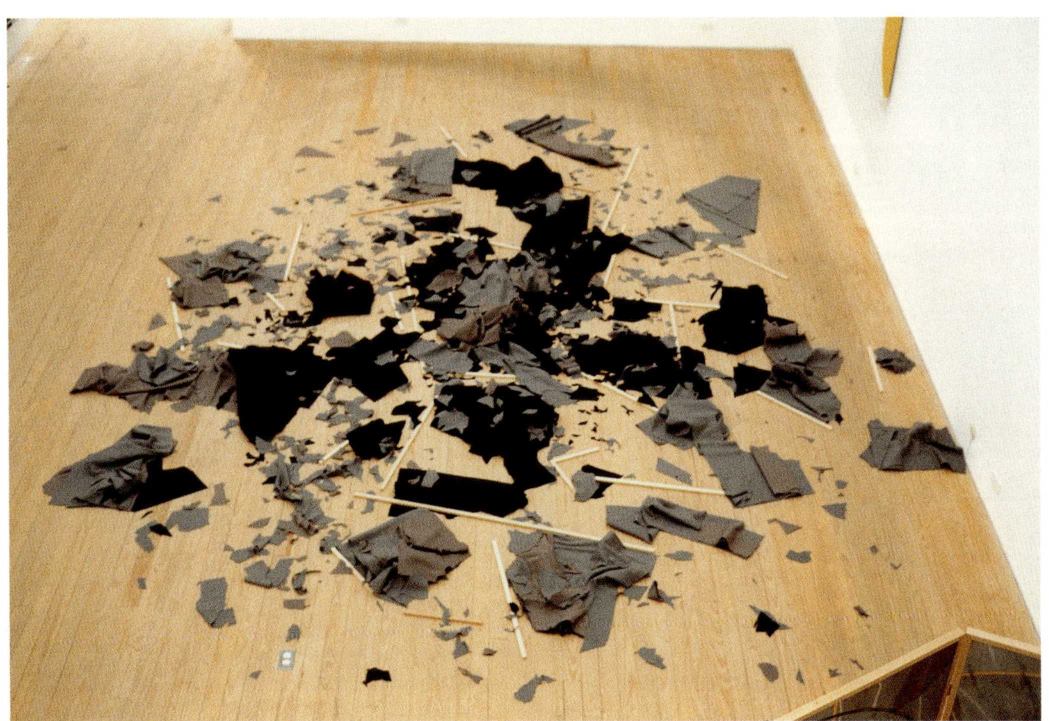

Barry Le Va, *Untitled*, 1967

Could purely visual concerns become the basis of the work? Decisions based on personal experience have been thought to becloud the clarity of intellectual intent; decisions based on objectively verifiable procedures or systems have formed much of the art of the past twenty-five years, including Le Va's. Many artists have sought the transparent logic of language; recently, however, more and more have come to realize that art may be weightless but it is not transparent.

In Le Va's work, choices of medium, size, scale, and placement (by chance and design) are, to varying degrees, determined by personal experience and preference. These choices are largely responsible for the work's believability. If there were no spatial tension or suspense, what would initiate the viewer's investigation? Could the work be drained of illusion and replaced by a diagram? Could it be written?

"Illusion," "spatial tension"—these are purely visual and psychological concepts. How are visual decisions made? Can they be communicated? The realm of the visual has become the primary (rather than secondary) focus of Le Va's most recent work. He seeks to make and analyze models of visual choice making. Since 1989, the work has been less about specific processes and more about "experience." With *Expanding Foundations: Eliminating Foundation, a Partial Exterior Plan with an Interior* (1981), the action begins to move back onto the plane of the floor.

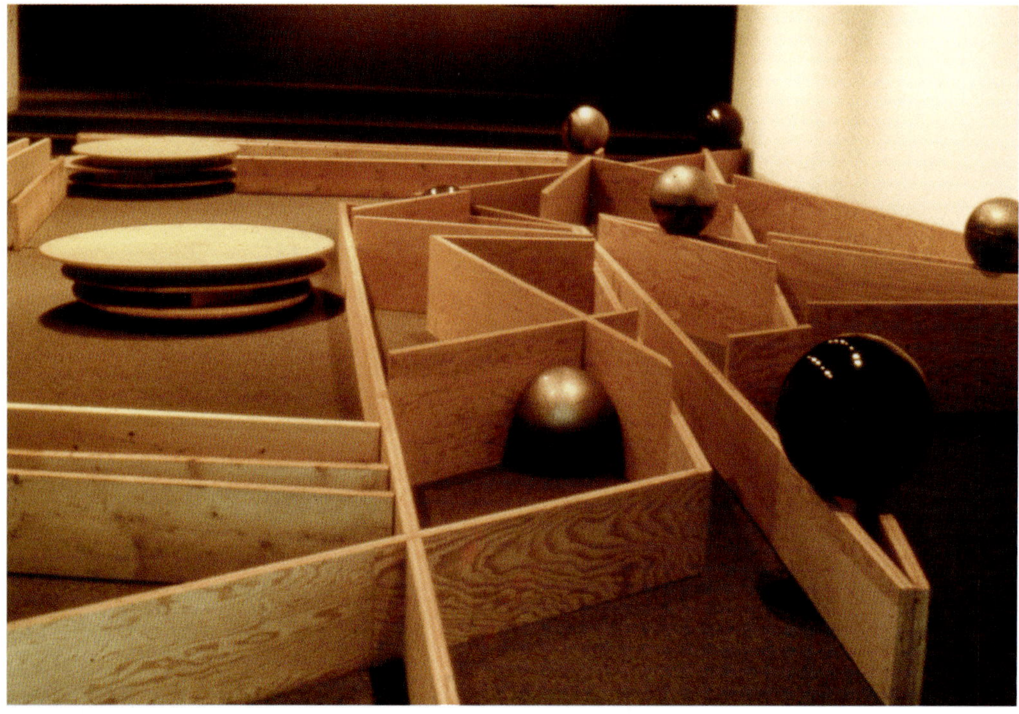

Barry Le Va, *Revolving Standards: Past Decisions, Present Revolutions, Future Drops*, 1982

"Gyroscope Roulette" suggests random rolling and rotation on a variety of planes of choice and chance. *Gyroscope Roulette: sketching a possibility* is the title of a work done in the winter of 1982, in which Le Va gambled with and abandoned himself to the totally visual. Like a gyroscope, the piece is simultaneously stable and revolving. The precariousness of shiny, ready-to-roll fiberglass balls on compartmentalized tracks, several sets of particle-board ellipses in staggered triplicate suggesting horizontal revolution, and sections of single, variously angled ellipses that seem to slice through the floor, all at about knee height, fan endless currents of illusion—illusion totally dependent upon material, shape, and placement.

What is an ellipse? Both a specific, complete geometric figure and an incomplete geometric figure, it falls short of a circle or appears to be a perspective projection of a circle. Its visual incompleteness seems to set it in motion. An ellipse is a perfect monogram for Le Va.

An ellipsis is a lapse of time or the omission of an element that is structurally necessary but understood in context. "Ellipses" is the plural of ellipse and of ellipsis. Ellipses populate and propel Le Va's recent work.

Two works done in the late spring and summer of 1982—one for Documenta 7, one for an exhibition at the DeCordova and Dana Museum in Lincoln, Massachusetts—are more demanding in both content and configuration than *Gyroscope Roulette*, although all three are composed of similar elements. The DeCordova installation is the latest, and most complex and disturbing, of the three.

In photographs, and at the first moment of viewing, the piece seems to be a uniform, maze-like structure incorporating ten spheres and two triple-tiered sets of ellipses. Barry Le Va the neo-Constructivist? Only for a second; almost immediately the structure becomes disjointed and the space uncomfortable. The paths that fill most of the room are scaled to the spheres and must be carefully stepped over or straddled—passage is awkward (as if one were on a miniature golf course). On inspection the maze-like structure breaks down into two separate sections: one side is made up of disconnected but parallel planks in a straight path ending in an angle, the other side of intersecting diagonals in two different scales.

The piece is titled *Revolving Standards: Past Decisions, Present Revolutions, Future Drops.* The roll of a sphere is an ambiguous measure at best, and an ellipse is an incomplete one. These "standards" are far more elusive than were the walked sticks; their placement by design seems almost as gratuitous as the placement by chance of the ball bearings in the felt pieces.

The placement and removal of the spheres and ellipses seem to have determined the structure of the paths, but the paths could as readily have determined the placement of the spheres and ellipses. Are the three different sizes and surfaces of the spheres the result of different standards or projections of the same standard? The piece goes round and round—the drop of a sphere defines an angle, an angle defines the ability of a sphere to drop. There is no solution, only flux and an endless, cyclical reciprocity. The work seems to be a record of the mind's erratic search for a reason to be.

The title of the Documenta piece is *Perspective Slot Drop/or Illusion/Delusion: Related Consequences.* This work has a simpler configuration, but also splits the room in two and builds a seemingly unified but ultimately disjunctive structure. As physicality and visuality become primary rather than secondary concerns in these works, decisions are generated directly by the self rather than through systems or procedures. There is less certainty, less verifiability, more doubt (self-doubt); standards are less "accurate," measure even more ambiguous than before. With self-doubt comes the specter of self-deception and the possibility that illusion is a delusion. The flux and vulnerability of much of the previous work now issue directly from the self.

Le Va would like to make an object but is painfully aware of the impossibility of making a self-confident one. Perhaps the only possibility is to continue the relentless laying bare of the problematics of sculpture, picturing more clues but finding no solution.

The body of work that Le Va has created is alarmingly uncompromising. His surgical awareness of the dilemma of sculpture is hardly endearing, but is as rewarding as it is instructive, especially at a moment when so much sculpture reverts to sheer mindlessness of material and reupholstering of Constructivist clichés. Object lessons are still in order.

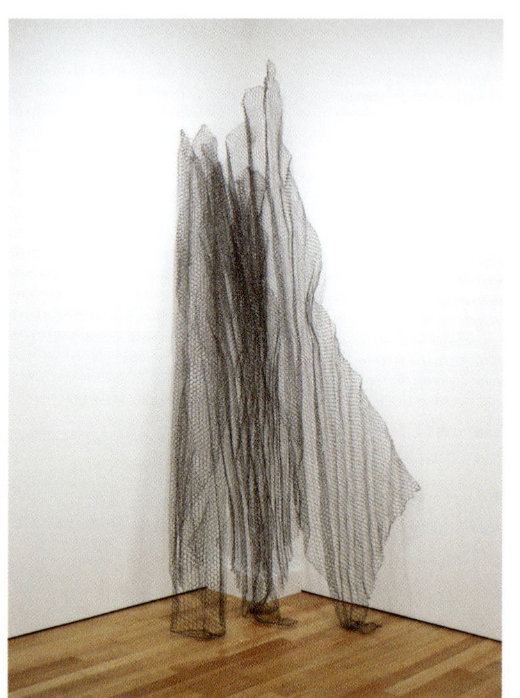
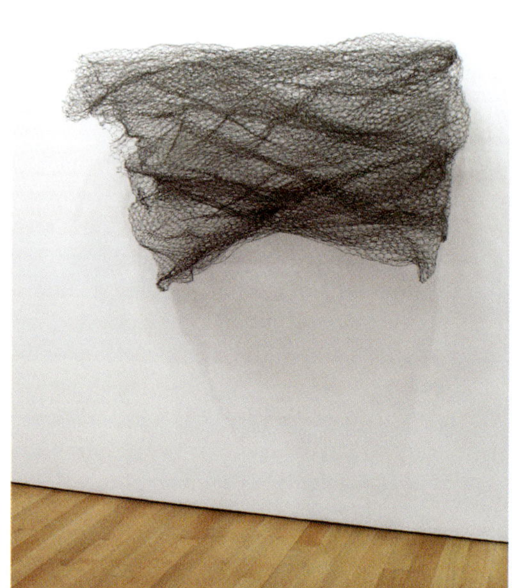
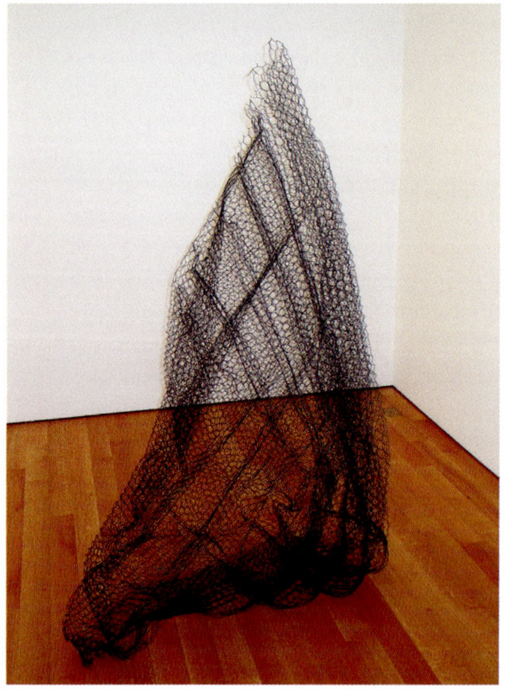
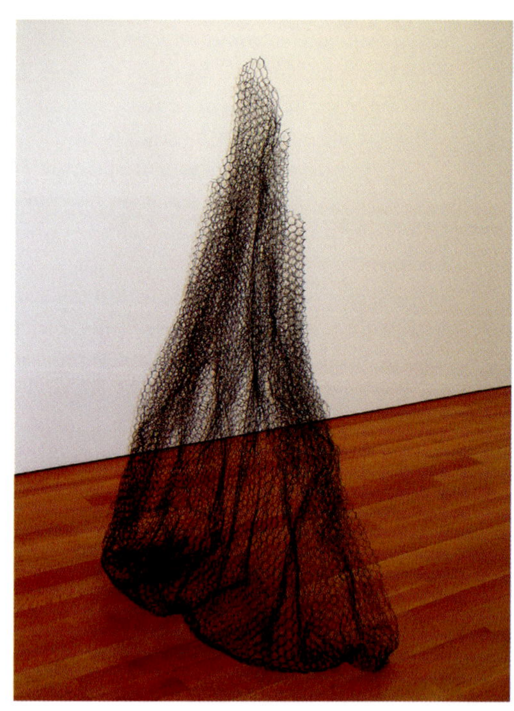

Alan Saret

Engineer of the Ethereal

Technology and the clarity of mathematics, attuned to nature, laid claim to Alan Saret's vision at an early age. He grew up in sight of the George Washington Bridge, more impressed by the harmony of the bridge's glistening spans with the craggy shorelines than by the implacable and inorganic staccato of New York City, visible to the northwest. Saret's sculpture, drawings, and architectural projects draw strength from the forces of nature; his first exhibition, in 1968, was titled *Mountains of Chance, Documents of Ruralism.* He draws organic images from industrial materials, molding and yielding to the structure of the material to "let matter present itself as spirit." [All quotations are taken from written statements by Saret.] Saret's work resolves and dissolves itself in a finely calibrated balance of contradictions: volume drawn from line, mass becoming space, the order of number disordered (re-ordered) by the mutability of natural forces, clarity of process turning into vapors of illusion. All conspire to transform the material into the skeleton of the immaterial. Saret constructs bridges to the spiritual.

Now, when pop stardom has become both subject and object of much art, the word "spiritual" hangs precariously on the page. Since "sublime" was expelled from the art vocabulary in the mid-1950s, flatter words and deeds have been preferred; nonetheless, Saret insists on "spiritual" in word and deed—he is anxious to protect and propagate the revelatory nature of art. His intent does not preclude but includes a refined and conscious formal intelligence.

Saret studied architecture at Cornell but came to sculpture through painting. The divorce of sculpture and architecture that occurred concurrently with the rise of the bourgeoisie and modernism led to a symbiotic relationship between painting and sculpture. Sculpture's solidity and mass began to dissolve in sfumato and chiaroscuro in the hands of Medardo Rosso and Auguste Rodin, and then flattened into a planar play of space and transparency with the advent of Cubism—drawing upon his painterly innovation, Pablo Picasso set about redefining sculpture, as did the Constructivists in Russia. The dissolution of mass into transparent planes and space was to dominate much of the sculpture of succeeding generations. Even the retreat from the painterly and a return to a greater specificity of form and objectness by sculptors like Donald Judd and Robert Morris, in the 1960s, still owed much to Constructivism and Cubism. In the late 1960s, a remarkable generation of sculptors emerged and renewed the bond with painting; but now it was to be a (re)view of Jackson Pollock, not Picasso, that submerged sculpture in a solvent of painterliness—a generation that included Alan Saret as well as Richard Serra, Keith Sonnier, Eva Hesse,

CLOCKWISE FROM TOP LEFT: Alan Saret, *Four Piece Folding Glade*, 1970; *Green Wave of Air*, 1968–69; and views of *Forest Close*, 1969–70

Bruce Nauman, Barry Le Va, and Lynda Benglis. Morris was to join them and become their self-proclaimed spokesman. Sculpture as object was submitted to a radical revision: gestalt gave way to process, form and mass melted into gesture and even transience. The nature of an astonishing variety of materials was probed and propelled into an active play with the forces of gravity. Materials generally noteworthy for their liquidity and/or pliability—molten lead, mineral oil, latex, chicken wire, felt, glass, flour, cloth, and others—were torn, poured, folded, or molded in configurations that revealed and congealed the behavior of the material and the marks of the maker (marks of process, not of personal touch).

Pollock's conversion of painting from the confined movements of hand and wrist to broad sweeps of the arm leaving layers of linear drips in their wake internalized and objectified human scale and measure as actual visual components of the work. The procedural clarity and the obvious interaction of paint and gravity of Pollock's drip paintings from 1947 to 1951 were seminal to many of the artists of the late 1960s: Serra's splashed lead pieces, Benglis's liquid latex released in multiple colors and poured from a pail directly onto the floor, and Saret's wire layers of linearity bowing and billowing with the memory of the movements of his body, all are clearly indebted to one aspect of Pollock.

Not surprisingly, the gusto that greeted this generation of artists blurred their individuality and encouraged a false homogeneity of intent. The critical emphasis on the phenomenological and the procedural was more germane to Morris and Serra than to Saret. In 1969, when Marcia Tucker and James Monte organized an exhibition at the Whitney Museum that included these sculptors, Saret withdrew upon learning its title was to be *Anti-Illusion: Procedures/Materials*. Then, as now, Saret insisted upon the freedom to investigate illusion as well as non-illusion. For Saret, the self-contained and the self-reflexive, so important to the modernism of the twentieth century, are not sufficient. His procedures are clear and transparent, but are further transformed and layered in meshes of metaphor and ambiguities of space and form that make vision a veil for the visionary.

Saret's early works set about subverting and converting the tenets of modernist painting. From the mid-1950s onwards, painting aspired to a more emphatic objectness (now approaching sculpture, rather than vice versa); in the hands of such artists as Kenneth Noland, Jasper Johns, and Frank Stella, the physicality of the painting's support took on increasing importance. Saret gave the support greater dimension and volume, pushing it into sculpture while simultaneously retrieving painting's lost illusions. He opened up the weave of canvas and unfurled it into the room.

Having first done studies for a group of shaped canvas paintings in the form of an elongated arch, Saret then extended the implications of volume into the round by substituting the open mesh of chicken wire for the closed weave of canvas, drawing the play of actual space and volume into the work. Moving from the wall to the floor, the chicken wire took on increasing complexity of configuration. *Hooke's Law*, constructed in early 1968, consisted of a cylindrical tube made of eight or nine layers of two-inch mesh chicken wire laid horizontally or stood vertically on the floor. The implied volume of shaped canvas paintings now became a real volume—but a volume that dissolved into a mirage of itself. The multiple layering and openness of the wire mesh create an oscillating moiré effect that blurs the edges and hinders the eye's retrieval of a specific form or shape. The clear linear configuration of the wire all but evaporates in transparence and vibrates with a painterly buzz; the viewer, literally and figuratively, sees through and beyond. Paradoxically, painting pushed into sculptural three-dimensionality has propagated an immateriality that fosters illusion.

While the cylindrical shape of *Hooke's Law* mimics the potential state of canvas and chicken wire when still in a roll, other works increasingly encourage the wire to surrender to and retain the gestures of process. The mathematical precision of the industrially fabricated grid of the chicken wire is subjected to the natural rhythms of hands and body—the measure of gesture choreographs the measure of mathematics in a cascading counterpoint. Like partners in a dance, both systems of measure are clear and independently visible, while interdependent in their partnership to create new formations uniting suppleness of body and of wire.

Like fossils, Saret's sculpture exists somewhere between memory and nonexistence. The wire's tensile strength and resilience holds the memory of the movements of the body—movements motivated by an urge to form—but a form in flux, no sooner composed than decomposed in its embrace of space. Seldom has sculpture achieved such an active exchange between space, form, and volume.

Saret seeks a sculpture that reflects and parallels the mutating forces of nature. The lightness and pliability of the wire subject it to constant change—there is no final and fixed configuration as there would be with a heavier, denser material or a congealing liquid. The sculpture is seldom as rigidly rooted as most of the work of Morris, Serra, and Carl Andre; it maintains a more open dialogue with gravity. The work settles and adjusts to its support, be it wall or floor. Saret has often shifted a piece from the floor to the wall or ceiling, permitting the configuration its own organic modification as it stretches or sinks into its new situation—like an air plant sprouting on top of a tree and drawing sustenance from rain and air.

The wire holds no false secrets; all is visible while all is variable. There is no confusion about the work being hollow or solid, no difficulty in seeing its density. The mathematical measure and transparency of the wire simultaneously blends formal clarity with an evanescent ambiguity. Order borders disorder.

By the spring of 1968, Saret's work attained its volition to volume, and by the time of his first solo exhibition in the fall of 1968, the sculpture took full and confident advantage of the wire's potential—the relative openness of the wire's weave, the weave's different shapes (hexagonal, rectangular, etc.). The weave's thickness and surface (shiny, matte, rubber-coated, spray-painted) are called into a panoply of varying density, mass, color, volume, and form.

The prevalent configuration of the works in the 1968 exhibition is mound-shaped and harks back to those early man-made shelters and sites that took their cues directly from nature—hand-hewn hills and megaliths that harmonize the artificial marks of the intellect with the organic forces of their surroundings—they can be open and airborne like a swelling, skeletal cloud, or approach the density of a pile of bristling antennae. One of the wall pieces was formed from a handmade mesh: *Into the Blue Field Galaxy* (1969) is made of several layers of wide-open webs of blue, vinyl-coated electrical wire with a sinuous linearity like a transparent, modular Pollock. *Galaxy's* hand-measured weave foreshadows Saret's sculpture done after 1974.

While wire is dominant in Saret's work, it is not the exclusive medium. The lightness, linearity, and flexibility inherent in wire are natural to materials like rope, polyethylene, cloth, and rubber—all have been called into service at one time or another. One floor piece in the 1968 show cloaked a bright blue, rubber-coated wire mound with the more liquid linearity of a web of thin, flat strands of brown rubber. In another work, a phantom mound accumulated out of folds and drapes unrolls from a bolt of black rubber. In still another piece, situated in a wall recess, Saret draped orange rubber from a door handle and half-submerged its ribboning cascade in the vibrant yellow of a pile of sulphur powder.

The dense look of the material and the activity of draping create the closest point of contact between Saret's sculpture and that of Morris, with whom he had frequently exchanged studio visits and ideas during the summer of 1968. While Saret's sculptures made from rubber have a less permeable presence than the wire pieces, they maintain a complexity of configuration and an ephemeral quality that hovers on the edge of slipping and sliding and melting away. The simplicity of procedure and almost smothering blunt-ness of Morris's cut, hung, and draped gray felt pieces, shown in 1968, insist on a more self-contained formal physicality.

Although related to Morris in process, Saret's work is much more intention-ally open to allusion and illusion—the rolling rhythm of layers of curving gestures

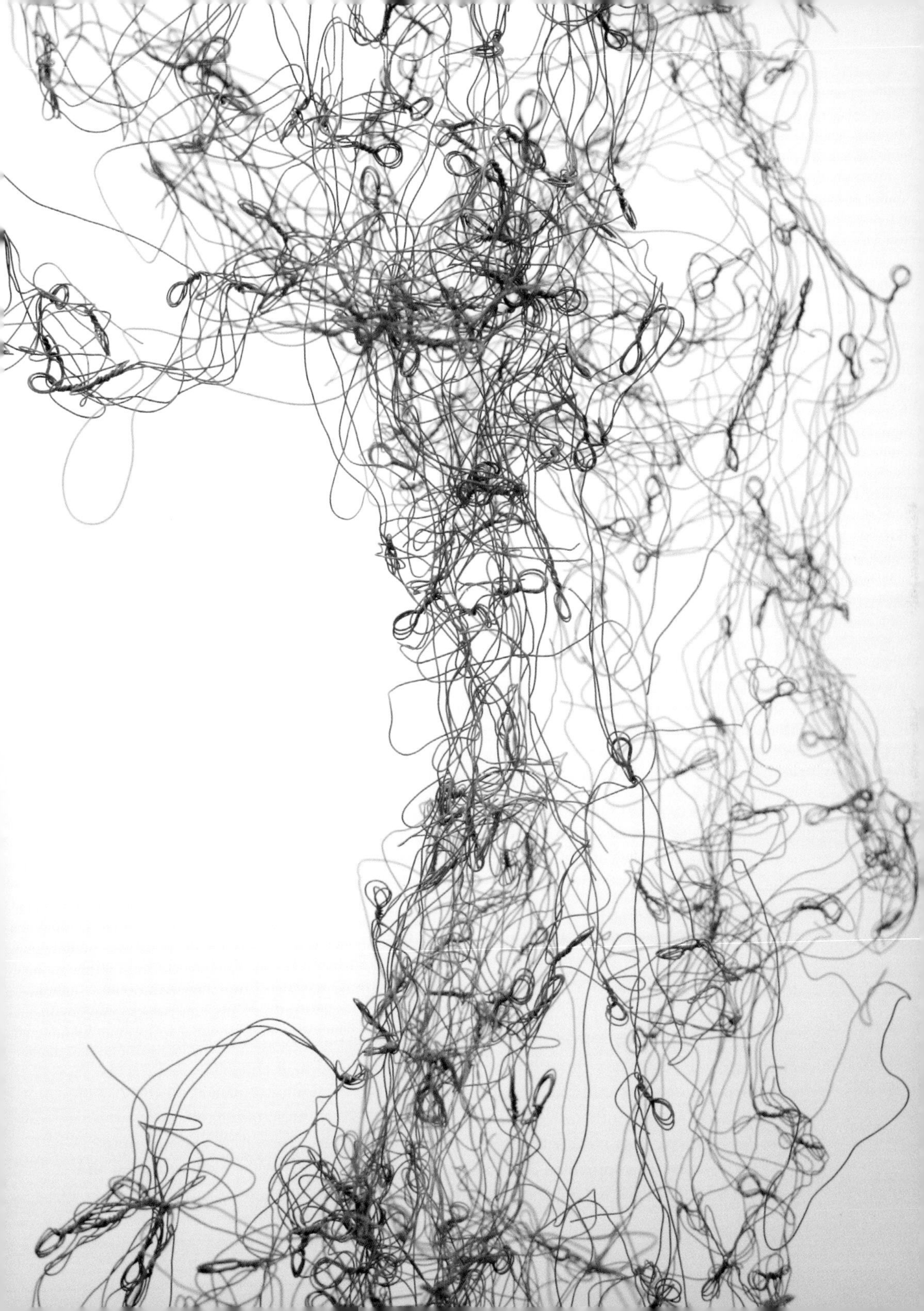

encourages reference to organic phenomena such as clouds, vines, wind-blown hair, cotton balls, and veils of seaweed shed by the ebb of the ocean. However, the work remains abstract; the supple swirls of the configuration almost never close in a completed form, and the industrial materials hold in check and contradict the natural references they simultaneously create. The images constantly fall away into a disembodied baroque that reveals the material as a reflection of the immaterial.

Any doubt about Saret's desire to take off beyond formal procedures was dispelled by the drawings shown in one section of his second exhibition, in 1970—drawings and gouaches of "imagined planets, landscapes, architecture, and beings." Some forty works, modest in size and execution, directly depicting existence on the border of the realms of the physically and psychically observable (for example, a tightrope-walking goddess in radical perspective, android-like figures, demons)—more remarkable for what they declared than what they did. They declared an interest in mythology, astrology, and fantasy, and a desire to appropriate them as legitimate concerns for art. What the sculpture alludes to now becomes specific—the figures that move in a landscape of Saret sculpture become hill and dale and vine—now utopian, now cataclysmic. In 1970, this was a bold act by a man in the minority; it is only recently that the mythic and the phantasmagoric have been invited to rejoin the mainstream. While these works illustrate more than they evoke, they make clear Saret's need for the freedom to exercise any one of the many options that form in his mind.

The drawings done prior to the imagined planets and landscapes were initially also intended to be representational (depictions of the wire sculpture), but they evolved into reinventions of the medium of drawing and became totally free of representation. They are called "gang drawings" and were done with a fistful of pencils drawn across the page, creating an organic arrangement of parallel lines simultaneously regimented and gesturally improvised, much as the sculpture is—the movements of arm and body now restricted to the sweep of the hand within the borders of the paper support—like a "neurological seismograph" recording the tremors of intent. The drawings have an effervescent delicacy and daring; changes in pressure, the number of pencils employed, choice and order of color and tone, and the type of gesture(s) permit a wide variety and complexity of formation in each drawing. Only a twist of grip is needed to distort the regular pulse of the parallels. Like the sculpture, the drawings approach an image but seldom close and complete it—the lines do not converge but are left open to air and allusion while retaining their real scale. Like the sculpture, formal power and innova-tion are revealed in suppleness and finesse. Organic irregularity has been retrieved and returned to the medium of drawing and counterbalanced with an order that prevents the vagaries and eccentricities of personal touch.

Saret's first "gang drawings" were done in 1967, and he has continued making them to the present. Likewise, the figurative drawings and, more recently (1979–80), even large paintings on canvas. The latest figurative work, achieving a greater scale and hieratic simplicity, was partially inspired by a trip to Egypt in 1981.

The second section of Saret's 1970 exhibition consisted of sculpture and extended and continued the concerns commenced in 1968. The sculpture became more expansive—now grace could approach grandeur. The mutability of structure was emphasized by subjecting a number of works to a variety of changes during the course of the exhibition. A very tight stainless-steel mesh was first folded into a Rayonnant budlike cluster, capped with an open mesh, green vinyl-coated wire arch, then rearranged, without the arch, to pop up into a shape approaching the point of a mountain peak. Another work—*Let Granite's Ethers Rise* (1969–70), made of a combination of rectangular and hexagonal wire meshes—achieved a buoyant volume as its forward lean accumulated more layers of undulating weaves of wire; its will to take wing needed to wait only a week to be achieved—it was hoisted and hung from the ceiling and permitted to spill a wispy trail of planes and process.

The 1970 exhibition's most imposing piece, perhaps because of its more implacably closed volumes, was *Triple Cornice with Windows* (1969–70). Three classicizing rolled zinc fragments of the cornice of a cast-iron building, salvaged from demolition, were laid on their sides and propped up in a step formation, the topmost end of which was embraced by the austere transparency of a screen of newly constructed windows—bringing a new and unexpected clarity to ancient forms. The ascending and descending spiraling curves of the volutes, and their visible hollowness, are directly related to the other sculpture but are more specifically mythic and monumental. Although totally composed of architectural elements, the structure achieves an abstract unity and reflects Saret's desire to reintegrate the forms and knowledge of past cultures—to make a new whole out of extant fragments. This piece predates, by nearly a decade, related attempts by postmodern architects to incorporate styles of the past in their buildings—attempts all too often motivated by a bankruptcy of invention unknown to Saret.

The watercolors in the 1970 exhibition were shown at the Bykert Gallery; the sculpture remained in Saret's studio, now renamed Spring Palace after its street location. Feeling a pall was cast by the commercialism of a gallery situation, he attempted to close the gap between the execution and the exhibition of art and turned his studio into an alternative space, both for himself and others. Saret's frustration with the homelessness of art and its frequent reduction to an object of commerce finally led him, in 1974, to start the Temple of Alael (an acronym of Alan Daniel Saret). As portentous as this sounds, the organization did not have elaborately codified liturgy or doctrine but quite simply proclaimed art as the religion and the artist as its revelator, leaving each person to be "his or her own experiment" and espousing "self-realization through art." The foundation of Alael's tenets was laid in India.

What theosophy and Madame Blavatsky were to Vassily Kandinsky, and Christian and Hebrew hagiology was to Barnett Newman, three years (1971–73) of travel and study in India were to Saret. He undertook no specific program of study but set out in search of a deeper understanding of the sources of his art. Saret's interest in astrology and predisposition toward a spirituality tuned to nature made India a relevant site for his search. His work, both before and after his trip, bears parallels most specifically to the tenets of Jnâna yoga: the emphasis on self-revelation, strength based on flexibility and endurance rather than developing musculature, discipline striving for a pacific bliss.

While in India and upon his return, Saret sought to reexamine and (re)ritualize elements of architecture. *The India Ramp* was built in 1971 for the Indian Triennale, New Delhi, and is quite simply a gently rising ramp to nowhere. A fifty-foot bamboo walkway is supported by hardwood scaffolding, with the lateral branches carried by three quadripods on either side. These quadripods return to one of the most basic of wooden structures that could be the skeleton of a shelter such as a teepee, or the support for a cauldron over a fire. More than a demonstration of basic building techniques with local materials, the ramp is literally and figuratively supported by the ascending diagonals of the skeletal scaffold—it seems afloat rather than anchored. The ramp becomes a bridge between the earthbound and the airborne; it is crucial to much of Saret's work. *The India Ramp* aspires to the ethereal. This aspiration is based on an understanding of the nature and structure of the material. The fragility of the linear components points to the immaterial, but is tied together in a web of superior structural strength—a strength that does not seek to overpower but to provide a space and place for self-intimacy.

The India Ramp was Saret's passport into India; its precursor is the stark stairway of a more functional nature built in the Spring Palace in 1970. The ramp was the only actual work created by Saret while in India, except for designing and supervising the construction of the more conventional structure of a wood and stone ashram with a tile roof, built for two swamis he met in his travels.

It was upon his return to New York, late in 1973, that Saret founded Alael in a loft space on Leonard Street and focused his attention primarily on architectural projects. Alael was more celebratory than celibatory, setting out to restore a sense of wonder and delight to the habits of daily life. Nowhere is this clearer than in *Bi-Column Temple and Water Arrangement* (1974–77), set up at Leonard Street. Again the literal and figurative become one as a bathtub is elevated, and cleaning becomes ritual cleansing. The tub extends into the room, its back atop a metal platform housed in a pointed metal canopy, its front held up by a single aluminum cylinder and framed by two cast-iron Corinthian columns anchored on a wooden beam. The ensemble becomes a counterpointing medley of straight and curved lines, volume and plane, container and contained, horizontal and vertical, smooth and rough, shiny and matte, that resolves itself in stark serenity. The gently bowed thrust of the form of the tub merits its elevated isolation and becomes a glyph for buoyancy—molded by and for the body. The bather cannot see the supporting cylinder when in the tub and so benefits from the illusion of being afloat while having his or her scale dignified by the elegant stretch of the guardian columns.

The symbolism of immersion in water, crucial to so many religions, is not lost on Saret; but now, ritual rebirth through immersion is self-administered. Like the cornices in *Triple Cornice,* the columns were taken from a local building being demolished, and represent a further attempt to integrate the spirituality of a past culture into the present. To build a temple, not a Tower of Babel, Saret is not a little proud that the tub is of an ideal height to be used as a basin for washing clothes and household wares. He is happy to marry the functional to the spiritual.

The artist ritualizes vision. The viewer looks out with the possibility that he or she might see more clearly when looking in. A window passively provides a view, art makes possible a re-view—not a hole but a whole. A (w)hole was made by Saret at Leonard Street and four other locations. Literally a hole in the wall: excavating through layers of brick and masonry, revealing the structure and finally breaking through to the outside, creating a miniature cave high up in the wall. The result is like breaking out of a shell, and seeing for the first time but seeing as though through the wrong end of a telescope. Like Alice, the viewer shrinks in scale and is encouraged "to be small and fly out." The hole provides another opportunity for rediscovery and a relief from the mundane regimentation of most domestic spaces. A house is a home is a temple.

An actual temple is what Saret undertook to build when invited to contribute to Artpark in Lewiston, New York, in the summer of 1975—well, more like a teepee of the sublime. Working completely empirically with only a small model to start with and the aid of Anne Wehrer and a few volunteers, Saret created *Ghosthouse,* a modular, portable shelter of remarkable lightness and strength—the thickest element being the eighth-of-an-inch diameter of 12½-gauge wire (only pneumatic structures are thinner). Saret worked as though making a sculpture, in collaboration with the tensile strength and flexibility of wire mesh, to create a habitable structure. Galvanized steel fencing was first folded, then pleated, to form a set of standard corrugated modules. Thirteen units were employed to make the basic structure: nine standard ones, twenty-four feet in height; three double ones, sixteen feet in height; and one double unit, twenty-four feet in height. Later, four sun and wind screens were added. The units were leaned together and tied with wire into a teepee-like structure, strong enough to be its own scaffolding and carry the weight of its builders, as well as resist a gale, and flexible enough to reveal both the acts of the constructing hands and the mutating forces of nature.

Ghosthouse, it was called—more absent than present. As transparent as some insects' wings with their structure imprinted like circuitry, its rippling pointed configuration readily harmonized with the surrounding trees and granite outcroppings, as well as with the grand sweep of the spans of the Lewiston-Queenston Bridge, visible to the south. Industrial materials constructed in an organic configuration so that "technology bows to the spirit of the natural world from which it derives its materials and inspiration."

Ghosthouse is closely related to Saret's sculpture. The individual modules bear a strong resemblance to the units of a floor sculpture leaning into the wall (*Four Piece Folding Glade*, 1970) and the shelter's fluctuating volume harks back to one of the earliest wire pieces (*Zinc Cloud*, 1967). As in the sculpture, the folding and layering of the wire creates a blurring of edges and shapes that frustrates the resolution into a specific form. The configuration simultaneously reveals the nature of the material (linearity, tensility) and dissolves it in a coruscation of essence.

From the inside, *Ghosthouse* became not only a shelter but an observatory. Its transparency revealed earth and sky, while transforming them and subjecting them to countless changes of order and scale in the kaleidoscopic shifts of its folded and layered grids of 180,000 rectangles.

Transparency turned to translucency when the onset of cold weather necessitated more protection. *Ghosthouse* was covered with shingles made of layers of wire and reinforced polyethylene, taking on a more defined conelike shape with a shiny crust on the outside and a diffused glow on the inside—a kind of radiant cocoon. In November 1981, *Ghosthouse* was dismantled and put in storage, where it awaits the possibility of another manifestation.

Ghosthouse's lacelike linearity and structure, dissolving in luminosity, relate it to the attenuated late Gothic of Sainte Chapelle, when the art of structure superseded Christianity's strictures. Both aspire to an aerated, abstract purity, but Saret's Gothic is more gazebo than church or cathedral—its human scale is geared to a more intimate self-illumination, a kind of peaceful pantheism. The ingenuity of the free-hand engineering and execution, and the sheer beauty and variety of its configuration, make *Ghosthouse* one of Saret's most impressive works.

As interesting as Artpark has proved to be, it provides but temporary sites for the possibility of potent public art. The distance between art and the world at large too often dictates a public art molded from the merely mundane. Like Richard Serra, Saret has made several attempts to bridge the gap between art and a larger public. A model for a public park project competition in Yonkers, later joined to the working model for *Ghosthouse*, recombines and summarizes Saret's architectural concerns. *The Three Archetypes: Curved Truss Platform Stair, Bi-Column Temple and Water Arrangement, and Meshwork Canopy* is the architectural resolution of the quest begun in India. *The India Ramp* now has a specific goal—a stairway similar to the ramp rises to a platform with an elevated tub emerging from a perforated copper arch in front of the giant *Ghosthouse* structure. Quest and ascent, immersion, re-emergence, and transfiguration in the shelter of a macrocosmic canopy: the spiritual symbolism in no way vitiates the sheer delight and wonder that this model promises—a promise unrealized.

Finding insufficient support and not wishing to waste endless energy battling with the IRS for tax-exempt status, Saret gave up the notion of Alael as a legal entity, but not its principles. The desire to focus exclusively on art as civilization rather than as commodity is perhaps naïve and certainly impossible to fulfill in our (or almost any other) culture; but, nonetheless, the desire is real and right, and has helped fuel Saret's work.

After 1975, Saret began to exhibit his work in more conventional spaces and focused more exclusively on creating sculpture. The work from 1974 through 1980 became increasingly insubstantial, the urge to objectness propelled by the clustering of glistening linear elements wholly dissolved (and resolved) by spatial currents. It was as though a spider set out to spin a Victory of Samothrace with its single thread—or even a mountain. Indeed, Saret's procedure is now like a spider whose seemingly rickety and random movements are ordered by the regularity of the logarithmic spiral. Saret has replaced the industrially fabricated planar mesh with a handmade mesh, spun from a single wire or wires. The mesh is now three-dimensional, not planar. The wire is gathered and twisted into nodes to form cubic or tetrahedral figures, or else wound into a bow-tie shape based on the human measure of the cubit or the span. Once woven, the wire is subjected to the will of the spirit's gestures—just as before, except the a priori decisions of measure, number, and structure are now all determined at will. Saret has become his own manufacturer. The handmade meshes gain new freedom for the forces of formation, permitting geometry's harmonic function a new set of options. The measure itself has now become more sculptural by taking on the third dimension. Volume is approached more organically. The single-wire construction permits more flexible manipulation. Wires of different color and thickness, and/or different systems of measure, can now more readily be woven into a whole, more varied in complexity of configuration, density, and scale. Simultaneously, volume and form more readily approach an agitated ambiguity. The almost infinite multiplicity of lines radiates out from the structural core into febrile single lines vibrating on the verge of evaporation. The slinky fineness of the wire and the single-strand multiplicity relate these works to the "gang drawings," now weaving their hand measure into volume—volume that envelops not only the clarity of number, but the mystery of number. Saret's configurations frequently conform to the occult combinations of numerology, adding yet another layer of possibility to their meaning.

If Saret's shelter was named *Ghosthouse*, his exhibition in New York in 1980 could appropriately have been named "Ghost Garden." A startling variety of color and configuration consumed the space and exhaled a soft fragrance of exotic reverie. If the metals were not precious, they looked it—the glow of copper, the lacquered luster of space-age coated wire, the sleek gleam of nickel—all coiled and woven in swelling whorls of light and doing the utmost to justify titles like *Reflected Aether*. The wires employed ranged from merely thin to hair-like filaments and gave the pieces an almost immaterial delicacy and bristling intimacy of scale. The configurations ranged from the simple, relatively contained and dense mound of *Annamalaxxy* (1980) to the open stretch of *Copper Connection* (1979–80), with its two copper mesh tendrils pulled from the ceiling to form an irregular triangle ending in a blossoming clump of geometry, to the endlessly looping and rolling lines that all but erase themselves in the multiplicity of the bow-tie shapes of one or another cone-line "Infinity Clusters."

No sooner done than changed. Having all but transformed metal into light and air, Saret turned to heavier surfaces to achieve greater scale and structural clarity. *Ascending Number Spirit Fountain* (1981) has a configuration much the same as *Copper Connection*, but its thicker wire surrenders more to the eye and the force of gravity. The tetrahedral geometry that forms the mesh of the two supporting arms is more clearly visible, as is the cubic geometry of the mesh of the bottom cluster. The piece is denser but hardly static—it is indeed like a fountain with its jets obeying the forces of its structure, yet constantly shifting and dispersing.

The most recent pieces extend the potential of single lines drawn into space—the lines move more slowly and deliberately as they become heavier and stiffer. In *Open Center Rising* (1982), stiff, straightened copper wire yields a large cube made up of cubic mesh

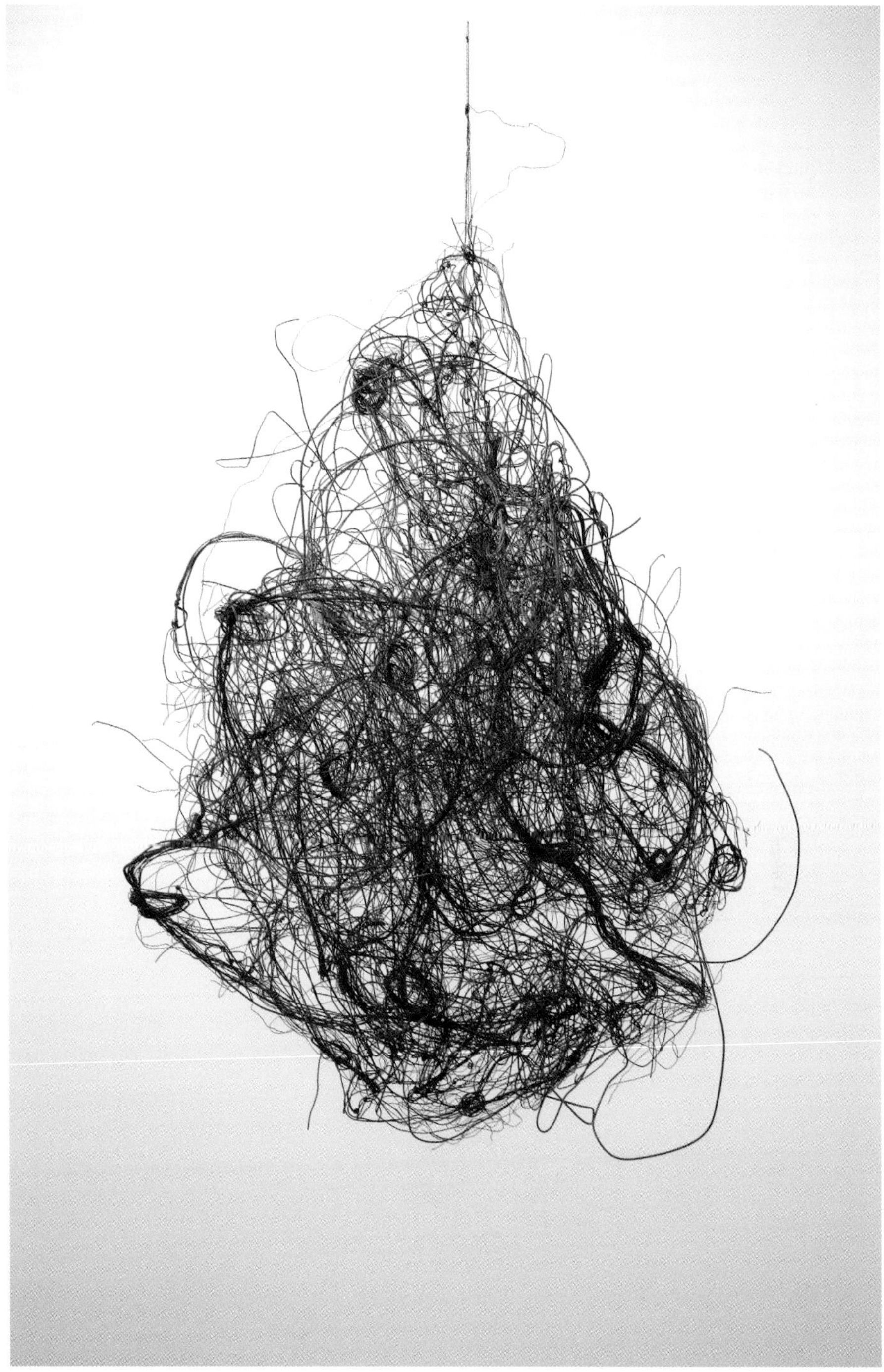

on the floor, with a smaller companion cube, (de)formed by gravity, suspended from the ceiling by four tendrils of tetrahedral mesh.

Weight and density play a visible role—the lavalike liquidity of lead sinks down into more languid loops in an Infinity Cluster than does nickel or steel. Different weights and thicknesses impose different sizes and scales—a lead Infinity Cluster, made up of wire with a diameter of a quarter of an inch, looks titanic next to an identical structure formed of nickel wire with a diameter of .0063 of an inch. However, even the weight of the lead piece slides into illusion. The lead's weight and malleability require larger loops, making the formation more open to space, while shifting its matteness into liquid shadow. The increase in the weight of the material is welded to an increase in the weight of the will.

The greater variety of measures and scale is fully exploited in *Had Heaven* (1982), with its congregation of seventeen different configurations, including a dense clump of cubic measure, the wide open, freely formed stainless-steel mesh of a spheroid, and a variety of Infinity Clusters. In *Icos Launching* (1982), a single icosahedral (twenty-sided) unit perches atop an Infinity Cluster like a cosmic insect about to take flight.

The new work brings yet another manifestation of the variety that culminates in the unity of Alan Saret's vision. A vision that folds the dictates of the material into the immaterial. The sonorous rhythms of the organic and the metaphorical roll through the regularity of number to make the visionary visible. The intent remains the same, as in the beginning, but the vocabulary has grown to form a new language more capable of exploiting the conjunction of chaos and clarity.

Keith Sonnier

Illuminations

Keith Sonnier, together with artists such as Eva Hesse, Barry Le Va, Bruce Nauman, Richard Serra, and Joel Shapiro, radically reinvented sculpture in the late 1960s, dissolving—even atomizing—sculpture's traditional mass and form in liquidity, pliability, and often transience. At the same time, they retrieved sculpture from its modernist homelessness and imbued it with a radical site relevance and/or specificity. Unlike the work of most of these sculptors grouped under the rubric of Process art, Sonnier has more often than not opted for a lyric eroticism and has been as beholden to the vagaries of his imagination as to revelations of process. Like Cy Twombly and Robert Rauschenberg, and like his peer Lynda Benglis, Sonnier's roots in the rural South have made their way into his work. In his many travels, he has found and explored parallels with the bayou landscape and Cajun culture, whether in stands of bamboo in India or Rio's Carnival.

With means as various as latex, satin, video, satellite transmitters, bamboo, and found objects, Sonnier's sculpture has seductively engaged the viewer and often transformed the sculpture's rectilinear, architectural site into pneumatic volume. Having directly engaged the architecture by such means as a strip of latex covered with tacky flocking, glued to the wall and partially torn away and left hanging like a hapless scab, Sonnier, in 1968, began attaching incandescent light fixtures to the wall, in combination with sheer fabric. He visually incorporated the light fixtures' hanging wires and transformer into the work. *Cloth, Neon, and Incandescent Set Piece* (1968) converts the wall into the ground for the painterly dispersal and play of transparent planes and light—making the space it is viewed in become an actual part of the work. The poetic conjunctions of Rauschenberg's Combines, which were a critical catalyst for Sonnier's work, have now become part of the architecture. Sonnier is prone to revel in a kind of sleazy beauty and tactility, and the sheer shiny materials of this piece long for touch. Its trashy eeriness, exacerbated by the scatological murmurings of the black stains soiling one of the pieces of fabric, seems to whisper whorehouse.

Later in 1968, not entirely satisfied with the projection of the incandescent fixtures and the need to use their standardized forms, Sonnier turned to neon. With copper tubing as a template for the fabrication of the glass-tubing–enclosed neon, Sonnier can create streams of color/light arcing and curving any way he chooses. Neon's gaseous, soft breath has a more atmospheric and voluminous diffuseness than incandescent light, making it more readily interactive with architecture's planes. And its utterly artificial, vivid palette, at once sexy and toxic, appeals to Sonnier. His work's beauty is often replete with thorns.

The looping doodles of the red neon seen in *Cloth and Light* (1968) emanate a kind of writerly insouciance that inhabits much of Sonnier's subsequent work. Pictured writing plays an important role in Sonnier's making, whether purely imagined, as here, or based on

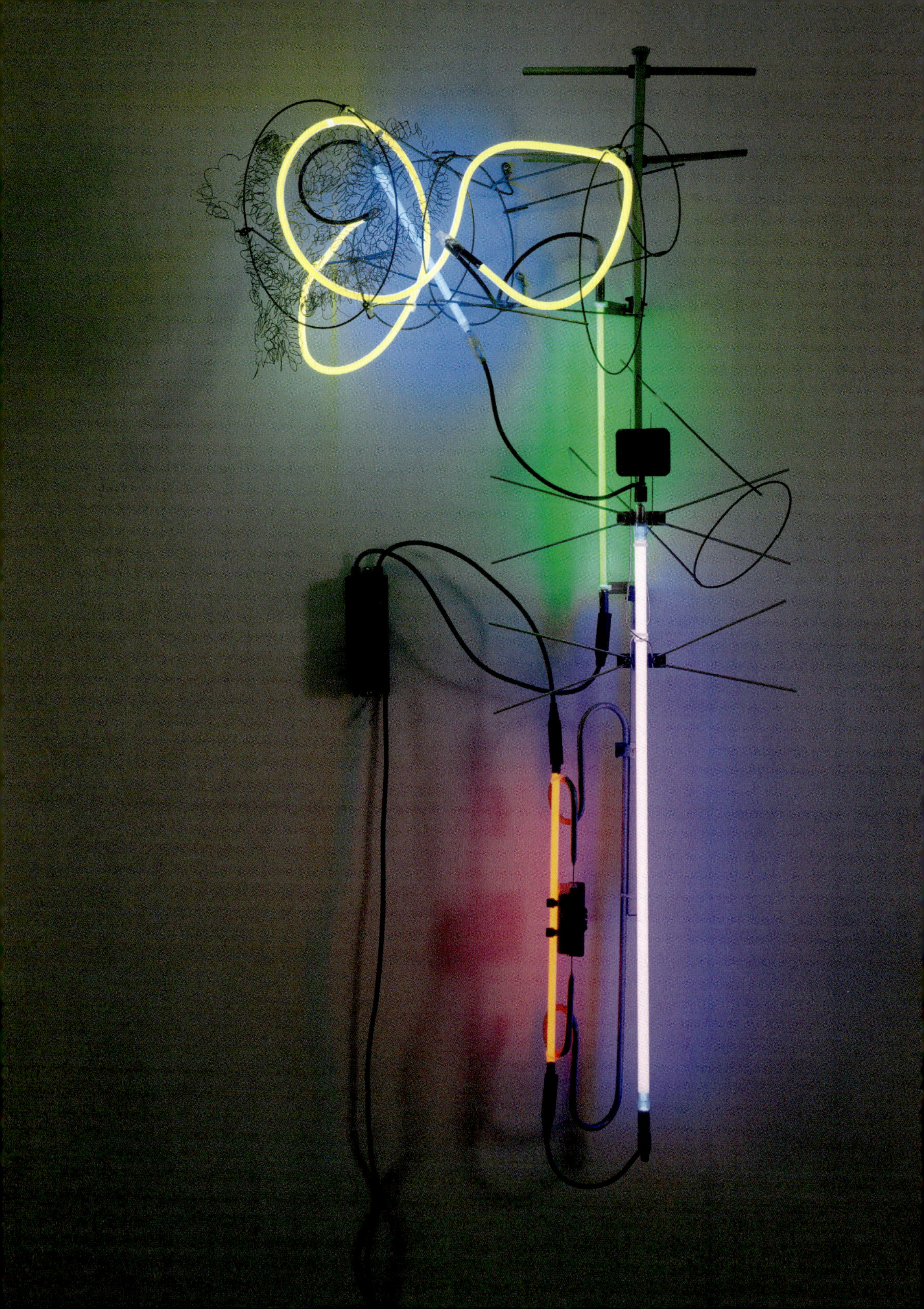

Keith Sonnier, *Dismantled Weapon*, 2004

actual forms, as in the 1977 Sel series, derived from an ancient form of Chinese calligraphy. In addition, the neon's linear arcing relates to the loosely draped electrical wiring connecting the neon to the source of its transformation into light—transformer and transformed become one. The sculpture is literally and figuratively plugged into and dependent upon the wall. Sonnier's formal brilliance is at once relaxed and acute.

While his peers Nauman and Serra have occasionally employed neon, it has been a regular, if not constant, part of Sonnier's sculpture from 1968 to the present. While this exhibition [*Keith Sonnier*, PaceWildenstein Gallery, New York, 2005] is devoted to a recent group of relatively small and intimate works incorporating neon, together with some of the group's forebears, Sonnier has also employed neon, largely since 1990, to create vast public commissions here and abroad, enveloping spaces in neon's voluminous breath that bathe the viewer and the space in the volumes of architected rainbows. While these public commissions exhibit a formal rigor beholden to their architectural ground, the smaller pieces are rife with idiosyncratic allusions more directly drawn from Sonnier's life.

Since 1994, Sonnier has more regularly returned to his native Louisiana, first to care for his ailing father and, after his father's death, to set up a foundation for artists on the land and buildings he inherited. His father ran a hardware store, to which Sonnier attributes some of his interest in technology. His father was, as well, a pack rat; while caring for him, Sonnier began to rummage through a shed filled largely with detritus. From this trove of castaways, he created his first sculptures incorporating found objects in 1994—the Tidewater Series. The subject of the first of these sculptures, *Doc Dudley J. LeBlanc*, is a healer infamous in Sonnier's native environs; he peddled home-brewed elixirs heavily spiked with alcohol. With its symmetrical tabletop structure holding various mysterious liquids in found containers (a pint vodka bottle, a plastic detergent container, etc.)—liquids that seem to be responsible for the red and blue neon emanations—this piece turns into a humorous ad hoc, votive altar. Sonnier continued these homages to his father and his own youth after his father's death and then returned to a vocabulary largely configured by the neon and its wiring. However, the Louisianian references continued to infuse much of his work.

Early in 2004, Sonnier created a group of sculptures, each incorporating the German word for "leaf" (*Blatt*) in its title. They grew out of drawings Sonnier made of leaves belonging to indigenous palm trees (palmetto and sawtooth) in a New Orleans garden. They are imbued with an open, elegant restraint limited to slowly arcing lengths of neon, almost all of a poisonous, artificial green that aggravates the loose beauty of their composition. Sonnier is smitten by the interface of technology and nature, and the toxic beauty of these virtually abstract works forms a meditation on exactly that.

Sonnier owns a house in Bridgehampton, Long Island, not far from the Atlantic Ocean, where he spends much time gardening and cooking for friends. He has no studio there, but this past summer he set about making a group of small works that once more incorporate found objects—now found in his own house or while scavenging on the beach. Four of these five sculptures reflect the war in Iraq that has impinged so intensely on our lives. *USA War of the Worlds* (2004) embroils Sonnier's daughter's discarded globe with tightly bound coiling neon, electrical wire, and metallic wire. These coils, as well as two straight lengths of white neon and two American flags, seem to pierce the globe and/or explode from it. This sculpture exudes an uncharacteristic cacophonous violence. At the same time, the warm glow of the globe, its circumference girded by red neon, draws the eye into becalmed reverie, like the flames of a fire. The equally unnerving *Dismantled Weapon* (2004), with its pointy phallic structure, resonates with the harshness of hostilities, while luring the viewer into the allure of its atmospheric glow.

Less direct in their referentiality, two other pieces perform meditations on culture. The symmetrical structure of *Baghdad Relic* (2004), centered on a curlicue spine of neon, offsets two relics—a cast of a large nautilus shell on the right and, on the left, a fragment, found on the beach, of a buoy that looks more like the remains of a very large shell. Each of these is a relic that has shed its natural state, one by partial destruction, the other by the replication of casting. They are violated fragments of Sonnier's culture that allude both to the alienation forced on cultural artifacts by artificial display and the more egregious violence performed on countless works of art by looters of Baghdad's museum left unprotected by U.S. military forces. Although *Baghdad Relic* is far from an unambiguous critique, it nonetheless basks in a lush calm. *Arabic Fringe* (2004) seems to be a comic but barbed send-up of our lack of knowledge of Arabic culture and our propensity to neutralize the threat of a foreigner with clichés. A belly dancer of a sculpture, its two lengths of red fringe look like the scant costume of a nightclub performer whose undulations are echoed by the curling neon behind the fringe and the lush volume, like a long torso, enfolded by the chicken wire to the right, as well as by the curvaceous play of the neon's wiring.

The fifth work in Sonnier's summer making, *Bundle Pack* (2004), is, if I may play upon its title, simply (and complexly) a bundle of joy that erupts from the wall in a lyric polyphony of linearity that unfurls lush volumes of luminosity—clear, mysterious, and illuminating. The airiness, fragility, sensuous ambiguity, aching beauty, and laid-back formal inventiveness of these works are the manifestations of a creator of brilliance in all the senses of that word.

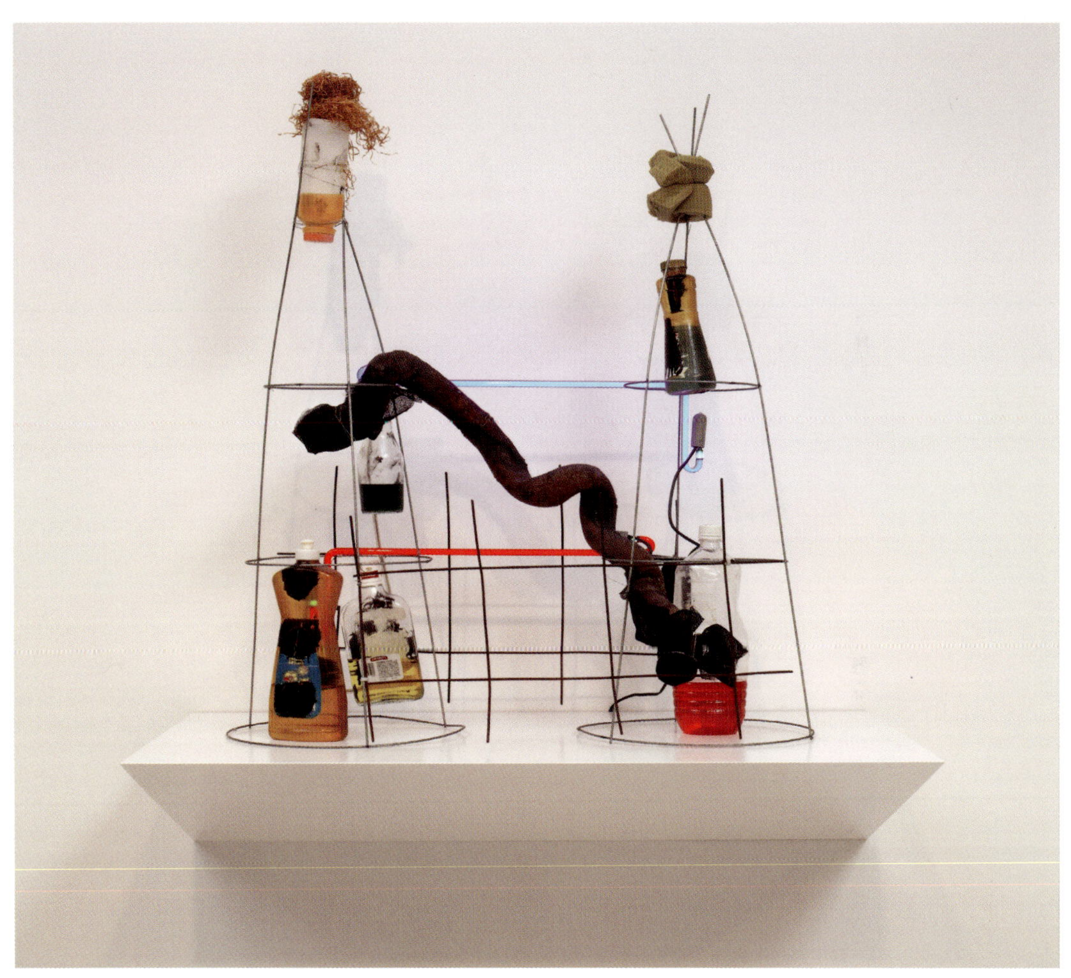

Keith Sonnier, *Doc. Dudley J. LeBlanc*, 1994

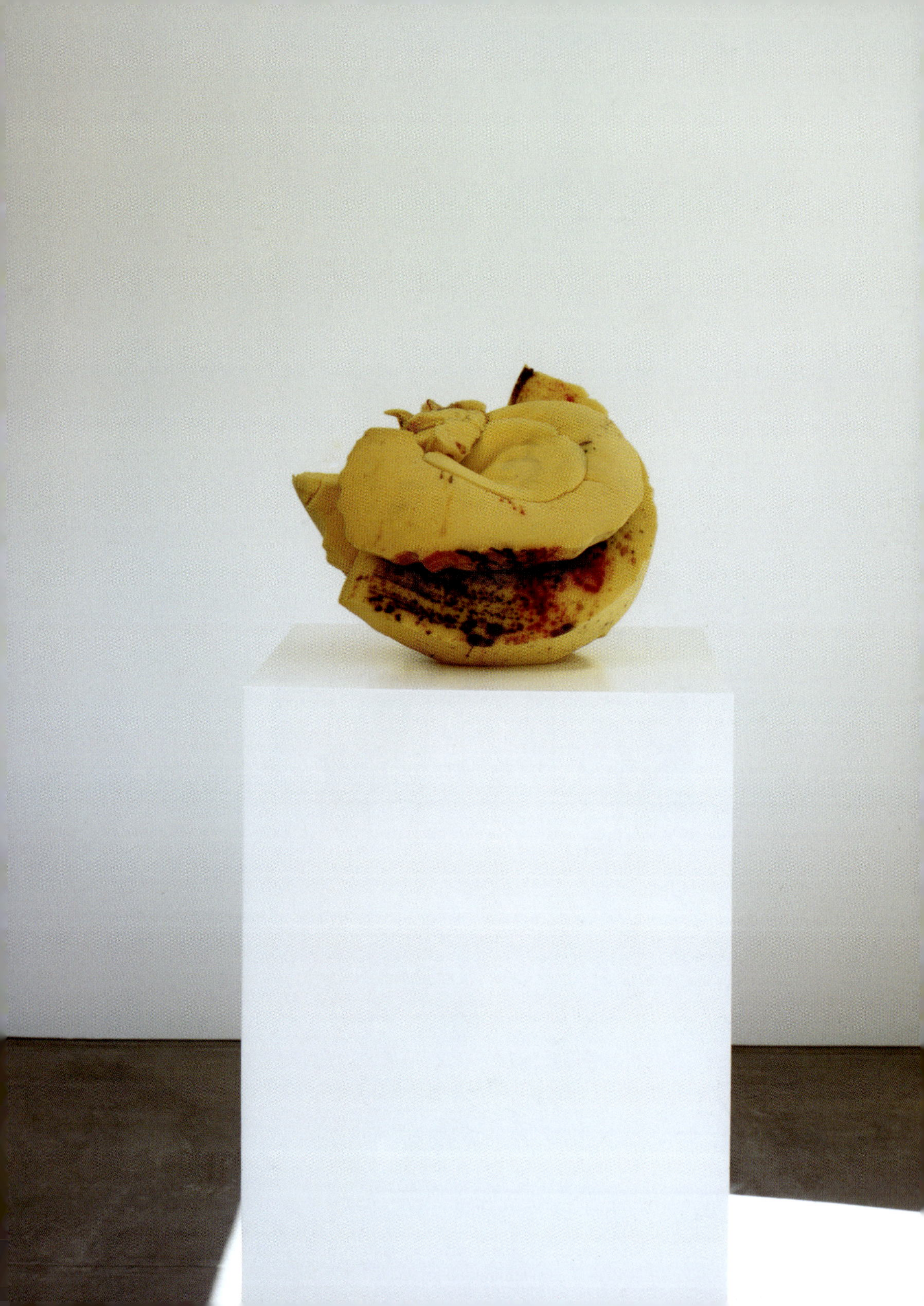

John Chamberlain

Squeeze Play

In 1966, some nine years after John Chamberlain, having momentarily run out of steel, spontaneously detached and twice drove over the fender of his friend Larry Rivers's 1929 Ford, he found himself in Virginia Dwan's Malibu beach house, just as spontaneously making sculptures out of small sponges and string. Annoyed at having his lavishly billowing layers of gently conjoined volumes referred to as car-crash sculpture, curious to try out some other materials, and perhaps seeking to more physically submerge his hands in his making, Chamberlain had been gathering various materials to test, household sponges among them. Sponges kept attracting him. Very soon the possibilities of transposing the pliability of thin steel to a material so willing to yield—and one so completely ordinary as that of a sponge—won him over.

Chamberlain said, "Everybody makes sculpture every day, whether in the way they wad up a newspaper or the way they throw the towel over the rack or the way they wad up the toilet paper." And squeezing/wadding a sponge some six inches in length, then tying it with string, led Chamberlain largely to ban painted steel from his making from 1967 to 1974, with the most notable exceptions being a group of predominantly white pieces made from discarded appliances, in Chicago in 1969, and twelve monumental works begun in 1972 in Amarillo. The simple act of wadding with his hands, instead of the mechanical wadding (crushing, compacting) of units that acted like volumetric brushstrokes congregating in a larger configuration, would dominate Chamberlain's modes of making for those seven years. Urethane foam and cord sculptures alternated with wadded sculptures in other materials, and urethane foam sculptures comprise the most in number during this time—in some part, no doubt, because of the relative ease and speed of their making. The vulnerability of urethane foam to light has kept many of these remarkable works out of sight and/or destroyed them. The exhibition of some forty urethane foam sculptures at Chinati, in 2005–06, curated by Marianne Stockebrand, restored these works to Chamberlain's oeuvre and made amply apparent the simplicity and directness of their making, as well as their revel in sensuality. The beauty of the obvious that Chamberlain championed is never more obvious than in his foam sculpture.

Chamberlain made some thirty small sketches with small sponges and string—referring to them as "instant sculptures." Amongst these is a piece tied with drapery trim with wooden beads, *Sylvester #234* (1966), looking something like a cross between an overstuffed hamburger bun and a large mollusk. The high visibility of the tying device in this and a subsequent work (also from 1966) is unique. Almost always the binding cord is rendered invisible by the resilient foam overflowing the restraining and shaping cord.

John Chamberlain, *Stuffed Dog 8*, 1970

Larger pieces followed the sketches; they are made with sections of urethane foam cut out with a knife, many of them named after provinces in China and exhibited in 1966 at the Dwan Gallery in Los Angeles. As the pieces of urethane foam got larger, so did the amplitude of the curves imbuing them with a buoyant monumentality. The porous, soft tactility and flesh-like tone of the urethane heightens what often appears to be a slow-motion eruption of flesh, as seen in *Lo An* (1966), *Ju* (1966), and countless other foam urethane sculptures. The curvaceous layering and folds already redolent of vaginal folds in the painted steel works become, in the urethane foam sculptures, such as *Kootan* (1966), still more specific—obviously, in large part, due to the nature and look of the urethane. Especially, when viewing details close up or in photographs, it appears Chamberlain purposefully sought to labialize urethane foam. During his brief tenure (1951 into 1952) at the School of the Art Institute of Chicago, he wrote a paper on Indian sculpture, which had impressed him strongly. Little, if anything, in Western culture can match the sensual purity and vivacity of the luscious curves and encyclopedic sexual acrobatics found in Indian temple sculptures, such as those swarming on the facades of the temples at Khajuraho; and this sculpture may well have seeped into Chamberlain's visual intelligence.

In 1967, while continuing to create urethane foam sculptures, Chamberlain, still forswearing painted steel, began a group of sculptures made from galvanized steel boxes he commissioned that were proportionate in size to the cigarette packs he was often seen wadding up at Max's Kansas City, where one or another late-night reveler hoped to carry home the crumpled treasure. Chamberlain literally galvanized these transpositions of everyday sculpture with a compactor and worked on them further in his studio—another form of wadding, now necessitating a machine and prone to sharper angles, folds, and bends than the more openly seductive, curvilinear folds and openings of a contemporaneous foam piece such as *Latback* (1967) with its succulent fluorescence into circularity.

The galvanized works are at once erect, unlike the more squat urethane foam pieces, and fold in on themselves. Their making visually acknowledges the whole out of which each was created. Might they represent the more masculine and/or be a comment upon and a challenge to the boxlike forms so prevalent in Minimalist sculpture, especially that of Chamberlain's friend and supporter Donald Judd?

Another mode of wadding was introduced in the Penthouse group created in 1969. Chamberlain would blow up a small brown paper bag, pop it, drip resin into some of the smashed folds to maintain the structure, and delicately drizzle on a bit of watercolor. A number of them look like blossoms of nostalgia in various stages of distress. Their modest dimensions—about the same as the first sponge sketches—enfold copious visual play. Their blossomlike forming and splashed color were carried over to many of the urethane foam pieces made between 1969 and 1970, especially the lyrical Stuffed Dog group, the first of which was started in 1967 (and probably splashed with watercolor in 1970) and the remaining eight created in 1970 (all exhibited in Stockebrand's exhibition). The urethane foam pieces, of course, rebound in rich curves as compared to the more squashed flatter resolution of the Penthouse works—urethane foam: resilient, bouncy; paper bag: almost completely submissive.

In 1970 into 1971, Chamberlain turned to baking/wadding. He placed Plexiglas boxes, again made to order in volumes proportionate to a cigarette pack, in a walk-in oven and cajoled them into lush slipping and sliding convolutions, just as the heat pushed the Plexiglas to the edge of dissolution. After cooling and removal from the oven, the pieces were treated with various mineral coatings with Larry Bell's vacuum coater; however, because of their rolling irregularities, they were hard to color.

A charged, intuitive directness has marked the best of Chamberlain's making. The stops and starts required to produce the Plexiglas pieces seem to have hindered their fluorescence into full presence. The procedures necessary to the production of the painted steel and urethane foam pieces were more seamless—as were the procedures performed in the final group of wadded works created during Chamberlain's hiatus from painted steel and begun in 1972. Made from industrial-weight aluminum foil formed into balls—much as you and I might do with lighter weight aluminum foil so commonly used in the kitchen—compressed, wadded, and, finally, sprayed with auto lacquer and polyester resin, these pieces have a shimmering, lunar glow that gives them the appearance of a rescued meteor. Exhibited at the end of 1973, many have since either been destroyed by the artist or lost their craggy form due to the flexible nature of the material.

The making of squeezed and tied urethane foam pieces—the most continuous activity pursued by Chamberlain during the period chronicled here—more or less subsided when he returned to painted steel on a regular basis in 1973 and 1974. Small groups were made in 1979 for an exhibition in Cologne. They relate in size and configuration to the Stuffed Dog pieces (1967–70). A 1981 work incorporating paper and paint looks back to the two early foam sketches bound by beaded drapery chord. Undoubtedly, others have left Chamberlain's hands without being properly recorded.

In addition, in 1967, in need of seating, Chamberlain gouged out shallow seating in one of the many pieces of urethane foam in his studio—yet another inspired moment of Chamberlain ad hocness. More couches, even a cradle, followed. When they extended to over ten feet in length, they were called a barge (for his 1971 Guggenheim exhibition, he created one some twenty-five feet in length to be placed in the rotunda). Chamberlain turned to furniture as sculpture before Scott Burton and contemporary successors such as Jorge Pardo. Chamberlain made them site-specific—dependent upon their placement and intended occupants—and they encouraged those occupants to revel and/or dream in horizontality. Furniture as sculpture as instant party.

The urethane sculptures should be counted as an important part of Chamberlain's polymathic pursuits (painting, film, and photography have not been mentioned here). The squeezed and bound urethane sculptures also deserve to take their place amongst the works of the so-called Process artists who came to the fore in the late 1960s and, like Chamberlain, performed everyday physical operations (throwing, folding, smashing) upon pliable, often non-art materials such as felt, molten lead, chicken wire, etc.—artists related to those gathered under the rubric Arte Povera (coined in 1967 for a group show curated by Germano Celant and including Alighiero Boetti and Luciano Fabro, among others) in Italy whose concerns, although often more overtly aestheticized and/or concerned with image making, also engaged ordinary materials and acts. Robert Morris, the self-styled spokesman and dogmatician for the Process artists in New York, ignored Chamberlain (both were represented by Leo Castelli), as did the curators for the museum exhibitions featuring these artists. Although he has never been anxious to be part of a group and seems allergic to anything programmatic, Chamberlain might well be counted as one of the earliest practitioners of Process art together with such artists as Eva Hesse, Barry Le Va, and Bruce Nauman. However, what surely counts most is the apparent ease with which Chamberlain has wadded the everyday into such singular erotics.

Peter Hujar

Lens Love

So directly did Peter Hujar confront us with the unique life of each of his subjects, whether a flower or a dove or the face of a friend, that the candor of his photographs seems to have bypassed art. Now lovingly, now unsparingly, the subject is most often centered in the foreground with little space to retreat from or to—and so are we. Hujar aimed his camera not at the perfect moment but at the vulnerable thereness he shared with his subject. He dared to risk empathy, indeed could seduce with it. Gradually we see what renders this empathy visually articulate is a highly sophisticated formal acuity and a deep understanding of the tools of his making—how the camera lens sees, how the developing fluids transform, how the camera and the naked eye conjoin, how inner vision and outer vision conjoin. The emotions shared with the subject are tempered by the love of the procedures of making that give body to those emotions. The moment fraught with vulnerability is coolly, meticulously constructed.

Hujar's two sojourns in Italy (1958–60, 1962–63) deeply impressed the works of Michelangelo and Caravaggio upon his vision, and imbued him with the resolve to expand his repertoire of subject matter beyond the portraiture and street photography that dominated his photographer forebears from August Sander and Lisette Model to the more recent work of Weegee and Richard Avedon. The silence of an isolated shoe, the humbled drapery of a thrown-out blanket, and landscapes bruised by refuse would take their place in Hujar's vision—so, too, would animals and nudes, who became, in Hujar's view, other forms of portraiture. He invested himself totally in these two subjects.

Around the time of Hujar's birth in Trenton, New Jersey, in 1934, his father abandoned the family; he was raised by his grandparents on a New Jersey farm. Speaking only Ukrainian until he entered school, he must surely have found his first companionship amongst the animals on the farm. After his grandmother died, when he was twelve, his aunts and uncles began to make life miserable for Hujar. On his grandfather's advice, his mother brought him to Manhattan to live with her and her second husband. The following year he received his first camera and began photographing the animals on the farm whenever he visited. This, his first subject, preoccupied Hujar throughout his maturity. The unconditional rapport he sought from and extended to animals catalyzed some of his most moving work. Hujar took many photographs at a farm belonging to friends in Germantown, Pennsylvania; other animal photographs he likely took serendipitously encountering a pasture during a drive in the country. For some two hours Hujar might literally talk an animal into communion with his lens and his feelings. Even the fowl seemed to respond to him.[1]

Intimately close up, generally one-on-one on an animal's turf, sharing intimacies and angles best revealed by the camera, Hujar engaged animals in a dialogue too direct,

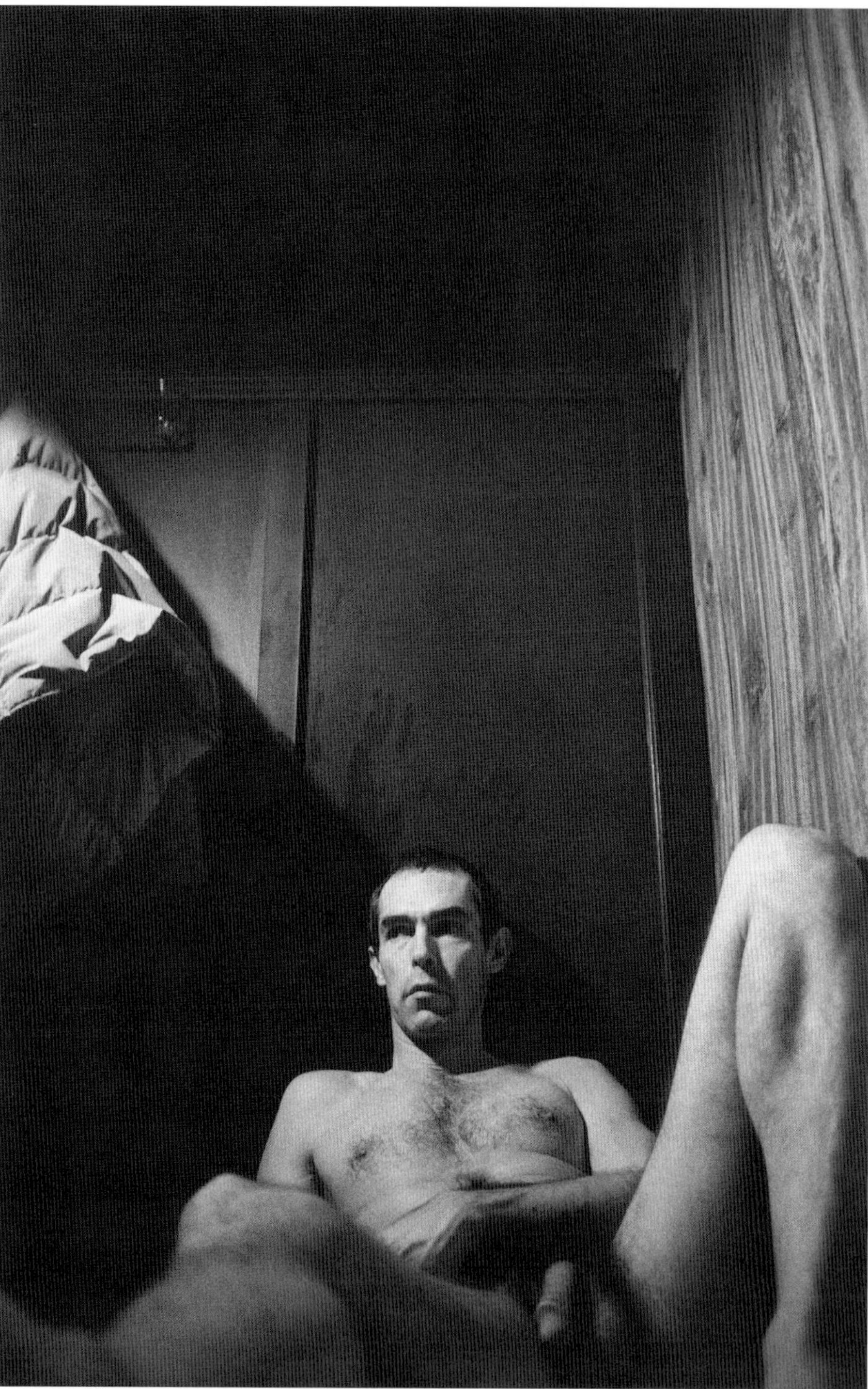

Peter Hujar, *Self-Portrait at the Baths,* 1979

unadorned, and centered to lapse into the picturesque or the emotionally gooey. All the while he turned the photograph into an essay on how differently the camera constructs vision from the naked eye. Except for the periphery of its field, our "natural" vision recombines and constructs our sensory impressions into seamlessly clear focus. The camera lens, however, sees more discretely; its focus ranges from sharpness to blur depending upon the lens and the intent of the photographer.

While Hujar preferred a stark and unstaged mise-en-scène, his intimate understanding of his camera's lens and visceral sensitivity to texture, touch, and pattern activated his planes with a shifting panoply of forming. In a beguiling portrait of one of those cows Hujar might refer to as a self-portrait, the linear play of highly focused, slickly surfaced blades of grass and the equally focused but dense, dry striations of a cow's cowlicked forehead—both in the foreground—against the gradually clumping blur of grass in the background, as well as the diaphanous screen of trees, undermine the viewer's initial efforts to see the entire view in the clear focus of natural vision with a tour de force variegation of mark making. Whether reveling in the groomed perfection of a princess lapdog's silken coat or playing twigs against feathers and woodgrain in the barnyard, the camera lens's touch infused each subject with a uniqueness of presence and place—a uniqueness that achieved its final state under the critical eye of Hujar in his darkroom.

Uniqueness and idiosyncrasy, as opposed to idealization/generalization, mark representations of mortality; and mortality obsessed Hujar. The cow so lovingly encountered lying in the pasture becomes beef. Hujar doesn't spare us the cruel intimacy of its flaying—more graphically than, but mindful of, Rembrandt's painted flaying. A dead cat, its body cut in half by the camera, lies on the border that separates high focus from blur—becoming a metaphor for its own passage. Unsparingly, the camera's angled close-up spills the cat into the viewer's space.

The raking close-ups, truncations, and seemingly unmediated encounters with his subjects reflect the influence of Model, the photographer Hujar perhaps most deeply admired. And, possibly, the emphasis Model placed on unconventional subject matter helped empower Hujar to pursue a subject so uncool, yet so personal as domesticated animals. Model reveled in the freedom granted her by a 35mm camera, whereas Hujar preferred the control, richness of detail, and fluidity of focus that his 2¼ by 2¼ Leica permitted. The shallow stage-like space and/or radically tilted horizon Hujar photographed his subjects in, as well as their untrained poses, tips those subjects into the spatial and psychological immediacy often as-sociated with 35mm practitioners from Henri Cartier-Bresson to present-day photographers. However, Hujar's stark, centralized compositions and meticulously nuanced flow of light, focus, and detail brilliantly embody the vision made possible with a large-format camera. And that vision unified the oppositions of immediacy and deliberation, emotional openness and aesthetic distance, spartan composition and richness of detail, grit and grace.

Vulnerable openness conjoined with aesthetic distance mark Hujar's human nudes much as they do his animal subjects. While Hujar's lens focused more frequently, and often more specifically erotically, on male nudes, he maintained a far remove from the classicizing, hyper-aestheticized homoeroticism practiced from the late nineteenth century to the present—from Baron von Gloeden's campy adolescents, to George Platt Lynes's balletic refinements, to 1950s beefcake photographers like Bruce of Los Angeles, to Robert Mapplethorpe's idealized S and M photos, to Bruce Weber's and Herb Ritts's couture pin-ups. The flesh of Hujar's nudes is warm to the touch and gaze, earthbound, and more often informed by Caravaggio and Egon Schiele than Greek or Roman sculpture.

Hujar shot most of his clothed and nude portraits in one of two studios he inhabited successively, from 1960 to his death, on Second Avenue in the East Village of New York City. Upon entering Hujar's loft you found yourself in the middle of his life—in the middle of his studio/bedroom/living room, an unadorned, funky space with little more than several straight-backed wooden chairs, a threadbare Oriental runner, and a bed, all serving as both furniture and photography props.[2] Most of the people he photographed played a role in his life, from casual erotic encounters to friends such as Candy Darling, Ray Johnson, Vince Aletti, and Lynn Davis, to the beloved compatriot of his last years David Wojnarowicz. Like Sander, whom he admired, he wanted to catalogue the world; but unlike Sander, Hujar focused almost exclusively on the world he played an immediate role in—a world his photographs helped create as much as document.

More overtly autobiographical than forebears like Sander or a peer like Diane Arbus, Hujar nonetheless generally avoided the unposed slice-of-life-and-plight shots favored by younger autobiographers like Nan Goldin and Mark Morrisroe. He preferred a one-on-one dialogue enacted and posed in his space. Hujar slowly seduced his subjects with his lens. His nudes, whether male or female, are frequently in a prone and vulnerable pose—arms behind head, or knees laxly bent, for example. They resonate simultaneously with eroticism and contemplativeness, openness and self-containment. Very odalisque, very post-coital, the intertwined circular and triangular disposition of their limbs relates more to the tradition of female nudes in Western art than to the tradition of male nudes that, if prone, are likely to be dead Christs, saints, or fallen warriors and, if standing, ready to do battle. These nudes are made vulnerably and viscerally available to us. Whether a softly fleshed round baby enveloped in a polyphony of angular blanket folds; or the languidly propped up, giant-angel–tattooed backside of the performance artist Ethyl Eichelberger; or an opulently curved and pregnant, Ingresque female; or the artist himself, prone and viewing us from the other side of the lens with an abundance of melancholy charm, Hujar's nudes, like his domestic animals, are urged without mediating barriers or contrapposto into the viewer's visual space. "The closest thing to waking up next to someone in bed."[3]

Abruptly, we find ourselves in an intimate situation, one that evokes the power of love. However, we don't become personally familiar because the subject remains an enigma to us, slowly revealing the artificiality of his or her stark pose and the meticulous lushness of the photograph's printing. The erotics of the figure become an analogue for the erotics of art—being alarmed into attraction by a subject we have had no prior relationship with and then subsiding into pleasurable contemplation.

While some of Hujar's finest photographs lovingly reveal his female friends, he was unabashedly drawn to the male body. His forthright examination of all its parts frequently embody literally and figuratively the autoerotics of making. He claimed no role in the sexual revolution marked by the Stonewall riots in 1969 but gained a following as one of its pioneering artists. His male nudes seldom celebrated conventional beauty and sought out instead a more mortal glamour and pathos. Slackness of flesh and thinning of hair engage Hujar's lens as passionately as the arrogance of youth. In one of his many self-portraits, we find Hujar slumped naked in a cubicle at the Saint Mark's Baths, sliding into shadow and blur at the bottom of the plane. The grim loneliness, occasionally the byproduct of anonymous sex, seems to flicker in the uneven light. We see the body at its most vulnerable, an icon of mortality. Hujar admired Weegee and expressed a desire to photograph, as Weegee had, in the morgue.[4] This photograph may be as close as he got.

Elsewhere Hujar was filled with forthright ardor and curiosity, nowhere more so than in his photographs of various acts of sexual self-gratification. One of his more startling images barely contains a contortionist twisted like a pretzel in self-fellation—part Caravaggio, part tantra. The viewer's eye is so close, one can almost feel the bristly scratch of the threadbare carpet on the performer's back. In another work, the subject simultaneously leans into and slides out of the front plane, giving us his backside as he penetrates his ass with a huge double dildo, the composition torqued as awkwardly as the act. Two of Hujar's closest friends have suggested this photograph is a self-portrait made in response to Mapplethorpe's self-portrait with a whip in his ass.[5] Perhaps the most stunning of these photographs places the camera and the viewer, literally and

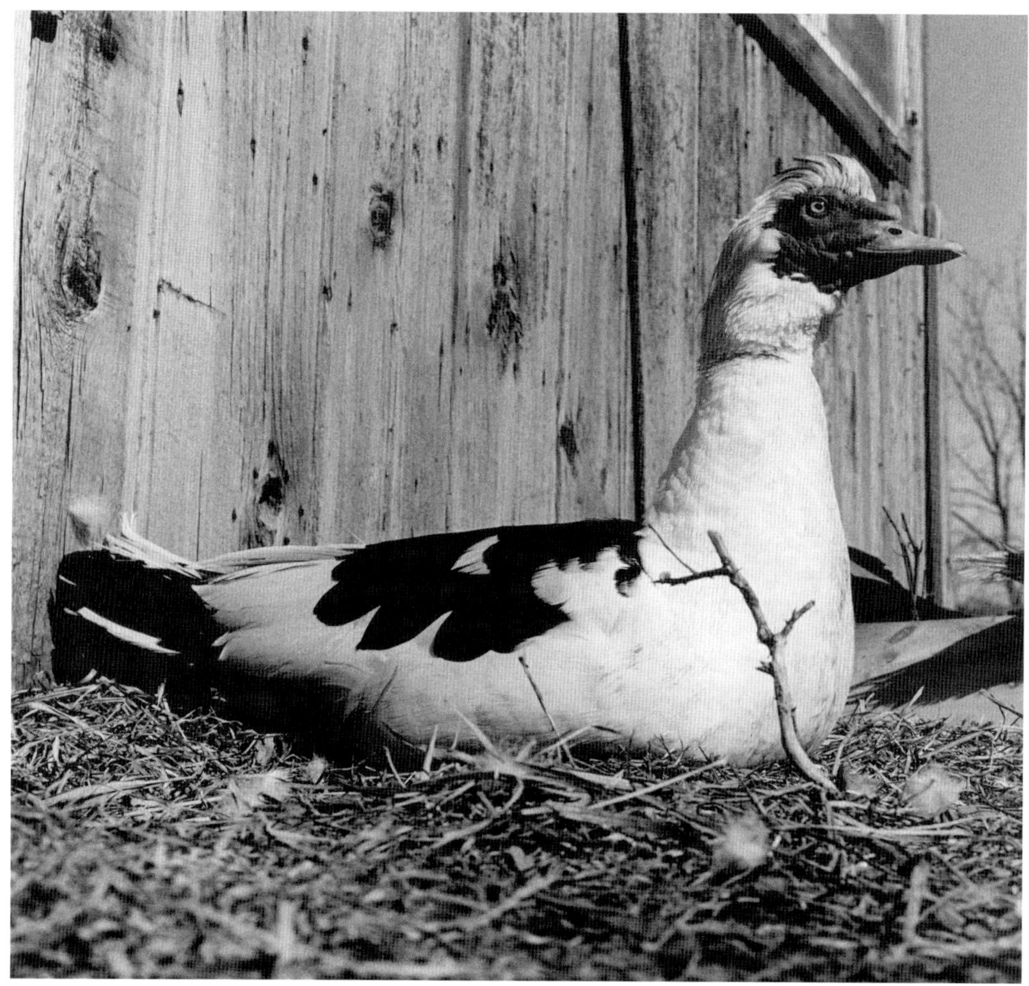

Peter Hujar, *Duck, Germantown* 1982

figuratively, in the same position as would be the missing head of a masturbating subject whose body is presented in radical monocular foreshortening that calls to mind Mantegna's similarly foreshortened dead Christ. And the camera has shot the ejaculation of the subject who has shot. Sexual self-gratification, aesthetic self-gratification, the eye of the camera, the eye of the subject, and the eye of the viewer are interchangeable. The erotic climax and the aesthetic climax are one. The eye's body housed within the camera becomes the body in the room.

Hujar kept alive the tradition of masterful touch in photography but reinvented traditional subject matter with his stunning conjunction of aesthetic restraint and emotional openness. He could identify with the animals he photographed to the point of thinking that he was creating a self-portrait—without irony or sentimentality. And few have seen deeper into the mortality of the nude, whether with joy, arousal, or tribulation—or shifting shades of all three.

1. Author's interview with the executor of Peter Hujar's estate, Stephen Koch, November 28, 2000.

2. Author's interview with the photographer Lynn Davis, December 12, 2000; and author's visit to Hujar's studio in 1985.

3. Ibid., Davis interview.

4. Author's interview with Vince Aletti, November 6, 2000.

5. Author's interview with the photographer Gary Schneider and the performer John Erdman, October 30, 2000.

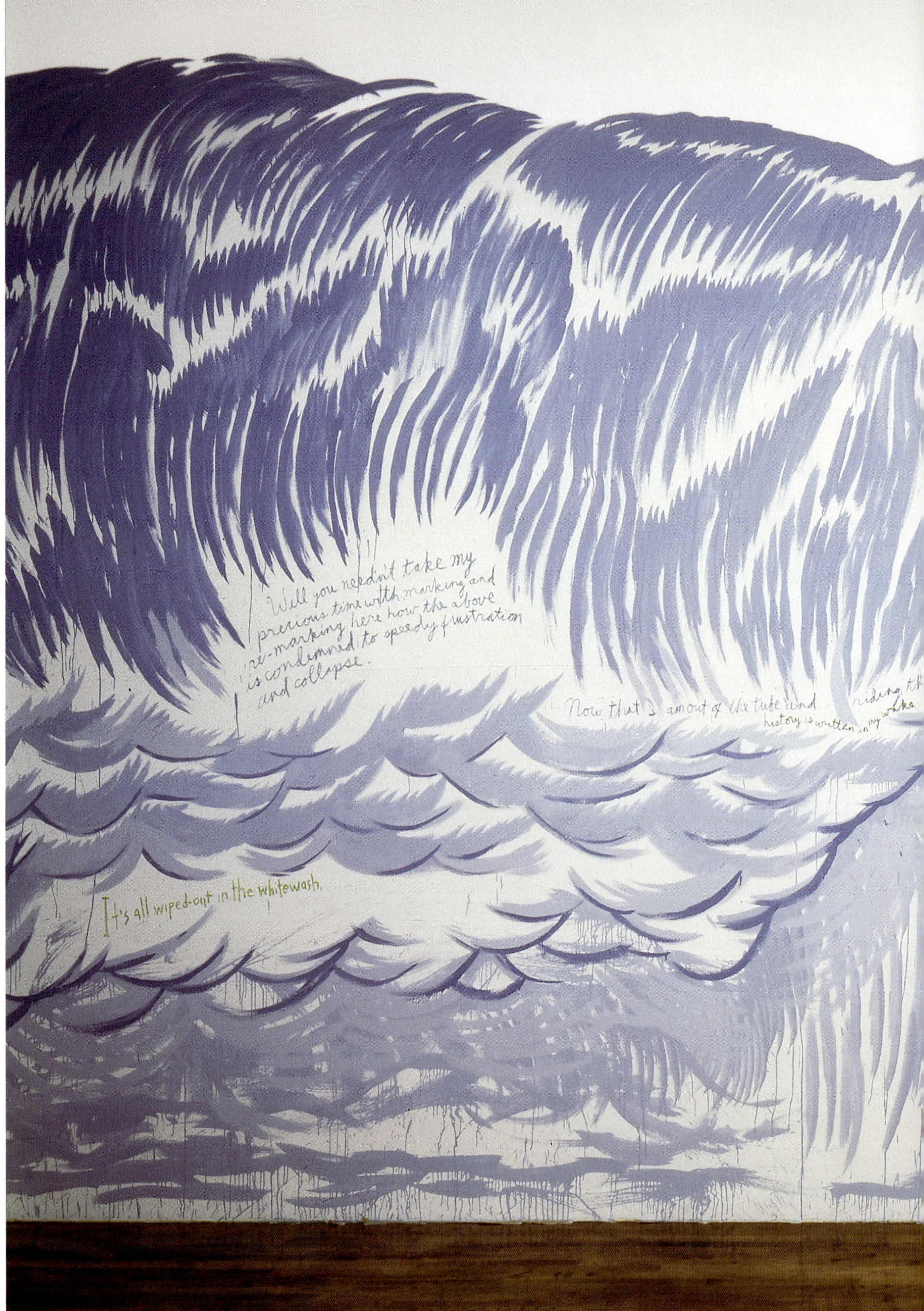

Well you needn't take my precious time with marking and re-marking here how the above is condemned to speedy frustration and collapse.
Now that I am out of the tube and riding it history is written in my wake
It's all wiped-out in the whitewash.

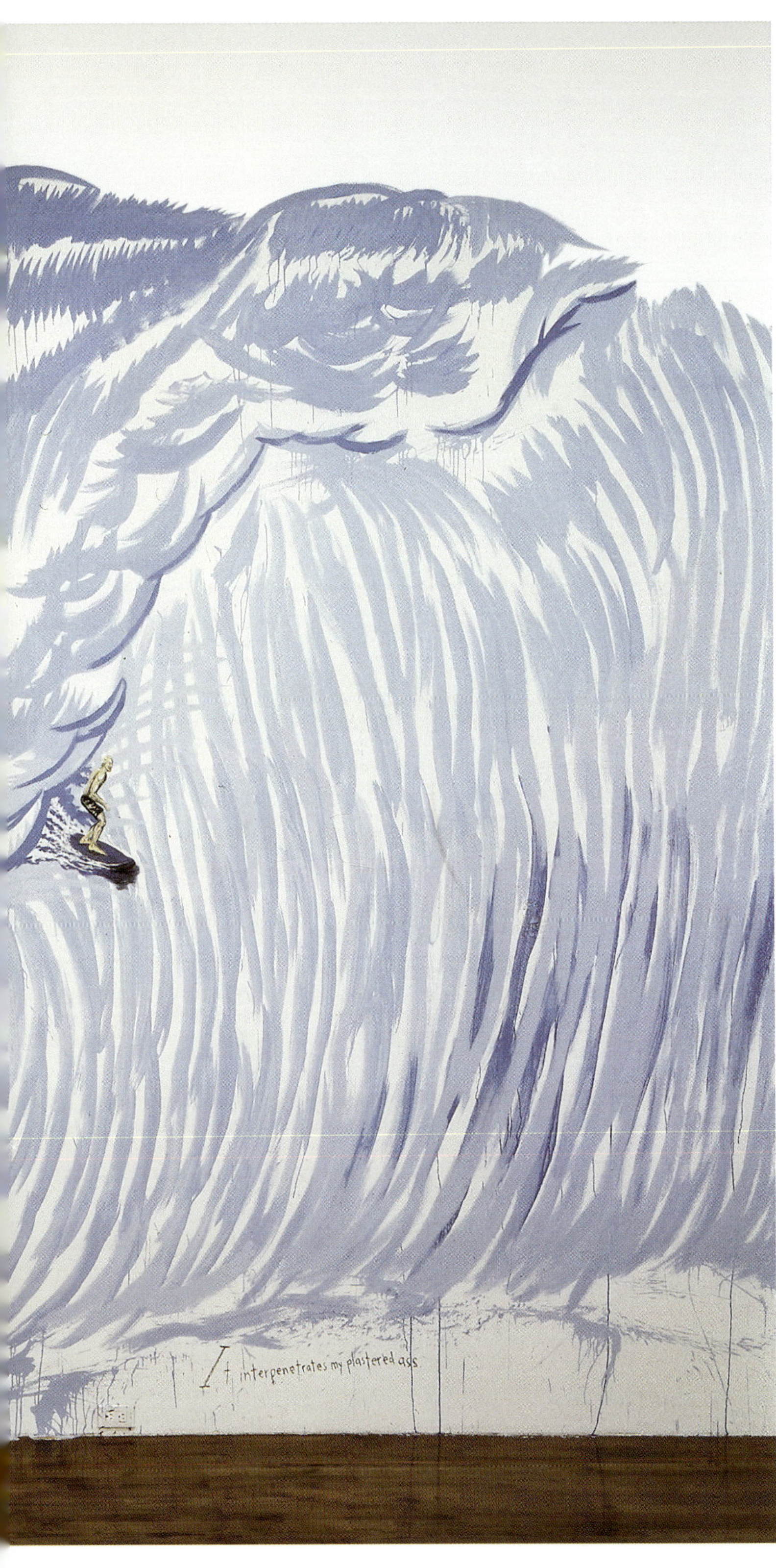

II. SEA CHANGE

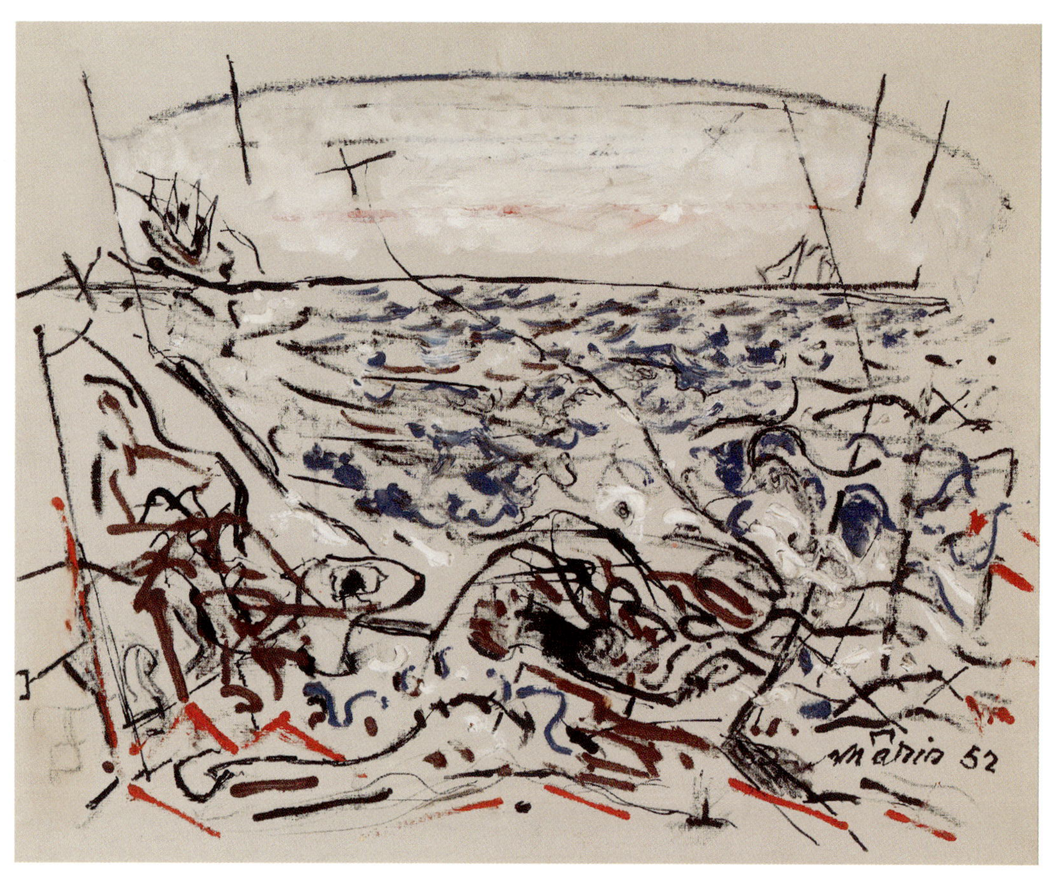

PREVIOUS SPREAD: Raymond Pettibon, *No Title (Well you needn't)*, 1997, installation view, David Zwirner, New York, 1997
ABOVE: John Marin, *The Written Sea*, 1952

Oceanicity

Full fathom five thy father lies
Of his bones are coral made
Those are pearls that were his eyes
Nothing of him that doth fade
But doth suffer a sea change
Into something rich and strange.
Sea nymphs hourly ring his knell.
— William Shakespeare,
The Tempest

In 1947, the poured paint that had sporadically marked Jackson Pollock's planes since the mid-1930s became the primary activator of his making. The literal and figurative sea change that fully transformed Pollock's painting began with his move to the environs of the ocean in 1946, when he and his wife Lee Krasner took up residence in the Springs, in East Hampton. Four of the nineteen works he created in 1947 bear ocean-referent titles (*Watery Paths, Sea Change, Full Fathom Five, Phosphorescence*) that herald his newly arrived-at resplendence of rhythmically wavering liquidity.

Like the title of the painting, "phosphorescence" is derived from Phosphor, the morning star—the first light. It is a luminosity occurring at a temperature below incandescence. It is a conundrum. In darkness, under certain conditions at the beach, hands or feet drawing in the wet sand bring forth tracks of phosphorescence, especially when the full moon silverplates the sea. And the luminous trails of light racing across the silvered depths of Pollock's surface imbue this phenomenon with a cosmic, painterly resonance.

Shortly thereafter Pollock would eurhythmically extend his trails of paint across larger planes to create a vagrantly overlapping calligraphy quite like that drawn upon the sand by the ceaselessly breaking waves. His paint-flinging arm would merge the flow of his body's consciousness with the phantom rhythms of the sea. Paintings like *Number 1A* (1948) rise up and over us suddenly, like a breaking wave. Pollock's "I am nature" can often be seen as "I am ocean."

The ocean's vastness, fathomlessness, and its clear surface rhythms and tides have been a major inspiration not only for Pollock, but for many of America's artists, especially for the American modernist painters who shared a growing urge toward a vastness realized in all-over rhythmic liquidity. Whether it is depicted as subject, as underlying metaphor for painting, or as both, the ocean's eminence is such that much of the history of American art since the mid-nineteenth century can be seen as reflections of—and on—its depths.

In European art, the ocean plays a far less consequential role. With exceptions such as the icy stillness of Caspar David Friedrich's occasional seascapes, the turbulent oceanic mists engulfing many of J. M. W. Turner's paintings, and the softly murmuring tide of geometry pulsing on the planes of Piet Mondrian's proto-abstract ocean and pier paintings, the bodies of water seen in European art are relatively contained and defined by land. The Seine River is to Parisian modernism what the Atlantic Ocean is to New York's modernism. But of course the United States is bounded east and west by ocean, and its early European settlers arrived via the Atlantic.

In spite of the upheavals of the Civil War, serenity-infused paint continued to flow into the vast horizons and meticulous detail of the Luminist painters' landscapes well into the second half of the nineteenth century. Martin Johnson Heade reveled quietly in the stillness where the ocean seeped into salt marshes and bays full of clear, empty space and contemplative water that not even the wind would dare corrupt. In *Gremlins in the Studio* (ca. 1865–75), his customary, subtle planar distortions of mimetic space are given a twist that undermines a sense of wonder with self-conscious artifice. The seamless illusion of water that merges with the canvas plane is interrupted at the bottom of the painting as we suddenly notice the shelf of an easel holding up the illusion we can no longer so readily believe.

Winslow Homer, one of the greatest seafarers of paint, turned away from his Luminist-influenced oceanside bucolics when he moved to the seclusion of Prouts Neck, Maine, in 1883. There his paint began to confront and battle with the elemental dangers often encountered on the sea—dangers that fishermen are more accustomed to than most of us, as they toil in one of the most hazardous occupations known to man. Oneness with nature gave way to threat and antagonism as furies of foaming ocean grayness embroiled Homer's planes, all but flooding the horizon and dissolving all thoughts of any security from gravity. Here, three boatmen, only their heads and upper torsos visible, are momentarily suspended and powerless between a wave that menaces the forward plane of the canvas and a cresting wave rising up and into the full moon—*Kissing the Moon* (1904). In the terrible beauty of Homer's late paintings, the paint's liquidity no longer simply describes, but palpably enacts and empowers the movements of the water. Paint dramatizes the sea, and the sea dramatizes paint.

If Homer merged his paint with vision, Albert Pinkham Ryder impelled his paint to materialize the visionary. Shakespeare, Wagner, and the Bible fueled his densely concentrated lunar broodiness, all sometimes lavished on a single painting over a span of ten years. Ryder's torturous love and arduous layering of the flow of his medium's viscosity, as well as his preference for a few simply massed forms and rhythmic repetitiveness, disposed his romantic imaginings to the movements of the sea—a sea glistening with moonlit moodiness. Whether a shipwrecked Jonah about to be swallowed by the whale, or Lord Ullin's daughter fleeing her father's wrath at her elopement into the fatal wrath of the ocean, or a dense black moonlit cove elegizing a flat plane of sky and ocean, Ryder's protagonists always materialize the sensual yearnings and strivings of his never-ending process—a process inexorably propelled into the unknowable.

The dramatically visible painterly process practiced by both Ryder and Homer had a crucial impact on America's twentieth-century modernism as tides of paint and ocean converged and flowed toward abstraction. While their co-pioneer modernist, Georgia O'Keeffe, was more inclined to the rhythms of flowers, mountains, and the dry sea of the desert, John Marin and Marsden Hartley continuously painted the sea. The aqueous cubism of Marin's watercolors was surely influenced by the Parisians he liked to disdain, and he more openly embraced Homer and James Abbott McNeill Whistler. Certainly the growing painterly vibrancy and brio of the oil painting that dominated Marin's art after 1930 was indebted not only to his increasing presence at Maine's oceanside, but also to Homer's equation of seaworthiness and paintworthiness. "In painting water, make the hand move the way the water moves," Marin wrote. While he always grounded his painting in the observed and often worked outdoors, Marin tilted the painted plane up still more into flatness than had Homer and gave his strokes greater freedom from their descriptive tasks so that they might more readily revel in (and reveal) the process of the painting.

Hartley, more willingly than Marin, assimilated early European modernism but also looked to Native American art and Mexican folk art, and especially to Ryder, whom he dubbed "moonlightist" and gravely portrayed in 1938. Indeed, the angular, abbreviated mountains and triangulated clouds of Hartley's late foreboding seascapes owe much to Ryder's forming and mood. In many of the late works executed between 1938 and 1943, Hartley's mutely expressive, monumental figures conflate homoerotics, Christianity, and the simple dignities and harsh indignities of fishermen's lives—most explicitly in drawings such as *Five Lobstermen* and *Christ Figure–Pieta Concept* (1940). Beach-bound leisure and sensuality are darkly ritualized by the somber beauty and iconicity of his male bathers.

The brighter light and more fluid openness and ease customarily associated with beach leisure were restored in the ocean- and Matisse-misted landscapes that Milton Avery so radically and gracefully pared down and flattened into his canvas plane from the mid-1930s onward. Like Hartley and Marin, Avery continued to rely upon observable place and space. At the same time, the surrealist-influenced early work of the Abstract Expressionists and their peers began to explore more internalized, purely subjective modes of abstracting, often seeking correspondence between the depths of the ocean and the unconscious depths of the psyche. Their forms and space depended upon imagined emanations arising from the flat rectangularity of the canvas plane.

Freud's and Jung's explorations of consciousness were joined by a growing interest in humankind's beginnings. The artists' search for the origin(al) often fused so-called primitive and archaic cultures with the cosmological quests of the various branches of science. Myth, microscopy, marine biology, automatic drawing, cave painting, tribal art, psychoanalysis, and more were stirred together in a hothouse potion meant to catalyze an art at once primal and new.

Notwithstanding the fact that the ocean covers more than seventy percent of the earth's surface, it remains the last great wilderness of our planet. The Dark Food Chain of the sea floor, so totally isolated and different from the Light Food Chain we know, may well be where earth life originated. And to these depths dived many an artist's imagination—for instance, that of Mark Rothko, who had studied biology and anatomy as a student. In the 1940s as he sought new ways to make his painting means reflect mythic ends, Rothko filled his planes with bottomless, shifting films of liquidity that frequently hosted mysterious marine forms with amorphous shapes and undulating tentacles. His friend Adolph Gottlieb began to loosely grid his planes and populate them with "pictographs," as simply formed as they are referentially permissive. We find lyrically glyphic marine forms often mixing with heads of Greek or Oceanic or African inclinations, isolated eyes, and a variety of abstract heraldry. Both Rothko and Gottlieb had earlier befriended Avery and had been influenced by the sophistication of his planar simplicities and the quiet splendor of his palette.

This subjectified space and search for the primal grew more fraught and apocalyptic with the horrific conclusion of the Second World War. Now Rothko, Pollock, Krasner, and their peers sought to dissolve the remaining vestiges of their pictorial descriptiveness and to infuse the very process of painting with the mythic. The radiance of the new painterliness that resulted readily lends itself to ocean referentiality, as of course to much else. Willem de Kooning, as profane as Pollock was pantheistic, knew how to make it impossible to know whether a lushly rising arc echoed a female breast or a cresting wave. Paint as flesh, paint as water, woman as water, woman as landscape—all are aswirl in ambiguities of painting and meaning. When de Kooning moved his raucously urban rages of paint from New York to East Hampton, the motions of his brush changed as much as the light those motions embodied as his art absorbed the new surroundings.

De Kooning's disavowal of his fellow Abstract Expressionists' metaphysics and his refusal to make distinctions between abstraction and figuration strongly influenced a younger generation of gestural painters who were seeking a more openly referential and secular painterliness. In her efforts to make her acutely calibrated whiplash strokes reflect her deep emotion-filled memories of the landscapes she inhabited, Joan Mitchell looked to de Kooning for inspiration. Although her preference was for lake and river, she too was drawn to the ocean. On the eve of her departure from New York to residence in France, she painted *To the Harbormaster* (1957), titled after her friend Frank O'Hara's 1954 poem. She marshaled her mutinous strokes into attacks and counterattacks of the ocean's conflicting motions and her conflicting emotions—a glorious tumult of departure and arrival.

Some, like Fairfield Porter, looked to de Kooning to energize their paintings' strokes and light but remained committed to the observed. While Porter painted the ocean not far from Pollock's studio and also in Maine, where Homer, Marin, and Hartley had painted, he took a more unassuming joy in the seen and the painted than any of those artists. Similarly indebted to Abstract Expressionism, Jane Wilson embraces the all-over atmospheric suffusions found in Rothko's 1950s paintings but subtly and painstakingly nudges her planar architectonics into ocean and sky.

The rolling organics to which the painting hand is so naturally prone and the synesthesia with the flow of the ocean in which those strokes so often evolved were more often than not held in high disregard after the mid-1950s. In the abstraction of the 1960s, autographic touch would be neutralized and regimented by the grid. Nonetheless, Frank Stella, one of the most rigorous and compelling of these spartan abstractionists, turned to the great ocean epic of *Moby Dick* in the 1980s, when he found the need to break out of his rectilinear strictures into the drama of baroque spatiality, albeit in high-tech fabrication. And the so-called Pop artists replaced cosmic vastness with comic-book frames and landscape with mediascape. Roy Lichtenstein turned his hand into an ironic imitator of mass-reproduction techniques and imagery. His *Seascape* (1964) gleefully mocks the seaboard strokes of his forebears and pseudo-mechanically mimics the clichéd sentimentality of the postcard sunset, although his compositional skill and flat, reductive silhouettes look back, like the older Avery, to Henri Matisse as much as they turn to the Yellow Pages.

If art's course is no longer so regularly charted on the sea, there still remain notable individual art mariners, though their vision, like Lichtenstein's, is not always drawn directly from the sea. Unique in his commitment to the ocean is Malcolm Morley. His early paintings contain seamless illusions of ocean liners that flaunted their artifice far more emphatically than Heade did, frankly revealing their photography-based, travel-poster origins. In time, Morley looked back to more painterly endeavors and turned from travel posters to traveling the world's water, seeking guidance for his rushing brush while keeping in view de Kooning, Marin, and Homer, as well as the model ships and reveries of his childhood.

Both Vija Celmins and Peter Cain enlisted the mediation of photography. In 1968, Celmins, seeking a way to extend the neutralized, no-color, no-composition, no-personal–mark making strategies of the Minimalists, turned to photographs of the ocean that she had taken while walking her dog in Venice, California, and then to the black-and-white images of the moon transmitted by Luna 9. Her hyper-precise renderings of the ocean's surface might have been the pride of any nineteenth-century Luminist were it not for her photo-based ocean's horizonlessness and colorlessness. More than they are about sea sorrows and jubilations, Celmins's obsessive poetics are about revealing simultaneously rote, absurd, and joyous acts of making as well as her acute awareness of the difference between looking and making.

Just like Celmins, the younger Cain was influenced by Andy Warhol's deadpan media-reproduction means and ends, as well as by Morley's early radical realism and the astringently empty abstraction of the 1960s. Like the work of many younger artists, Cain's is at once remote and personal. In *Sean Number One* (1996), Cain blew up his lover's beach-inclined head to billboard dimensions and turned head and horizon perpendicular to their customary location on the plane. Yet this formal self-consciousness and publicness is combined with an intimate, loving account of the unique features and idiosyncrasies of Sean's face and neck, details that can only distract from his bearing as a fabricated media image—more specifically personal and public than are Hartley's bathers but just as enigmatically concealing.

The return to illusionism practiced by Frank Moore looks not to photography but to the nineteenth century and such artists as Heade, who painted America's Edenic expanses. But Moore's pristinely painted forests harbor dollar-sign leaves and fake Native American teepees; his Niagara Falls give off lacy vapors that are filled with the symbols for the chemicals in the industrial waste polluting their waters. The more refined and luminous his paint becomes, the more barbed his eco- and AIDS-activist humor becomes. The subject of his *Birth of Venus* (1993) bears a penis and has been washed upon the beach into medical and/or drug-addict waste. Is Venus more exotic or more ordinary than coral, which looks like a rock but is an animal and can be both male and female? How long can Venus endure this polluted sea? Is Venus radioactive, like the sponges absorbing measurable amounts of plutonium in waters where nuclear waste has been dumped? Could Venus survive the algae

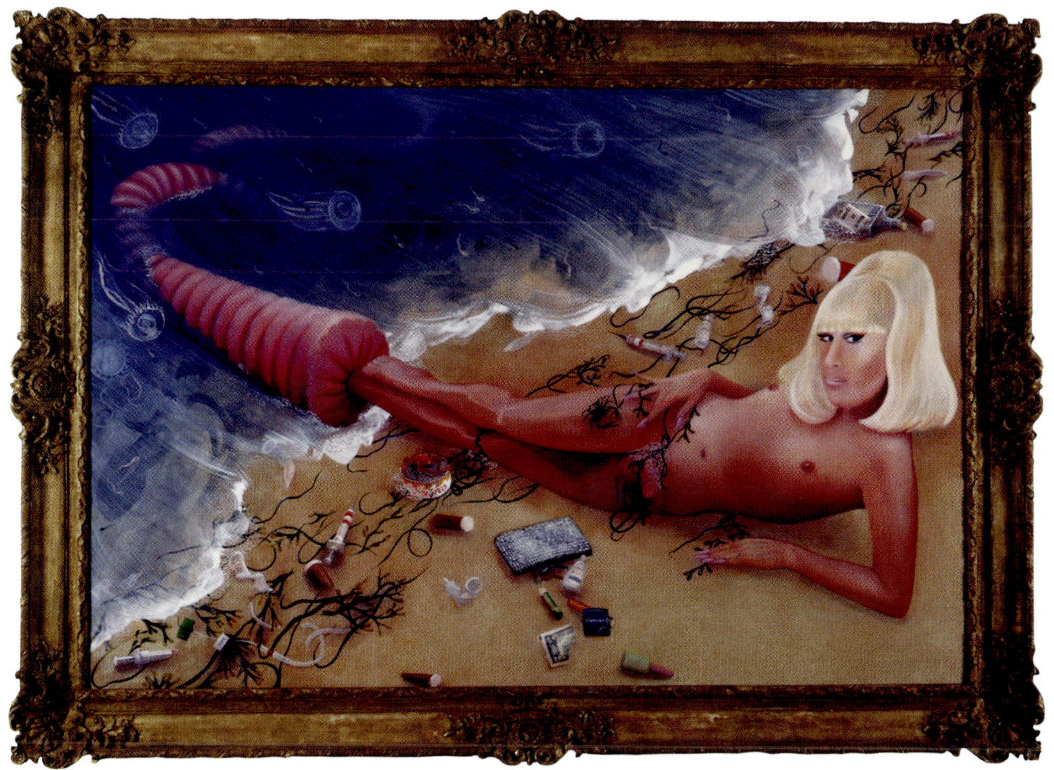

Frank Moore, *Birth of Venus*, 1993

bloom that has on occasion in recent years suffocated the local bay-scallop population? And is the metaphor of sea change harder to come by since the pearl shortage caused by the recent death of 150 million Akoya mollusks in Japan?

Raymond Pettibon practices a more absurdist humor than Moore. With off-key brilliance, his zine-inspired drawings exacerbate and challenge images with seemingly unrelated phrases. Erudite, highly literate, fanatic of Hollywood noir, now scabrously and hilariously reflecting our culture's violence, unexpectedly drawing and/or writing a grace-filled haiku, he seems an unlikely surf enthusiast; but draw surfing he does. His California dreaming is hardly blond and buffed and carefree, however. His waves are chilled and thrilled by murder mystery plots. And, with this dark bow to the ocean, this essay ends, in the hope that this brief survey of the confluence of American art and the ocean might increase our understanding of these two life-giving, powerful, and fragile resources.

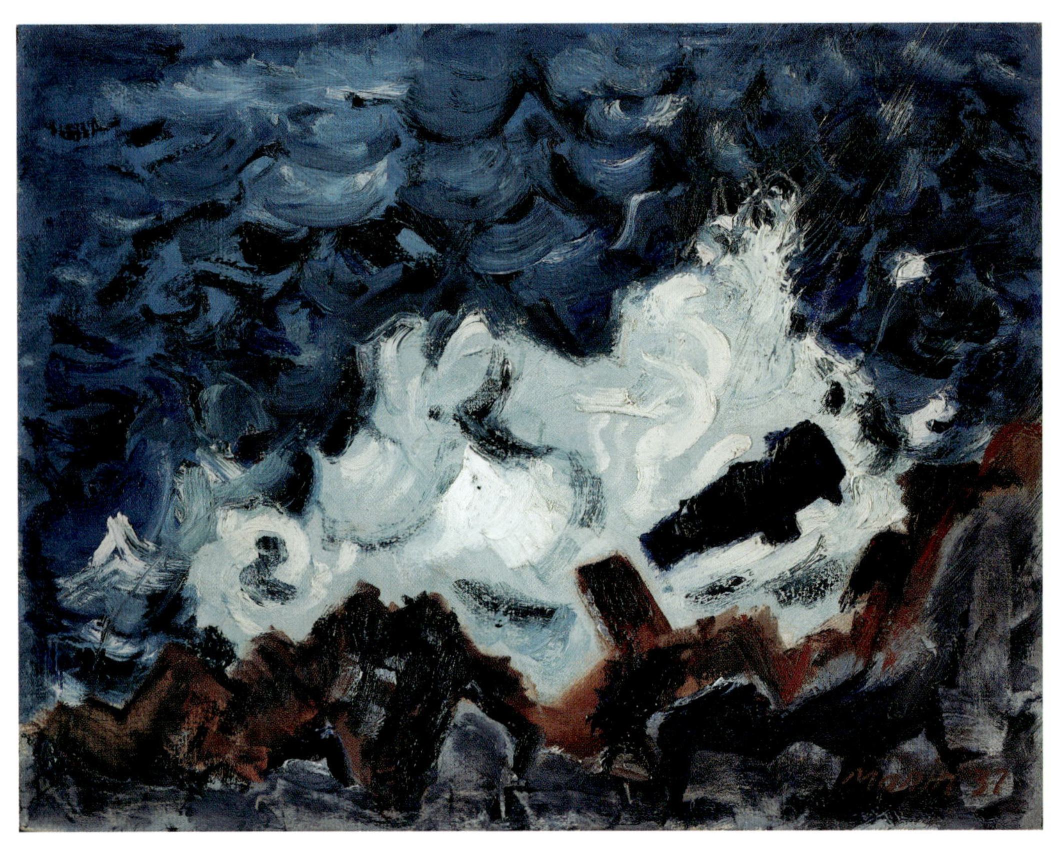

John Marin, *Wave on Rock*, 1937

John Marin

Marin in Oil

Born in 1870, John Marin became one of the leading early American modernists; like many of them, he sojourned in Paris to absorb the lessons of Paul Cézanne, Henri Matisse, and the Fauves. Marin arrived in Paris in 1905 and was soon taken up by Edward Steichen, who was a major enthusiast of Constantin Brancusi and Matisse—although his own paintings remained enshrouded in symbolist and Whistlerian mists. In association with Alfred Stieglitz, Steichen became the major conduit for transmitting Parisian modernism to the frontiers of the American art scene. In 1908, he rallied his young compatriots, Patrick Henry Bruce, Arthur B. Carles, Alfred Maurer, Max Weber, and Marin to form the New Society of American Artists in Paris. Marin had already exhibited in the Salon d'Automne and the Salon des Indépendants in 1907; and, in 1909, together with Maurer, he exhibited at Stieglitz's 291 in New York. In 1910, Marin was given his first one-person exhibition at 291, and he was included in the legendary Armory Show in 1913.

Unlike his fellow American artists in Paris, Marin was initially not so anxious to add "new" to his vocabulary. In 1907, the year the younger Pablo Picasso painted his brutally beautiful and pivotal *Demoiselles d'Avignon*, Marin was creating etchings of Venetian and Parisian views influenced by James Abbott McNeill Whistler. However, by 1910, his preoccupation with line had begun to increasingly extend into watercolor, now reflecting the freewheeling bravura of the Fauves' paintings in oil and a kind of liquification of Cubism's crystalline planes. Marin's visually evident joy in his subjects and the liquidity of his medium, as well as in the procedures of his making, resulted in some of the most compelling watercolors created in the twentieth century and earned him a reputation as one of America's greatest painters.

The uniqueness of Marin's almost Oriental, liquid Cubism was nurtured and promoted as an indigenous phenomenon by Stieglitz, America's first and foremost impresario of modernism. Stieglitz promoted Marin as a watercolorist, but neither he nor America was fully prepared to accept Marin as a painter in the denser medium of oil. Marin had sporadically painted in oil from the outset of his career; but, after 1930, oil painting became his major preoccupation. Going back to and expanding upon a singular group of small oils that he had painted in 1916, he started painting with an intense visceral and physical agitation, as well as a painterly clarity that, with the exception of Chaim Soutine, were unparalleled in Europe and in America until the advent of Abstract Expressionism. If the frenetic energy of New York's rapidly rising skyscrapers had sparked Marin's watercolor dynamics in the second decade of the twentieth century, the ocean's rolling rhythms took precedence in the oil paintings. In Marin's final paintings of the late 1940s and 50s, he conjured a breezy and open synthesis of his watercolor and oil paintings.

Marin's turn to oil came at a time when his reputation as a watercolorist had reached all but epic proportions. In 1925, Stieglitz started a new enterprise, the Intimate Gallery, with Marin and Georgia O'Keeffe as his major stars (he had married O'Keeffe in 1924, with Marin as witness). It was not mere hyperbole when, in an introduction to the catalogue for his artist's 1927 exhibition, Stieglitz referred to "Marin's established and ever-increasing prestige as probably the world's foremost watercolorist." The energy Stieglitz had invested in Marin was devoted almost entirely to his abilities as a watercolorist and would largely continue to be so. But while Stieglitz's charisma remained compelling, his own development was now virtually complete, while Marin's unceasing intensity would push his brush into the unknown until his death. His scarce public appearances made Stieglitz his surrogate, while he, like most of Stieglitz's artists, became shrouded in mysterious seclusion and self-containment. No one stepped forward to champion the oil paintings, and Marin's reputation as a vanguard modernist, as a great American artist, as a watercolorist, and as a painter in oil were often seen by critics to be in conflict.

The 1920s witnessed the formation of a modernist-dominated art establishment: the Phillips Memorial Collection opened in Washington, D.C., in 1921; the Barnes Foundation was chartered in 1922; and the Museum of Modern Art in New York was inaugurated in 1929 with an exhibition of Cézanne, Paul Gauguin, Georges Seurat, and Vincent Van Gogh. At the same time, the need to define a specifically American art was becoming increasingly acute, not only in conservative circles, but in liberal ones as well. This goal frequently entailed denying, ignoring, or vilifying the manifestations of modernism in American artists. Abetted by Stieglitz and by Marin himself, many critics who admired Marin ignored the contribution that Fauvism and Cubism had made to his work. Enthusiasts such as Waldo Frank, Lewis Mumford, the German art historian Julius Meier-Graefe, and Paul Rosenfeld all sidestepped Paris and tended to focus on Marin as the foremost practitioner of the peculiarly American medium of watercolor.[1] Thomas Craven, beginning in 1924 a retrenchment from modernism that would become shrilly racist in the 1930s, bemoaned both Marin's new expressiveness and "intellectual design." He praised the earlier work, which he claimed had emanated from Cézanne, when Marin had, Craven said, "quite simply abandoned himself to nature."[2]

Stieglitz's artists had little to unite them but some of their common roots and a general commitment to modernism. America's search for identity in the 1920s was exacerbated by the fact that no monolithic style or group could claim the spotlight. Marin did indeed stand alone, as did so many others, yet he did not emerge from a cocoon of his own creation. He was unique in his ability to merge Cubism not only with the organic irregularities of the rhythms of nature but also with the organic irregularities of the rhythms of paint. From the mid-1910s through the 20s, when Cubism spread out from still life back into landscape, both in Europe and America, it generally took a crystalline sculptural form—the stained-glass Gothic Cubism of August Macke, Lyonel Feininger, and, occasionally, Paul Klee; the cylindrical and tubular constructions and construction workers of Fernand Léger; the steely staccato of the Futurists; the slide-ruled regularity of Le Corbusier's and Ozenfant's Purism in France; and Charles Sheeler's and Charles Demuth's Precisionism in America. Marin's more internally impulsive liquidity separated him from hard-line Cubism, but his painterliness also had little in common with that of his friends Marsden Hartley and Arthur Carles. He was alone, in America, in his strong commitment to the revelation of the painting's making. He had little influence on fellow artists except as role model (especially for practitioners of watercolor, such as Demuth). What was peculiarly American, and what Marin did share with Hartley, O'Keeffe, Sheeler, Demuth, and others, was a need to ground painting in specific observation—the sites of European paintings were usually more generalized and abstracted—and the merging of this empirical observation with the more romantic realm of intuition. Unlike Arthur Dove, Hartley, and O'Keeffe, Marin eschewed overtly spiritual symbolism. His openness, intuitive directness, and refusal of the programmatic: all could be labeled "American," but all had gained much of their momentum and vocabulary from Europe.

The issue of Americanism escalated into rancor in the 1930s, spurred on by the political confusion and the economic disasters caused by the Depression. Many viewed with deepest suspicion anyone deprived of Anglo-Saxon heritage or appearance. On the art front, bitter battles would be fought between modernists, on the one hand, and Social Realists and Regionalists, between abstractionists and representationalists. Marin, in spite of his French-Spanish name, would increasingly be referred to as a Yankee, apple-pie American. His reputation continued to grow, but largely on the basis of his watercolors. Although an empathic look back to American nineteenth-century painting was highly visible in many of his oils, they were largely viewed with circumspection or negativity.

Stieglitz could insulate Marin from the deprivation of the Depression, but apparently he had neither the energy nor the desire to wage the kind of battle for Marin's oils that he had mounted for the watercolors. Plagued by his own financial woes, he closed the Intimate Gallery in 1929, but quickly rebounded to open what would become his final venture. With the help of photographer Paul Strand and aspiring photographer Dorothy Norman—who became not only his most devoted financial backer but also his Boswell—Stieglitz opened the all-too-aptly named An American Place in 1930. To inaugurate the Place, as it came to be known, Stieglitz presented first a group show, and then a Marin watercolor exhibition.

Meanwhile, Marin himself inaugurated the decade with a revival of the vitality of the Weehawken Sequence. Of the nine oils he painted in 1930, eight comprised a series of small (ca. fourteen-by-eighteen- or eighteen-by-fourteen-inch) landscapes moving from fall through winter (Fall, nos. 1–5, Winter, nos. 6–8). *Fall of 1930, No. 1, No. 2,* and *No. 3* are virtual curtains of crackling color that spread over all or almost all of the flat, horizonless surfaces. Differing lengths of choppy strokes thrust up and down in the irregular clotted verticality of the wooded, hilly landscape. The strokes move from virtual independence to coagulating bunches, from dryly pulled thinness to fuller-bodied wetness, from scumble to shrub-like clusters. Ochre, orange, bright yellow and red, and greens moving from yellow to blue hum the acid harmonies of fall. Chronologically and stylistically, these paintings are situated between the frenetic energies of André Derain's and Maurice de Vlaminck's Fauvism and the harsh, crusty monumentality of Clyfford Still's autumnal abstractions of the late 1940s.

The last two Fall paintings encourage the paint to breathe in more representational space; also more representational are all three of the Winter paintings, suffused with the season's chalky muteness. The last oil painting done in 1930 is of the sea. The grayed blues and broad, relatively modulated stillness of stroke, as well as the horizontal bands of outcropping rocks and an island barely squeezed between the high horizon and the top edge of the canvas, are combined in a muffled, reductive composition reminiscent of Whistler's soft-voiced seascapes. The firmer strokes and the high horizon are pure Marin. The seascape was a quiet beginning, in oil, of a relationship that would grow in depth and intensity to become responsible for some of Marin's most compelling paintings.

In the 1930s, Marin would unite the medium of oil with the subject of the ocean to create deeply moving medleys of paint. The rhythmically charged flatness and openness, the willed surrender to paint's liquidity, and the entrancement with the workings of nature so crucial to Marin become totally compatible and congruent with the movements of the ocean. Its incalculable repertoire of flux, flow, and reflectiveness moving into and out of flatness would bring Marin into full mastery of his newly favored medium. The weight and lustrous density of oil is a better match for the ocean than is the thinner-bodied translucence of watercolor. With notable exceptions (such as the four Off York Island, Maine, works of 1922), most of Marin's watercolors of the sea from the 1920s are stabilized and centralized by sailboats or dominated by the rocky shore. Often they were motivated by the movement of light and the currents of air rather than by the more palpable currents of the ocean itself. In oil, Marin immersed himself not in its ambiances but in the nature of the ocean itself.

In 1931, the ocean configured more than half of the some twenty oil paintings Marin completed in Small Point, Maine. Generally, an uneven diagonal of irregularly coruscated strokes anchors the painting on a rocky shorefront and counterpoints the insistent, overall horizontality of the rumbling sheet of sea that rises (more than it recedes) almost to overflow the thin strand of sky at the top of the canvas. Occasionally Cubism rises to the surface, but more often it is dissolved in more organic configurations. Here a pine moves out of natural shape to rise up in a pointed stack of thickly painted planes; there an island or rock outcropping becomes a band or zigzag that reflects the canvas rectangle more than the subject. In one painting of Small Point Harbor, with a lower than customary skyline, densely painted floating bars and rectangles bring the sky back into unity with the surface plane and seek their reflections on the sea—ambassadors of flatness perhaps more Oriental than Cubist.

"In painting water, make the hand move the way the water moves," Marin wrote.[3] Marin set about making his brush simultaneously seaworthy and paintworthy, synchronizing the ocean's surface with that of the canvas. The strokes vary with the tide and weather. Choppy strokes react to the wind wrinkling the surface; more smoothly modulated strokes mirror placid clarity; strokes of rolling regularity follow the tide; bundles of pointed strokes are pushed into each other as they bounce off rocks that have been pressured into shapes by thinner, scratchier marks. Marin's pleasure in the rich viscosity of oil now brought the churning physicality of paint into greater tension with the canvas support and urged the flow of oil into a compositional clarity that had frequently been lacking in the more experimental Weehawken paintings. He now had good reason to write about "the paint job which is a lusty thing."[4] By the end of 1931, he had established the painterly principles that would guide his hands into the next decade.

In 1933, Marin rented the house on Cape Split in Addison, Maine, that he would buy the following year and paint in, during the warmer months, for the rest of his life. Here his new power in oil reached its apogee. In *Off Cape Split, No. 1* (1934), the daring diversity and boldness that mark the boulders in the foreground play against the greater regularity of the glistening green and blue of the ocean. The monumental simplicity of the boulder shapes grants vastness to the painted sea that covers but a tiny piece of canvas. *The Ladle* (1934) beams and revels in more intimate pleasures of paint. A low, splashed rectangle of sea is topped by a slathered scoop of paint that is in the island named in the title. The island rides the sea with porpoise-like playfulness and plasticity.

Marin's Maine is not a hospitable bather's resort. (The politer side of the ocean's shore is visible in the soft sand- and front-filled painting done at Jones Beach in 1931, where Marin seems to have paid his respects to Eugène-Louis Boudin, whom he openly admired.) The Maine coast invited drama more than dalliance. The rugged, often brooding pine- and rock-bound shoreline is reflected in Marin's dark palette: deep blues and greens that are offset by a limited range of earth tones. Black takes on a breadth as color and shape that it had seldom been permitted in the more regularly linear role it played in the watercolors of the 1920s.

The forcefulness of oil's density and the highly activated accumulation of strokes into the great massing of the seascape rock formations are pushed into a more orderly urgency in the new oils of New York City. In New York, the boulders become Cubist canyons; once more, Cubism holds sway in the city. The watercolor-dependent linearity of the 1928 cityscapes gains in weight and planar tension. The dark tones glide and collide in density rather than thinness. Light is no longer so exclusively derived from the whiteness of bare canvas, but shines through and is derived from the paint itself. A nocturnal, lunar clarity most often pervades the urban scenes, but a garish yellow sun can also be called into a daytime play. Marin's increasing compositional complexity and sureness are more than visible in the packed, pulsing stacking of planes and shapes in *Lower Manhattan from the Tip End* (1931). The almost chaotic escalation of Cubist checks and balances moves into and out of spatial depth in oppositions that are clearly calibrated to come to rest in the canvas's flatness. In *Study, New York* (1934), the more open and decoratively flat lateral dynamics are decelerated by a broad, fretted interior frame that mimes Art Deco skyscraper detailing.

Marin was now obviously becoming more reliant on finishing some work in his Cliffside studio. And most of the paintings of human figures that he was producing were now not only finished in the studio, but started there. The figure, which had first reappeared in a 1920 watercolor, and then among the oils of 1928, began to make increasing appearances in oil after 1931. At first it evinces none of the gusto so evident in Marin's other subjects; the figures are part of a peculiarly American race that is naively simple and stiff and seldom embodies any sensual or psychological pleasure or pain, yet still resists a purely formal abstractness. They are literally and figuratively a race suspended in animation. Members of this race also populate the paintings of Maurice Prendergast, Louis Eilshemius, and Milton Avery, among others. Many of Marin's figures of the 1930s seem to be unintended victims, rather than motivators, of the transient, urban planes that surround them—subways, waiting rooms, restaurants, and so on. The four participants in *Figures, Street Movement* (1935) are among the few that Marin successfully integrated into the city's space and paint. The clattering of transparent rectangles from which the figures barely emerge makes a giddy hieroglyph out of the uneasy anonymity of the urban pedestrian. More at home on the plane are the figures at the sea: first, more and perhaps most successful in their planar integration, the mundane bathers at Jones Beach in 1931; then, starting in 1932, nude bathers that become increasingly acrobatic in the late 1930s and finally rambunctiously ethereal in the 1940s and early 50s. These arcadian New England naiads, at least in their later manifestations, may well be one of Marin's few direct debts to Cézanne—specifically to his *Bathers* (1906), which Marin saw around 1941 for the first time and is reported to have admired.[5] Nevertheless, even the figures' openness to the ocean does not always prevent them from seeming like an afterthought; at best, their presence appears to be a happy coincidence.

Almost without question, Marin's strongest achievements in the 1930s were at the ocean. Since until quite recently the subject has been relegated to mothballs or to the tourist trade, to claim that Marin is one of the great seascapists, if not the greatest one, of the twentieth century seems rather faint praise. But excluding Piet Mondrian's radically reductive, sea-inspired abstractions of the early 1910s, only the more brooding and sculptured beauty of Hartley's Ryderesque late-1930s seascapes can vie with Marin.

Marin's and Hartley's devotion to the sea as subject reveals the still-strong roots their painting had in nineteenth-century American landscape—Albert Pinkham Ryder for Hartley, and Whistler and Winslow Homer for Marin. While Ryder was a direct influence on Hartley, as Whistler was on Marin, Marin's relationship to Homer is mostly one of parallels and affinities. The generous fluidity of Homer's watercolors may have had some influence on him, but more likely they simply and importantly set a precedent for the credibility of the medium. Homer bemoaned the public's preference for his oils to his watercolors; Marin bemoaned the reverse. Homer, too, loved the drama of the sea, Maine, and paint, but his thinner application of paint and more representational space find no reflection in Marin's impassioned flatness. Marin's ocean paintings of the 1930s are related to Homer in the heroic ruggedness of their sites and mood—a mood that, for many, made each a pioneer of one of America's last frontiers. At the moment when Cubism was shattering previous notions about painting, Homer, in his old age and traditional technique, was generally considered the most important painter in America. And at the moment when Abstract Expressionism would again shatter previous notions about painting, Marin, in his old age, would generally be considered the most important painter in America.

In the 1930s, modernism was besieged as never before since its first introduction to American art. The right as well as the left accused it of excluding meaningful subject matter. The right sought a populist comprehensibility and looked to the Farm Belt for art's salvation, while the left sought to replace aesthetic radicalness with political radicalness, reviling the formal elitism that failed to protest visually the poverty at home and the terrifying rise of totalitarianism abroad. The decline in Hartley's reputation that began in the late 1920s was, at least partially, caused by the suspicions aroused by his continuing trips to France and Germany; the very titles (locations) of his landscapes offered his detractors evidence enough. Yet Marin's reputation continued to grow. His supporters searched their closets to find yet another American flag to drape him in; even his harshest critics bowed to his skills (generally in watercolor).

The Regionalists, with Thomas Hart Benton the most prominent among them and Thomas Craven their evangelist, sought to atone for the sins of European excess committed by the modernists. Benton, who had been to France (1908–11) and had absorbed Cézanne, Neo-Impressionism, and Fauvism, rejected modernism in the 1920s in favor of trying to transplant El Greco to his native Missouri soil. Craven celebrated the prodigal son's return to "strong representation and clearly defined meanings which may be shared and verified by large groups of people."[6] Stieglitz he labeled a "Hoboken Jew hardly equipped for the leadership of a genuine American expression."[7] Marin he still credited with "poetic insight" and "talent," but he decried Marin's inability to escape from Stieglitz's permissiveness.[8] Craven found that George Grosz, Diego Rivera, and José Clemente Orozco, together with Benton, were returning art to the people and declaring the tenets of modernism dead.[9] Neither Craven nor anyone else could guess at the radical American modernism that would burst forth in the following decade, with one of Benton's most avid students in its vanguard.

If the Regionalists and the Social Realists (largely led by the Eight) were vying for credit in the purging of French influences from American art, the beleaguered supporters of modernism were only slightly less anxious in their denials of France. Marin's rising reputation was confirmed in 1935 by the first monograph to be published on him, by E. M. Benson. With Marin's collusion, Benson went out of his way to insist that "Marin's plastic solutions are generally the result of being catapulted into them by the sharp impact of an experience with nature."[10] After condescending to Cézanne, Benson continues his often-sensitive descriptions of Marin's development without a single mention of Fauvism or Cubism; the framing devices of the 1920s are merely referred to as "cloud enclosures." Benson's book set the basic mold for most of the succeeding efforts of Marin supporters—a mold formed almost entirely by nature, America, and watercolor. The oils, especially throughout the 1930s, would be greeted with ambivalence at best.

In 1936, Marin was honored with a large retrospective at the Museum of Modern Art; the show included 160 watercolors, 32 etchings, and 21 oils, the last all done between 1931 and 1935. Stieglitz, who had difficulty with all institutions other than himself, was made director of the exhibition, and catalogue essays were contributed by Henry

McBride, Hartley, and Benson. Any retrospective at this time would perforce have to reflect watercolor's majority in Marin's output, but neither McBride's short, chatty essay nor the deep warmth of Hartley's words touched on the oils. Benson acknowledged their new importance to Marin, but assigned any cogent judgment of them to the future. Again, Fauvism and Cubism were bypassed, and Marin was proclaimed "an isolated figure in American art."[11] Marin was indeed now quite isolated, but he was hardly building on a foundation composed solely of Whistler and nature. As his friendship with Hartley and Carles continued, so too did his dialogue with modernism.

If Marin himself had any doubts about his oils, they were not visible in the paintings. In the late 1930s, oil continued to gather in force and physicality; the increasingly turbulent ocean fumes and foams across some of his most successful paintings. In *Wave on Rock* (1937), the entire canvas is swamped by short, peaked, muscular strokes that lap and layer as they gather in on the central spume of frothy white. Such paintings as *Sea After Hurricane* (1938) and *Heavy Sea* (1938) continue this tumultuous overallness and rejoice in the drama of the power of paint to turn the emptiness of canvas into a vast polyphony of rhythmically coherent mark making. "As for message—as for story—The very doing—the very way it is done—the very what is being done—by they the parts—lead to this message—to this story—in fact is the message—is the story."[12]

Marin's work and his words bear strong connections with the Abstract Expressionism of the late 1940s and 50s, but his vastness remained contained within the confines of easel painting. Until the end, twenty-two by thirty inches would remain the almost standard size of his oil paintings. The compositional checks and balances retained but radically flattened by the Fauves and the Cubists would always stay a part of his vocabulary. Even in his most frantic paintings of the ocean, the strokes surrender some surge to the rectangle, whether in a narrow band of horizon, or in their sporadic flattening out in confirmation with the rectangular edges of the canvas. "Order" and "boundaries" are as important to Marin's vocabulary as "movement," "forces," and "disorder." In *Lobster Boat, Cape Split, Maine* (1938), the short, choppy strokes—of the ocean and the thinner, longer flurry of strokes of the sky—are driven leftward with gale force. But the clouds gather to a near halt in the upper left corner, and the overscaled triangle of the lobster-boat prow is firmly anchored in flatness to the bottom edge of the canvas.

The frames Marin frequently carved and painted, from 1930 on, for his oil paint-ings—rarely for the watercolors—simultaneously reinforce the view inside and its resolution into objectness. The conventional frame's task of punctuating and isolating the view into the canvas is subverted with colors and configurations that relate to the painting and help pull it back into flatness. The frames often extend interior framing devices to the exterior edges of the canvas. They were carved and painted with a simple directness—something like a restrained folk art rococo. The panoramic objectness that dominated painting from the late 1940s until quite recently renounced all frames and exulted in making Marin's quite difficult to accept. The recent revival of more pictorial space has brought frames back into play and now offers a better climate for Marin's harmonic intentions. When they are not troubled by a certain artiness, the frames do indeed add an extra dimension to the tension of the painting plane. Conceptually they are closer to early Cubist devices and to the occasional frames Hartley had made as early as 1914 than they are to the more traditional window-view framing made by Whistler in the nineteenth century.

Marin's dialogue with flatness, a dialogue that would again become more specifically Cubist in the 1940s, relates him (as well as Carles) to a whole new group of modernists who were coming to the fore in the 1930s. European modernism was once more gaining momentum. The American Abstract Artists Association, including such artists as Josef Albers, Burgoyne Diller, and George McNeil, banded together under the umbrella of abstraction that had been formed by the influences of Picasso, Matisse, and Piet Mondrian. Stuart Davis's jazzy rearrangements of mundane Americana were breathing new life into synthetic Cubism, and two émigrés from Europe, Arshile Gorky and Willem de Kooning, met and began an exchange with each other and with both Picasso's and the Surrealists' work. Gorky, first with his brazen 1920s pastiches of Cézanne and then those of Picasso done in the 1930s, was the earliest to embody the new and more willful confrontation with European modernism that would lead into the great American abstraction of the late 1940s.

In spite of Marin's professed wariness of the French, until well into the 1940s he was regarded by many artists living in New York as America's major carrier of the torch of modernism. It is unlikely that he had any direct influence on the younger generation, but he was certainly strongly admired by them, especially by de Kooning.[13]

Marin's increasing prominence notwithstanding, the painter in oil remained an embattled figure. The Stieglitz group grumbled about the oils and Stieglitz himself showed little of the fervor he continued to evince for the watercolors. (At his death, Stieglitz owned some two hundred Marin watercolors, but barely a handful of the oils.) It has been reported and denied that Stieglitz, who had started exhibiting the oils together with the watercolors in 1931, tried in 1938 to dissuade Marin from the darkness of his pursuits in oil.[14] Marin responded to the many criticisms of his oils with a rather hilariously defensive introduction to his 1938 exhibition. Addressing his "Oil Kids," he concludes by observing that "there be those who have said—may still say—You should never have been born—Give them not a thought."[15] The critic Jerome Mellquist, who had already favorably reviewed the oils included in the 1936 Museum of Modern Art retrospective, was one of the few to praise the oils in 1938.[16]

If Marin's impasto was not as wild and thick in its viscosity as that of Chaim Soutine's paintings, his painterly physicality was nonetheless quite singular in America. Perhaps only Edwin Dickinson's wispy Whistlerian seascapes and figure studies of the 1930s can match Marin's ardor in exposing painting in the making. But the trenchant physicality and somber tonalities of his oils evoked negative reviews from the critics of the day, whose orientation was more closely geared to the smooth gyrations of his watercolors. (Many of the watercolors of the 1930s actually followed oil's lead into brooding gravity.) Not until the paint began to thin and the colors to brighten would Marin's oils be met with favor.

Marin's role as precursor and precedent-maker for the budding new modernism would become increasingly distanced by differing intentions, but many striking parallels would continue. He had preceded the younger artists in his liquid enlivening and loosening up of the Cubist grid, but he would continue, to varying degrees, to be dependent on his observation of nature. Many of the future Abstract Expressionists were becoming more and more engaged with the aleatory procedures of Surrealism and the Urwelt of the unconscious. In addition, the Mexican muralists, whom Craven had praised for their popular subject matter, were now instead being studied for the possibilities they held out for modernism to achieve a new, heroic scale. This interest in scale was reinforced by the work on murals done by many of the artists who joined the Works Progress Administration to survive the Depression (both Pollock, who had studied with Benton at the Art Students League, and de Kooning joined the WPA in 1935).

Marin's 1936 retrospective took place in the same year as *Cubism and Abstract Art*, but that same year the Modern also staged *Fantastic Art: Dada and Surrealism*. Surrealism was renewing and modifying the modernist dialogue with Primitivism and spurring a new American interest in myth. These concerns were reflected and influenced by some of the Modern's other exhibitions: for example, *American Sources of Modern Art* (including Aztec, Mayan, and Incan art) in 1933, *Prehistoric Rock Pictures in Europe and Africa* in 1937, *Twenty Centuries of Mexican Art* in 1940, and *Indian Art of the United States* in 1941 (the same year that a Joan Miró exhibition was presented). The new abstraction being partially catalyzed by these exhibitions drew further encouragement from the large selection of Wassily Kandinsky's work available in New York with the opening of the Museum of Non-Objective Painting (now the Guggenheim) in 1939.

Marin's love for the observation of nature would, in the mid-1940s, give way increasingly to studio conceptualization and the memory of nature rather than its direct experience, but until his last breath he disavowed abstraction. In 1939, he still turned to nature directly to breathe life into his paint: he looked again at the wooded landscape and mountains that had previously activated his brushes. In thirteen small (twelve-by-sixteen–inch) paintings of spring, each a different view of mountains and foliage, a lightening of touch and brightening of palette began to set in. The lower horizon line of many of the paintings challenges the flatness of the canvas, and the predominant overallness of the ocean paintings is interrupted with the more independently isolated configurations of the woods. The strokes bristle and stipple rather than speed; turbulence subsides into sunnier joy.

This renewed interest in mountains hardly spelled the end of the ocean for Marin. His rushing brush would never stop seeking synchrony with the organic excitement of the sea. Gales and hurricanes continued to race across his canvases; but here, too, dark drama began to ease more and more into evanescence. *My Hell Raising Sea* (1941) was painted with much of the party rowdiness implied by the title. The festiveness is underscored by the increasing appearance of playful nudes by the sea, as well as by a new interest in circus performers, both human and animal, which had made their first appearances in his work in the 1930s. The boats, so frequent in the watercolors, now begin to move more regularly through oil, and they, like the nymphs and the frequently included islands, make shapes that counterbalance the surge of the sea.

After 1937, the frequent move of the watercolors toward the opacity of oil was arrested, and the medium's inherent transparencies were fully restored. Some of this transparency began to seep into the oils of the 1940s. Marin began to show more concern with the reflection and refraction of light. The oil was thinned, but hardly to watercolor consistency; hues grew more lucid or were lightened with white. The layering of wet strokes created a more complex modulation of light. The sea's and the canvas's surface, as a mirror of light, became more pronounced; the dense, dark blues and greens surrendered to a greater variety of not only hue and tone but also thick and thin paint. Bare canvas returned, but now to achieve a greater dynamism than in the earlier watercolor-dependent oils. In *Maine Sea with Island* (1940), the heavy black marks begin to thin and fade and the frantic strokes to subside; light and color are invited in to play a more significant role: green shimmering with white bobs up and down on the ocean's blue. In *Pink Rocks and Green Sea*, painted in the same year and at the same site, the surface is bleached and thinned by mist-shrouded sunlight. By 1944, the impasto had moved into a new collusion, with lilting immateriality. Only the insistence of the broken green horizon line and the schools of wriggling and rippling blue-green strokes separate the striated sky from its reflections on the ocean surface in an untitled seascape of 1944. The clarity of counterpointing strokes, light, and space assume a blissful ease.

The passage of Marin's oils into energized grace found more favor with his critics, but the oils were still often overlooked. The *New Yorker* profile of Marin by Matthew Josephson, published in 1942, gives evidence of his increasing fame, but makes not one reference to the oils.[17] Mellquist, however, continued to praise the oils and made Marin the final chapter ("The Master of Equilibrium") of his book on American modernism, which he began with Whistler.[18]

The continuing attempts by Mellquist and his generation to isolate the Americanism in modernism is in marked contrast to the new internationalism that was growing in New York in the 1940s—a new Americanism that was openly assimilating European modernism and pitting itself directly against it. The monstrousness of Hitler's war caused few disturbances on American shores (the pain suffered by the loss of loved ones notwithstanding); indeed, the disastrous dislocations taking place in Europe were a major ingredient in establishing New York as the new capital of the Western world. The arrival of artists like Breton, Max Ernst, André Masson, Roberto Matta, and Mondrian heightened the cosmopolitan tension and augmented the experimentation and the growing confidence of a younger generation. The year 1942, when both Mellquist's book and Marin's profile in the *New Yorker* were published, also marked the inauguration of Peggy Guggenheim's gallery Art of This Century. Advised by the likes of her husband at the time, Ernst, and Breton, Marcel Duchamp, and Alfred Barr, she had put together a major collection of Surrealism, and the gallery became a magnet for younger American painters. Jackson Pollock, who had been so influenced by Ryder before turning to Picasso and Surrealism, had his first exhibition at Art of This Century in 1943. Stieglitz's American Place now depended solely on Marin, O'Keeffe, and Dove for its exhibitions; Hartley, who died in 1943, had previously severed his relations with Stieglitz. Stieglitz's extraordinary enterprise was going into eclipse, and his death in 1946, as well as Dove's the same year, put a virtual end to the Place. The gallery itself continued until 1950, when its remaining functions were assumed by Edith Gregor Halpert's Downtown Gallery.

Marin, who had already suffered the loss of his wife in 1945, was now quite alone. He was stricken with a heart attack in 1946, but with the encouragement of Paul Strand, and later of his son, John Jr., he continued to work. The figurative isolation that had been thrust upon him for so long was now literal. His reputation continued to grow, but as an institution more than as a living force. Yet the vitality of his continuing development belied the stasis so often assumed with fame.

Starting in 1944, the hovering planes and fractures of Cubism took on a revived importance that would continue for the rest of Marin's career. These final paintings first preceded by several years and then were concurrent with various proto-Abstract Expressionist attempts to relieve the rigidity of the Cubist grid and blend it with a fluid physicality. Picasso himself had already moved beyond his earlier strictures, and for Matisse and the younger Miró, Cubism hardly mattered anymore. The Cubist framing devices Marin introduced in the 1920s literally become a window in *Related to Hurricane* (1944); the storm is seen on a window's plane rather than through it. The suspension of planes in a transparent liquid solution continued in such subsequent paintings as *Boat with Blue* (1945), where one rectangle frames the boat and two rectangles in the sky are reflected on the water and bend the surface in vacillating flatness. So, too, do many of Rothko's 1946–48 watercolors and oil paintings move, though more abstractly than those of Marin, out of landscape into a painterly, aerated rectangularity that respects the boundaries of the support.[19]

In *Tunk Mountains, Maine* (1945), the planes and angularity are integrated into the subject to create a flowing, crystallized landscape. One year after that work, painting the same subject, Marin thinned the oil to near watercolor consistency and took generous advantage of the bare canvas without relinquishing oil's more emphatic materiality and resilience. The viscosity of the medium is fully exploited as the brushes push the paint from the immateriality of sky to the stippling of shrubs. The merging of Cubism with the more organic forces of paint and nature that had so frequently preoccupied Marin are similar in intent to the irregular, curvilinear planes of abstracted body parts with which de Kooning began to layer his canvases in 1945. Although by 1948 de Kooning would have moved to a more insistent and homogeneous abstract overallness than Marin would accept, he retained a loosely folding and unfolding structure beholden to Cubism. Like Marin, de Kooning always eschewed the programmatic.

Movement–Sea and Sky (1946) dances in and out of Cubist planar distillations, but in *Movement in Greys and Yellows* (1946), Marin felt free to return to a quasi-representational solution: all is ruled by wondrous wetness. The sunset's shifting radiance oozes through broad strokes of clouds, and the grayed sea is awash in rolling and rollicking whitecaps that scatter the sun's reflection. The "movement" of the titles calls back to Whistler and marks Marin's increasing reliance on the more abstracted acts of memory and imagination that were taking place in his studio. By 1947, the similar dynamics of linear angularity in the sea and the mountains could make the subjects all but indistinguishable from one another, and Marin could justifiably title a painting *Movement: Sea or Mountain As You Will* (1947).

"I'm calling my pictures this year 'Movements in Paint' and not movements of boat, sea or sky, because in these new paintings, although I use objects, I am representing paint first of all and not the motif primarily," he wrote in 1946.[20] But Marin stopped short of abstraction, which he continued to consider self-indulgent; he was as critical of Mondrian as he was of the new abstraction taking hold in New York. Not only did "motif" remain important to him, but also the boundaries of the canvas. He always retained the small easel format of the early Fauves that still favored the subject as a view, although the view was made more and more to coincide with and conform to the flatness and the contour of the canvas. By 1947, Pollock, Newman, and Still had all, to varying degrees, achieved a new, self-consciously heroic abstraction that broke the boundaries of Cubism with a seamless painterly homogeneity. The sheer size of many of their works aspired to "wallness" and engaged peripheral vision. They replaced the rectilinear regulation of Cubism with an open and palpable vastness. Now it was not the view that was vast, but the actual painting. Pollock did not represent nature; instead, in an existential leap, he became nature. The luminous flatness of late Claude Monet's paintings, the flowing openness of Matisse, and the boundlessness of Miró's automatism all played a role in this new modernist abstraction that rendered "old" the solutions of Marin and many of his peers. In modernism's continuing round of revolutions, Pollock would challenge Marin's leadership.

In 1947, Marin's work was celebrated with a second retrospective, at Boston's Institute of Modern Art. (It traveled to the Phillips Collection in Washington, D.C., and the Walker Art Center in Minneapolis.) The exhibition was drawn from Marin's own reserve that had been selected by Stieglitz. The proportion of oils (nineteen) to watercolors (forty-five) was now more equitable, but one of the catalogue's essayists, Frederick Wight, credited the watercolors with more charm.[21] The other essayist, MacKinley Helm, found more favor in the oils but continued to extend the image of Marin as a billiard-playing loner, "as purely American as Buffalo Bill."[22] This image was more elaborately perpetuated in Helm's book on Marin, published the following year (it was here that the Weehawken Sequence was mentioned in print for the first time).[23]

Marin's awareness of the Abstract Expressionists is made clear in his foreword to Helm's book. In one of his more peevish utterances, he refers to "the so-called non-objective approach" as "quite too often a disease approach."[24] This defensiveness, so similar to that expressed earlier toward French painters, certainly was not grounded in any current lack of attention for his own work. In a 1948 survey of art critics and curators conducted by *Look* magazine, Marin was voted America's number-one artist, leading a group that included Max Weber, Stuart Davis, and Edward Hopper, among others (none of the younger Americans were included).[25] Clement Greenberg, the major champion of the emerging Abstract Expressionists, found reason in 1948 to praise Marin's oils over his watercolors: "His oils, however, tend to be stronger, ampler, even more temperamental than even the best of his watercolors."[26] In the same year, Greenberg pitted Pollock against Marin, "with whom Pollock will in time be able to compete for recognition as the greatest American painter of the twentieth century."[27] Indeed, the global ambition of Pollock and Abstract Expressionists would shortly overshadow the more modest, epigrammatic modernism of Marin. When Alfred Barr was asked to choose three of the six artists to accompany Marin's retrospective of watercolors and oils at the 1950 Venice Biennale, he selected Gorky, Pollock, and de Kooning: all would soon reverse places with Marin.

Perhaps Marin's return after 1947 to the writerliness he first enlisted in the mid-1910s was hastened by an interest in Oriental calligraphy and possibly even by a reaction to Pollock's new work. Line activates and agitates the lyric delirium of thinly painted planes that spreads across his final works in a synthesis of drawing, watercolor, and paint. The sweep of line and plane in paintings such as *Full Moon over the City No. 1* (1949) is at once thinner and more daringly free and spatial than in previous cityscapes. The calligraphic shorthand of the watercolors and oils of 1914 takes on a breathless speed and assurance in *Movement in Red, Blue, and Umber* (1950). The black that was so prominent in the 1930s, and that began to be thinned in the early 1940s, was now further pared down and limbered up as it moves through multiple changes of direction, density, and configuration. To give his lines a more liquid urgency, Marin frequently applied thinned black paint with a syringe.[28] The line moving in and out of plane and contour turns *Tunk Mountains* (1951) into a breezy imbroglio. The same line transforms the transparent rectangles that so frequently hung over or on the sea into an exquisite haiku, awash in pale gray and a few patches of blue in *Movement, Grey and Blue* (1952); Whistler, the Orient, and Cubism dissolve in a Marin solution. *The Written Sea* (1952) is just that—all is line, now spelling rocks, now spelling boats, now simply taking pleasure turning in and around on itself.

In its intimacy, its single color, its sheer joy in movement and rhythmic vitality, and its variations of line traveling in and out of conformity with a configuration, *The Written Sea* is strongly related to Chinese and Japanese calligraphy. Although one can be quite certain that Marin was familiar with Oriental landscape painting,[29] his awareness of the lesser-known calligraphy cannot be so readily posited.[30] Nonetheless, the resemblances are striking and obvious, and Marin was included with Mark Tobey and Morris Graves, who had both studied in the Orient, in a 1956 exhibition titled *Contemporary Calligraphers*.[31] Marin's calligraphy is freer and more energetic than Tobey's "white writing," although both remained mindful of Cubism.

Marin and Tobey were hardly alone in their strong preference for line. The paintings of Pollock, Franz Kline, Bradley Walker Tomlin, and early de Kooning are all grounded in the activation of line into paint and painting. If Marin's line was still partially ruled by conforming to the configurations of subject and canvas, its organic spontaneity and speed bear strong resemblance to contemporaneous Pollock—especially to some of Pollock's intimate drawings of the 1950s. Nonetheless, Pollock's more insistently programmatic engagement of chance in his "drip" paintings and the almost total immersion of his body movements in his paintings remain at a far remove in intentionality from Marin's use of both hands and a syringe. Marin's intentions are closer to those of such painters as de Kooning and especially Tomlin, who did not altogether disavow Cubism. The off-white planes shot through with a web of whiplash black lines in de Kooning's *Attic* (1949), though they are more intense and implacably frontal, are akin to the rustling linear planes snapped in and out of flatness in such Marins as *Sea Fantasy* (1952).

Tomlin was much the gentlest of the Abstract Expressionists, and perhaps the one whose work was closest to Marin's. With the encouragement of Robert Motherwell, the early Cubist compositions he painted from 1939 to 1945 gave way first to Surrealist-derived automatism and cryptic symbolism and then to a purer, more painterly calligraphy (around 1948). Like Tobey (and occasionally Marin), Tomlin often referred to his paintings as being written, and he may well have been aware of Chinese calligraphy. The glyph-like meanderings of his line are more controlled and far less volatile than the movements of Pollock's line; their lyric intimacy and implicit reliance on the interior push and pull of the Cubist grid, although again more abstract, are closely related to Marin's paintings of the late 1940s in both composition and mood. The calligraphic dynamism and rawness of Kline's driven swaths of black paint have the heroic toughness and bigness so often associated with Abstract Expressionism, a toughness quite alien to the intimate mode of Tomlin and Marin.

Marin's final paintings are euphoric concertos of consciousness. Their lucidity and seeming modesty are grounded in the complex sophistication of his lifelong commitment to the workings of paint and nature. The vigorous grace of *Spring* (nos. 1 and 2, 1953) narrows paint down to its primal mark making functions—marks as units of space, plane, color, and contour, paint as paint as nature. The movement from pasty opacity to thinnest transparency; from whispering, febrile straightness to more spontaneous, organic irregularity; from emphatic red to muted washes of gray to bare canvas—all are redolent of a life well remembered. In the blond grisaille of *Circus* (1953), mark making is freed of almost all its duties so that it may parade in a glyphic panoply of pleasure in itself.

Marin died in 1953, at a time when the Abstract Expressionist hegemony had already been fully consolidated and passed on to a younger generation. Regardless of the existential heroics and emotiveness that would shortly be subjected to modernist ironies and subversion, the Abstract Expressionists' variants of painterly overallness and frontality dominated many of the vital intentions of painting through the 1960s. Marin and peers such as Hartley and Dove became virtually obsolete for succeeding generations. His name was seldom mentioned outside of art schools or in the conversations of older critics and collectors (Fairfield Porter was among the few artists to praise and seek encouragement in Marin's version of painterliness). Marin's watercolors and oils, seen regularly through the 1930s and 40s by the developing Abstract Expressionists, were seldom credited as precursors or possible influences. Perhaps Marin became the victim of the same defensiveness he and many of his fellow artists (and critics) evinced toward the French modernists. For just as the need for an independent American art had seemed to require discrediting the importance of the Fauves and the Cubists, so later did the need for a more international Americanism seem to require the dismissal of the allegedly provincial earlier American modernists. The more willful self-consciousness and the frequent grandiosity—some of it indeed real—that became part of American painting with Abstract Expressionism would make the more modest forthrightness of a Marin or a Dove seem minor.

Since the late 1960s, increasing numbers of artists and critics have come to question modernism's relentless revolutions, upheavals that have been instigated by the quest for an ever-greater self-referential abstractness. While it is still often guided by modernist strategies, painting has once again embraced representation and referentiality. Early American modernism has been reviewed and revived and has even become an influence on a new generation of artists. Besides Ryder, Hartley and Dove have made noticeable contributions to Bill Jensen's development, for example. Malcolm Morley has come to admire Marin, and the agitated expressiveness of his paintings has much in common with some of Marin's paintings of the 1930s. New retrospectives and catalogues raisonnés have helped restore the role of the early modernists. Sheldon Reich's excellent catalogue raisonné (published in 1971) and his accompanying stylistic analysis have done much to see through the obfuscations that so frequently clouded the Stieglitz circle. Much remains to be done: Dove's paintings must be seen with Kandinsky's, Hartley's extraordinary late figure paintings must be viewed with and compared to those of Georges Rouault and Soutine. The larger context eschewed by many of the early modernists themselves must now be attempted. Marin's oil paintings, so scantly praised during his lifetime, deserve far greater prominence in the story of his own development and in the broader history of twentieth-century painting. If not the equal of Matisse, Picasso, Pollock, or de Kooning, his forceful vision in oil paint is nevertheless that of a major artist. He was equally blessed and cursed by the modesty of his format, but the ambition that strives for masterpieces was not part of Marin's constitution. Of his peers, only Weber had the will (but not the way) to challenge and emulate Parisian leadership directly. But the singular clarity of Marin's intentions often assumes a sweeping authority that belies his unassuming side. The smallness of his lyric mode is quite capable of bigness. His oil paintings need more time and exposure to find their proper place. It is hoped that this essay will help to restore and reveal the painted pleasure and intelligence Marin hoped for himself when he wrote of that "artist—releasing the different folds of his seeings at periods of his many livings—He—be he working on a flat surface reforms his seeings on this surface to a seeing of his own choosing so that which he chooses shall live of its own right on this flat—"[32]

1. See Waldo Frank, "The American Art of John Marin," *McCall's* (June 1927): 37; Lewis Mumford, "Brancusi and Marin," *The New Republic*, vol. 48 (December 15, 1926): 112–113; Julius Meier-Graefe, "A Few Conclusions on American Art," *Vanity Fair*, vol. 31 (November 1928): 83ff; and Paul Rosenfeld, "An Essay on Marin," *The Nation*, vol. 134 (January 27, 1932): 122-124.

2. Thomas Craven, "John Marin," *The Nation*, vol. 118 (March 19, 1924): 321.

3. In a 1932 letter from Marin to Stieglitz, quoted in Dorothy Norman, ed., *The Selected Writings of John Marin* (New York: Pellegrini & Cudahy, 1949), 149.

4. In a 1931 letter from Marin to Stieglitz, quoted in Norman, *Selected Writings*, 139.

5. MacKinley Helm, *John Marin* (Boston: Pellegrini & Cudahy in association with the Institute of Contemporary Art, 1948), 88.

6. Thomas Craven, *Modern Art: The Men, the Movements, the Meaning* (New York: Simon & Schuster, 1934), 313.

7. Ibid., 312.

8. Ibid., 326.

9. At the time Craven's book was published, Rivera, having refused to remove the depiction of Lenin from his Rockefeller Center murals, had to suffer their destruction.

10. E. M. Benson, *John Marin: The Man and His Work* (Washington, D.C.: The American Federation of Arts, 1935), 20.

11. E. M. Benson, "John Marin—and Pertaining Thereto," in *John Marin* (New York: The Museum of Modern Art, 1936), 19.

12. John Marin, "A Few Notes," in *Twice a Year* (Spring–Summer 1939) reprinted in Norman, *Selected Writings*, 185.

13. This was confirmed in the author's conversation of July 8, 1986, with Elaine Fried de Kooning, who first met her husband in 1938 and shared a painterly dialogue with him.

14. Sue Davidson Lowe, *Stieglitz: A Memoir/Biography* (New York: Farrar, Straus & Giroux, 1983), 353. Dorothy Norman, in a conversation with the author on December 12, 1985, vigorously denied any interference by Stieglitz in Marin's work.

15. John Marin, "To Paint My Children," in the catalogue for his *American Place* exhibition that opened February 14, 1938; reprinted in Norman, *Selected Writings*, 179.

16. Jerome Mellquist, "Marin and His Oils," *The Nation*, vol. 146 (March 12, 1938): 308–309. Mellquist proclaimed 1938 as "the year of Marin's oils" and concluded, "Marin is richer than he was before, and so are we."

17. Matthew Josephson, "Leprechaun on the Palisades," *The New Yorker* (March 14, 1942).

18. Jerome Mellquist, *The Emergence of an American Art* (New York: Charles Scribner's Sons, 1942).

19. According to John Marin Jr., in a conversation with the author on May 15, 1986, Rothko found much to admire in *Related to Hurricane* when he saw it, around 1966.

20. Marin, quoted in 1947 in Helm, *John Marin*, 101.

21. F. S. Wight, "Pertaining to Marin's Style," in *John Marin, a Retrospective Exhibition* (Boston: Institute of Contemporary Art, 1947), 32.

22. MacKinley Helm, "John Marin: A Portrait," in *John Marin, a Retrospective Exhibition*, 14.

23. Ibid., 33.

24. Ibid., foreword.

25. "Are These Men the Best Painters in America Today?" *Look*, vol. 12 (February 3, 1948): 44ff.

26. Clement Greenberg, "John Marin," 1948 article reprinted in *Art and Culture* (Boston: Beacon Press, 1965), 182.

27. Clement Greenberg, "Jackson Pollock," *The Nation* (January 24, 1948): 108.

28. "I fill up a glass ear syringe with diluted oil paint, usually black paint, and while I press on the plunger I draw." Quoted in Helm, *John Marin*, 72.

29. In one of the many references made by various writers to Marin's Oriental influences, Mellquist, describing the work of the mid-1910s, writes of Marin as "not forgetful of the ancient Chinese whom he came more and more to appreciate." Mellquist, *The Emergence of an American Art*, 397.

30. In my conversation with him on May 15, 1986, John Marin Jr. remembered his father purchasing a book on calligraphy, but to this date he has been unable to locate it.

31. The exhibition was held at the Contemporary Arts Museum Houston. In his catalogue essay, Frederick S. Wight gives no documentation of any direct involvement Marin may have had with Oriental calligraphy.

32. John Marin, "Marin Writes," in *John Marin, a Retrospective Exhibition*, 10.

Willem de Kooning

Drawing No Conclusions

Willem de Kooning was always drawing, never making a drawing—"finish" and "closure" were not part of his vocabulary. He often drew on his canvas before starting to paint; in the course of his making, he sometimes drew with charcoal into wet paint; he drew endlessly on paper, with little regard for the differences between a preparatory sketch, a breathless notation, and an individual work. De Kooning was not averse to tearing up a drawing and recombining some of its sections with those of other torn-up drawings. Tearing up could be drawing. First on pieces of tracing paper, later on large sheets of vellum, he made tracings of one or another section of his finished paintings that he might wish to integrate into one or another stage of a subsequent painting. One or many of these tracings might as readily be momentarily stuck onto the gluey viscosity of a painting in process as become an independent drawing on paper. And he drew and he drew, clustering pencil lines as incisive and finely honed as the sharpest razor, or urging an ink-loaded brush into freely splashing pirouettes and arabesques, or encouraging soft, ashen drifts of charcoal to luxuriate in the nap of the paper. Drawing gave breath to the body of de Kooning's art.

In both the generation of an individual work and that of its overall development, de Kooning's process unfurled like the spiraling secretions of a volute shell making the pattern of its evolution materially visible. Each layer reflects, expands, and depends upon its predecessors while simultaneously responding to the vagaries of the surrounding environment. De Kooning constantly and visibly excavated and reinvented his past, almost always working in groups, the beginnings of which are as difficult to determine as their completion. Few if any other artists have made the starts and stops, joys and woes, and trials and errors of the procedures of their making so transparent and visual.

By focusing here on four groups of drawings, we can begin to see again the multivalent flow of de Kooning's process that has inevitably been slowed down, halted, and/or interrupted by his canonization and by the assigning of "masterpiece" to many of his works. Seldom seen or published in depth, these drawings span some twenty years (from the late 1950s to the early 80s) of de Kooning's artistic maturity and have been selected to reveal the wide range of his endeavor.

While his peer Jackson Pollock sought to merge his identity with and reenact the forces of nature, de Kooning, more profane than pantheistic, declared the content of his work to be a "glimpse." If in part this simplism sought to deflate the metaphysical pretensions of many of his fellow Abstract Expressionists, it also referred specifically to the tides of forming and de-forming that ebb and rise across de Kooning's planes from the late 1940s throughout the remainder of his career—not a "glimpse" of the seen but of the act of seeing. De Kooning made radiantly visual his concrete bodily experiences in the throes of complex cognitive forming. A passing glimpse of a shifting cloud, a rising wave, a brazenly squatting nude—all interact with the unfathomably dense neuronal flow of consciousness. Suddenly the nude devours the landscape and vice versa; the wave calls to the shape of a dune, the cloud to a breast; the landscape's flatness begins to resonate with echoes of de Kooning's native Netherlands; the nude leers at the memory of Peter Paul Rubens, then recoils in a cruel rush of mortality; and on and on and on, as the desire for resolution is constantly undermined by another wave of interchangeable associations of woman, water, flesh, and paint. De Kooning drew (and painted) seeing as metaphor.

Like his Dutch genre-painting forebears and like the Cubist painters of still life, de Kooning had a lively interest in the everyday world around him. In the mid-1940s, words ("art") and letters (ZOT) casually took their place in his paintings and were followed by the ghosts of newsprint serendipitously left behind by the pages of newspapers placed on top of paintings in progress in order to slow down drying. A few years later he might look to 1940s airflow automotive design (*Florida Trailer*, 1950–51), or collage a mouth cut out from a magazine advertisement for cigarettes onto a woman's face study. In his *Folded Shirt on Laundry Paper* drawings (1958), this utterly mundane subject is transformed into a series of dazzling gyrations of an ink-loaded brush shifting from folded shirt to giddy glyphic abstraction to comedic torsos writhing and struggling to unfold themselves to shirt collars inflating into bulbous breasts bursting from their décolletage.

De Kooning turned the plane of the paper into a cocoon metamorphosing wetness. The brush glides and slides into and out of the rectangular restraint of the rectangle, now fully loaded and emphatic, now dragged into a dryness that leaves behind slowly disappearing trails of bunched bristle marks, now yielding to impetuous speed, now lazily drifting into immateriality, constantly pulling arcs, diagonals, and wavering rectangularity toward a coherence he knew was unobtainable. This desire for completion and the knowing that only incompletion is possible animate these drawings, as indeed they animate all of de Kooning's mature work. As full as each work is when seen individually, the ambiguities beguile still more as they evolve and revolve in a series.

In their suave economy, openness, and, for de Kooning, uncustomary punning on the rectangularity of the support, this series relates directly to his Parkway paintings created in 1958. Broad bands of paint merging with and emerging from variegated clumps and splashes of green, blue, and yellow allude to the blur of high-speed glimpses experienced from a car on the highway. These configurations literally and figuratively led de Kooning out of the gritty, urban turbulence that congested and ravished his planes from the late 1940s through the mid-50s and into the more pastoral ambiguities of the eastern end of Long Island and the *Rosy Fingered Dawn at Louise Point* (1963). The allusions to torsos and breasts emanating from the Folded Shirt drawings also look back to the organics of the more furiously fragmentary drawings and paintings created in the 1950s, after the raging bitch/goddesses exploding in the *Paintings on the Theme of the Woman* (1951–53).

De Kooning was prone to see his virtually sublime abilities as draftsman as much a bane as a boon. He challenged himself constantly with new movements of the drawing hand and new obstacles for it to surmount, in order to keep his making vivid—racing, erasing, defacing, or looking not at the page but at television while drawing. He also drew with his eyes closed (documented in a photograph taken in 1963).[1] The eyes-closed drawings were created and reproduced in 1966, accompanied by de Kooning's testimony: "It is true that I made them with eyes closed. Also, the pad I used was held horizontally. The drawings often started by the feet…but more often by the center of the body, in the middle of the page. There is nothing special about this, and I am certain that many artists have found similar ways…but I found that closing the eyes was very helpful to me."[2]

But for their documentation, these drawings are indistinguishable from de Kooning's other contemporaneous drawings, some of which are undocumented eyes-closed drawings. Most of the twenty-four eyes-closed drawings are devoted to the subject of woman, to which de Kooning had once again returned in 1963, when he moved to the Springs on Long Island. The thunderous Woman of the 1950s now deliquesced into water nymphs in unabashed disarray, naked and frequently flashing their genitalia. In Long Island, a lighter touch came into play, and these nymphs ravel and unravel in a loopy, writerly mode. The softness of touch and the softness of the charcoal medium conspire in gusty wisps of smoky strokes. The center of the page, the center of the body, the hand stroking the page, and the (imagined) hand stroking the body are interchangeable.

Was this uninhibited narrowing of the gap between the erotics of art and the erotics of the body encouraged by de Kooning's newfound joy in nature, by the more urban excitation of the sexual revolution of the 1960s, or by the wishful vanities of an aging man (although the sixty-two year old artist suffered from no lack of female companionship)? When a flurry of strokes actually produces an act of coupling, both faces and bodies betray youthful, hilariously awkward shock at such self-exposure—very unlike the incisive line, form, and the urge to control that guided the dominating hand of Pablo Picasso in so many of his erotic drawings at this time.

So seductive and engaging is the vigor of their presence that we hardly think of these vamping figures as having been deprived of the seeing of their creator. But, of course, we have been told so. That which art students have often been instructed to undertake as a learning exercise and which may later be employed as warm-up practice, de Kooning choreographed into a tour de force solo for the hand. Gradually, we might conclude that, for de Kooning, the act of drawing was indeed seeing. So totally was he able to imagine his bodily experience onto the plane of his making that eyesight could be ignored. The body in the mind permitted the hand to see.

Like all of de Kooning's art, these drawings provoke and embody more questions than answers. What is the relationship of the learned reflexes and the handwriting that become unconscious to conscious premeditation and invention? What is the difference between seeing and imagining? How spontaneous are the chance procedures so often claimed as a hallmark of much Abstract Expressionist art? The trap and/or embrace that bind body and mind in inextricable oneness provide the only unquestionable certainty.

The fugitive nature and fragility of the charcoal medium, as well as the wavering incompletion of the drawn configurations, impart a transience to these figures that soon temper their joy with pathos. Almost as tenuous as a windswept cloud, their presence hovers on the brink of evaporation. The afflictions of mortality agitate de Kooning's surfaces as much as the jubilations of the flesh.

One of the most exuberant of these nymphs leaps from the page, arms and legs wildly distended in a rush of welcoming. The extended arms also render the body unprotected, however, and so extreme is the pose, with all four limbs extended beyond the edges of the paper, that the figure might easily be read as uncomfortably pinioned to the page. A similarly hilariously contorted figure, with arms again extended beyond the edges of the support, but now with legs down and with a little squiggle added to the wobbly W that is de Kooning's glyph for the vulva, becomes a crucified male with testicles and penis, becomes Christ on the Cross. This slippery transformation makes the frolicking nymphs almost interchangeable with these drawings of Christ, comically contorted by his suspension on the paper plane.

Until he stopped drawing on paper, in the early 1980s, de Kooning continued to occasionally draw crucifixions [approximately thirty such works created between 1964 and 1980 were included in the exhibition that is the subject of this essay].[3] With the exceptions of Georges Rouault's and Alfonso Ossorio's frequent depictions, Christ has been a rare protagonist of twentieth-century vanguard art. Marsden Hartley's homoerotic fisherman-savior seen in some of his paintings and drawings created in the 1940s; Henri Matisse's Chapel of the Rosary (1950) in Vence, France; and Francis Bacon's *Crucifixion* (1965) are among Christ's more noteworthy appearances. In de Kooning's art, male figures occurred only sporadically, most prominently in the Jean Auguste Dominique Ingres and Le

Nain–inspired paintings and drawings completed in the late 1930s and early 40s. In many of these works (e.g., the drawing *Self-Portrait with Imaginary Brother*, 1938), de Kooning employed himself as model. After a long hiatus, male figures began occasionally to appear in his paintings in the 1960s and 70s (e.g., the painting *LaGuardia in Paper Hat*, 1972). Christ, who seems to have remained exclusively a subject of drawing, is first to be seen in 1950, in a conventionally posed, Picasso-influenced *Lamentation*.[4] He returns some fifteen years later in several drawings predating but related to the crucifixions found among the eyes-closed drawings and then continues to appear sporadically on de Kooning's paper plane. Why Christ?

Emerging at the bottom of a vaporous wash of orange in the painting *Sphinx* (1964) is a crouching figure with a large head: high of forehead, flat of top, with big intense eyes and a wide mouth. A very similar head appears in one of the two flailing-lined, charcoal crucifixions very similar in size and execution to a drawing signed and dated 1964 (*Woman*, 1964, Hirshhorn Museum). Both the head of the sphinx and the head of Christ look remarkably like de Kooning. And an increasingly caricatured version of this head tops Christ in some of the documented eyes-closed drawings, as well as in some subsequent crucifixions. While he was certainly not known to be a devout, churchgoing Christian, de Kooning clearly identified with Christ. At this time, when Barnett Newman was painting his severely abstract *Stations of the Cross* (1958–66) and Mark Rothko was creating his elegiac abstract murals (1965–67) for the chapel commissioned by the de Menils in Houston, de Kooning might also have smilingly thought to himself, "Why not show them the real thing?"

"And remember having coffee with my old friend Spaventa...telling him the difficulty I had in sustaining the tragedy of painting (someone on the Cross...and he looked rather surprised...and said You mean to tell me that you think of Him... in the flesh?? Boy are you kooked!"[5] With grammar as inconclusive as his drawing (all elisions and absent closing parentheses are de Kooning's), he conflates Christ, flesh, and painting. In almost all the crucifixion drawings, one and usually both of Christ's extended arms are cut off by the physical edge(s) of the paper, thus crucifying quite literally the capacity to draw and paint.

Six charcoal crucifixions (ca. 1966), the same size as and indistinguishable in manner from the documented eyes-closed crucifixions, as well as six further, related crucifixions (ca. 1966) all depict Christ in a pose that makes the top-heaviness imposed by crucifixion ridiculously apparent. With his sunken head, swollen chest, and distended arms, Christ is on the verge of toppling over and out of the plane. The cosmicomics

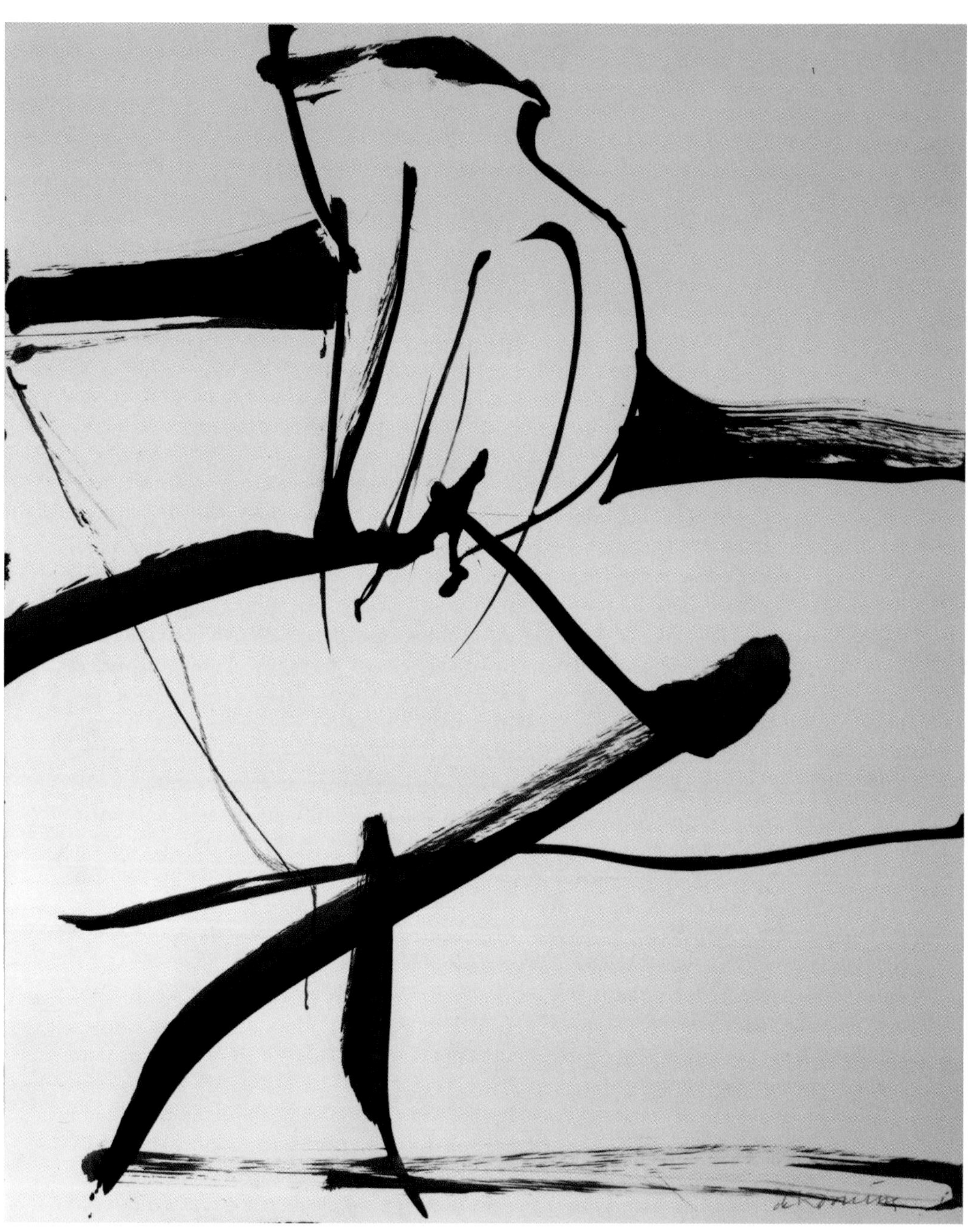

Willem de Kooning, *Folded Shirt on Laundry Paper*, 1958

of Christ's condition, caused by the slippery, quivering linearity, incomplete contours of bodily contortions, and placeless instability call simultaneously to the placeless alienation of Alberto Giacometti's eviscerated bodies and to the blurred abrasions and painful twists inflicted upon his painted figures by Francis Bacon. Both artists were admired by de Kooning.

In a succeeding group of crucifixions, starting with a *Charleston Pose* drawing (1969), Christ almost evaporates in windswept drizzles of fine lines, now in pencil, now in charcoal, as he takes his place in four apparent versions of the Lamentation that now gave de Kooning the opportunity to riotously update Hieronymus Bosch's grotesquerie. Christ is lamented by a variety of street-wise nudes, including an exhausted, blowzy type collapsed in an armchair. In the wildest of these Lamentations, in both drawing manner and pose, we find a reclining nude confined in a boat (reprising a group of 1964 Woman in Rowboat works), together with a mooning nude seemingly bent over Christ's nether region, threatening to make quite literal the Lamentation as foreplay of the Resurrection.

A totally different way of drawing propels *For Santa Emilia–Six Tears for Six Saints* (1972). The gender and identifying attributes of the six saints have been dissolved in liquid swaths of ink and oil emulsion, twisting and turning into calligraphic figures that give meaning and body primarily to the movements of the brush. The body is reflected in the liquidity of the medium (the tears of the title?), rather than vice versa. These writerly characters may well have taken some cues from the traditional Japanese drawing methods de Kooning sought out and observed during a trip to Japan in 1969.

By the mid-1970s, de Kooning's figures had almost totally melted into the rhythmic currents of paint as nature as flesh. In a crucifixion drawing likely to have been created at this time, only the top of the cross resists the charcoal current that pulls and disperses the body across the surface. When soft drifts of charcoal marks once again begin to conjoin in an isolated figure, they do so as the whispering memories of corporeality.

Amongst the 1966–67 crucifixion drawings are two that are nearly identically posed and drawn, except for their differently reacting mediums: charcoal on paper and oil on vellum. The strong diagonal torque of both cross and legs and the harrowing facial expression work to make this one of the most compelling images of the series, an image that de Kooning seemed to want to repeat. On the right side of both drawings, the cross and arm are cleanly cut off before reaching the paper's edge; nor does the bottom of the cross meet the bottom edge of the paper. This arbitrary truncation suggests that both drawings derive from a third work on a smaller support, upon which arm and cross would have been drawn out to intersect with the corresponding physical edge of the

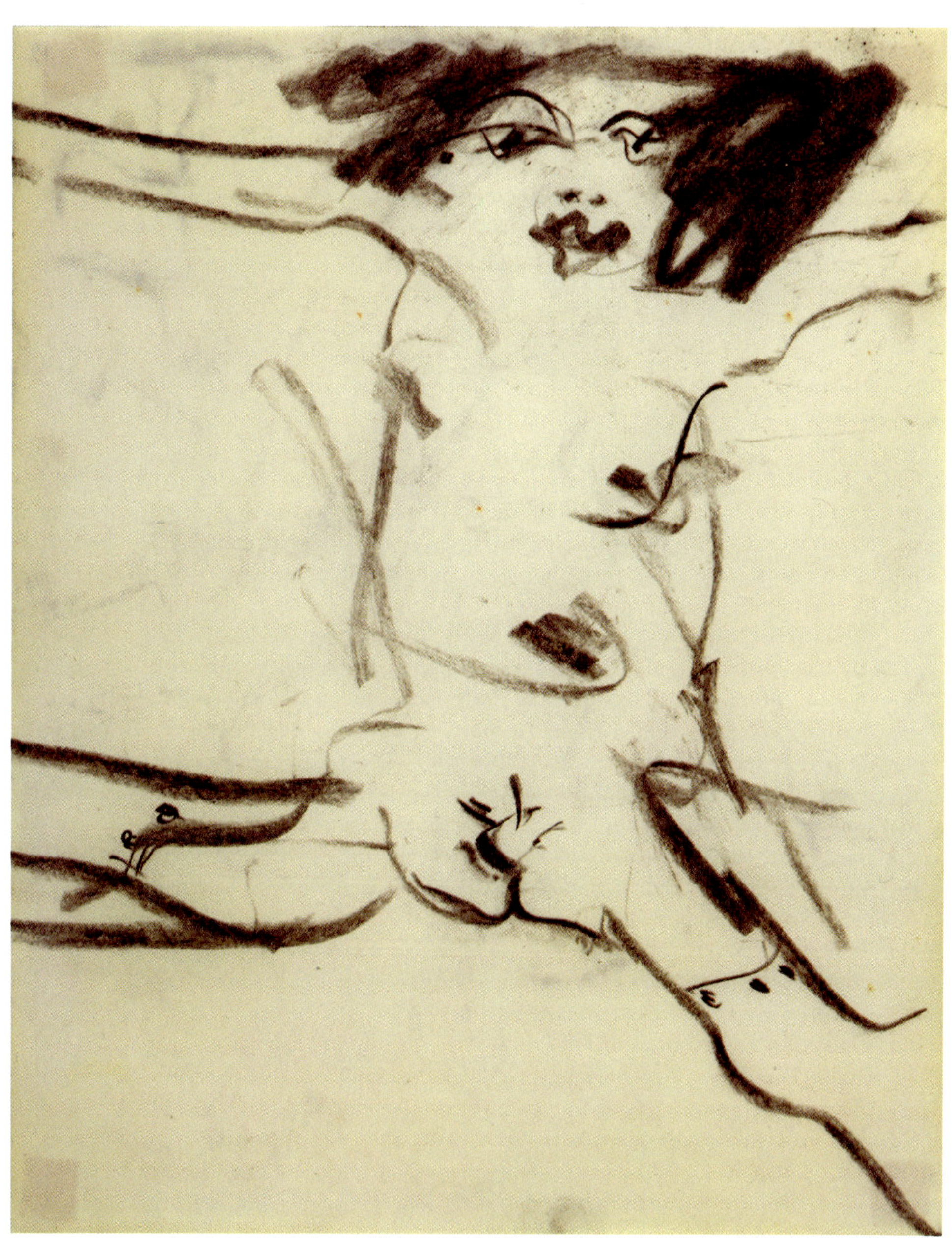

Willem de Kooning, *Untitled*, 1966

plane. In addition, the paint smudges on the vellum suggest this image found its way, in some form, into a painting, possibly to be swept away by succeeding layers of process.

As early as the 1940s, in his growing urge to confound the flow of his painting and keep it constantly in motion, more than to focus and stabilize it, de Kooning might partially cover a painting in process with a barrage of tracings on standard sheets of tracing paper.[6] After he moved into his new studio in 1964, he started making these charcoal tracings on large sheets of vellum cut from a roll. The model for each tracing was a section of one or another of the finished paintings, mostly created in the 1960s and 70s, that de Kooning kept around his studio to help catalyze his self-dialogue. Occasionally, when he arrived at a configuration he might wish to employ in the future, a tracing was made from a painting in process. More often than not, the subject was part of a painting that visibly incorporated a figure, just as the preliminary charcoal drawing on canvas almost always contained a figure, no matter how abstractly that painting might evolve. Many of these tracings were made on both sides of the vellum so that de Kooning also might be able to revive their mirror image. The side chosen to be transferred to canvas was drawn over from the reverse side onto a section of bare canvas, to become part of the beginning of a new painting. A tracing might also be introduced into a painting in process.[7] On occasion, both sides might be inducted into the formation of a new painting.[8]

Given the amorphousness that prevails on the surfaces of de Kooning's 1960s and 70s paintings, and given the clarity of line and contour necessitated by a tracing's potential for legible transferral onto another surface, a considerable amount of the "copying" would require modification or partial reinvention of the original configuration. Surely, the satyr-like figure seen so readily in one of these vellums was not as clearly defined on the surface of the painting from which it was traced. Hardly surprising, for no matter how seemingly clear, no act of de Kooning's making was devoid of ambiguity.

These vellum tracings, started in the mid-1960s, played a visually prominent role in the paintings de Kooning created in the 1980s. The lines and interacting, open contours of the vellums, as well as those of his preparatory charcoal drawings on canvas, were executed with a distinctness of definition that calls back to the precisely delineated contours found in the lunar organics of such mid-1940s paintings as *Pink Angels* (1945) and in the black-and-white abstractions of 1948, created before de Kooning began to flood his paintings with more visceral, shifting states of liquidity. In his vellums and preparatory drawings on canvas, he was quite literally retrieving his past to become the foundation of his new work in the present; in his use of the tracings, that past also became an active participant in the shifting stages of a painting's development. In the 1980s, de Kooning's past rose up closer to the surface of his work. Painting layers were thinned down, diminished in number, compressed, and made more transparent to reflect the taut linearity billowing into and out of the pneumatic forms of the 1940s in a new light, with a new and restrained mode of painterliness.

The vellums beg still more questions. Tracing from painting, tracing into painting, tracing as drawing, drawing into painting—what is the difference? Can a studio tool be a work of art? What is a beginning, and what is an end?

1. See photograph and caption ("De Kooning drawing with his eyes closed, July 1963"), in *Willem de Kooning, Works From 1951–1981,* exh. cat. (East Hampton, New York: Guild Hall, 1981), 14.

2. *De Kooning Drawings* (New York: Walker & Company, in association with M. Knoedler & Co., 1966).

3. With his unwillingness to declare anything "finished," de Kooning almost never signed or dated works until they left the studio. Some of the Crucifixion dates are inferred from directly related, dated work, such as the eyes-closed drawings. Some dates are known; *Charleston Pose* is part of a group of drawings, some of which are dated 1969–70. The date of 1972 was given to *For Santa Emilia–Six Tears for Six Saints* by Emilie Kilgore, for whom the drawings were made between the summer of 1972, when she and de Kooning traveled together in Italy, and Christmas 1972, when the drawings were given to her by de Kooning. Other dates are more tentatively proposed on the basis of purely visual speculation that is obviously risky considering de Kooning's constant recycling of his means and images.

4. For an illustration of *Untitled (Women and Crucifixion),* 1950, see Thomas B. Hess, *Willem de Kooning Drawings* (Greenwich, CT: A Paul Bianchini Book, N.Y. Graphic Society,

1972), 128, plate 43. Hess relates the composition of this painting to a Grunewald painting in Karlsruhe, Germany.

5. De Kooning to Emilie Kilgore, November 13, 1976, in a letter faxed to the author by Kilgore, April 15, 1998.

6. *Willem de Kooning,* exh. cat. (Paris: Centre Georges Pompidou, 1984), 185, illustration showing de Kooning working in his studio in 1946.

7. This account of de Kooning's tracing on vellum is based upon the author's phone interview on May 5, 1998, with Tom Ferrara, who started assisting de Kooning in his studio in 1980.

8. For a discussion and illustration of the recto and verso of a vellum being employed in the making of a 1982 painting, see Richard Shiff, "Willem de Kooning: Painting's Potential," in *Willem de Kooning: Paintings 1983–1984,* exh. cat. (New York: Matthew Marks Gallery/Mitchell-Inness and Nash, 1997), 12–13.

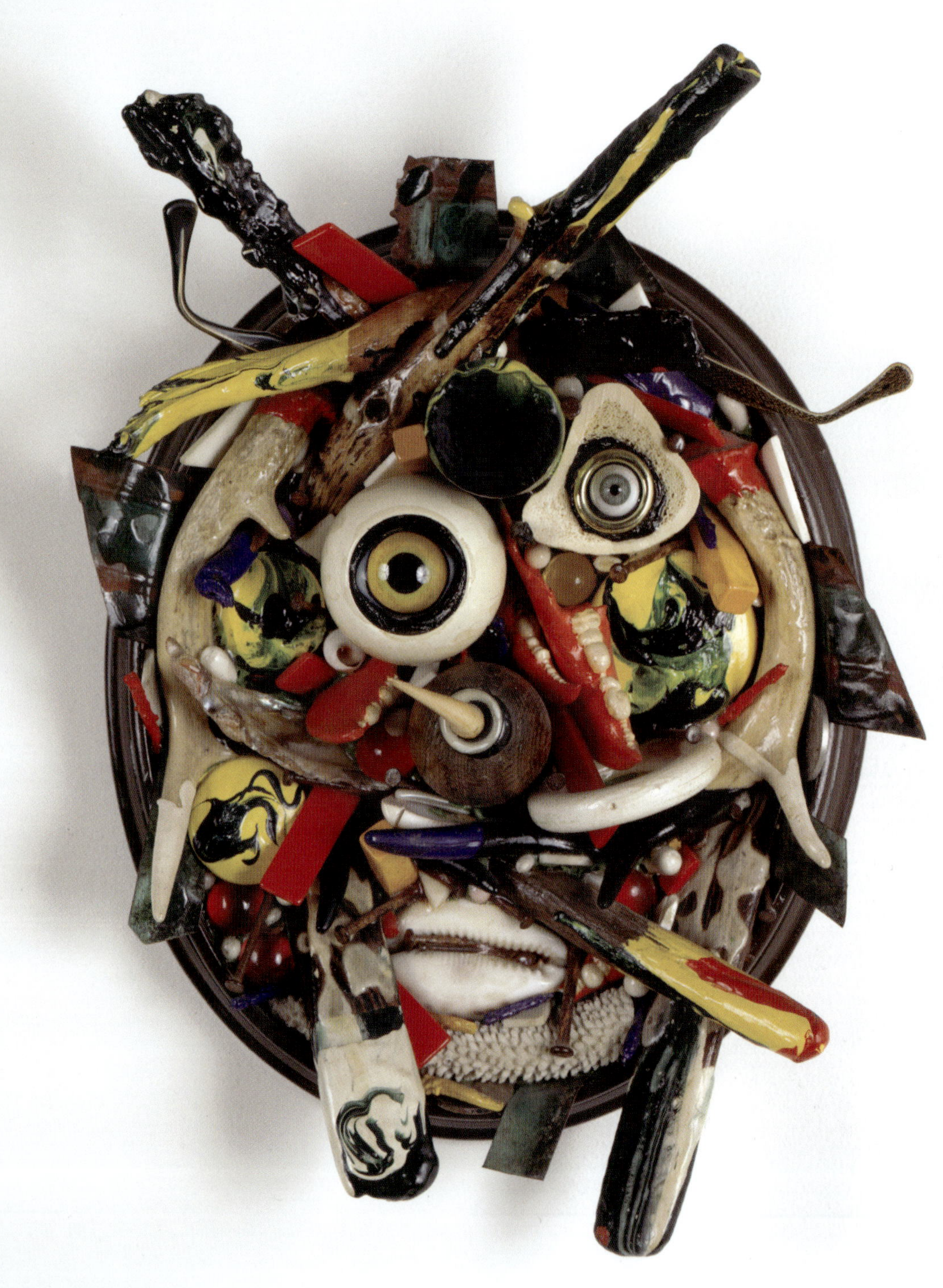

Alfonso Ossorio

Eyewitnesses

From 1955 through 1958, Alfonso Ossorio's oil paintings stormed with furies of liquidity that vacillated between invocations of the ultimate deluge and the fitful throes of genesis. The excoriated organic forms being dissolved and/or resolved in linear flings of paint and oozing coruscation materialized, in large part, out of Ossorio's assimilation of the fraught, painterly physicality found, in totally different states, in the work of his friends and mentors Jackson Pollock, Clyfford Still, and Jean Dubuffet. Ossorio's palette, prone to the lurid—often to a miasmal phosphorescence—and his drive, more openly conflicted and frantic than Pollock's related one, to make visual the interdependence of chaos and order, merge the harrowing spirituality already visible in Ossorio's earlier work with the lessons of Abstract Expressionism and Dubuffet.

By 1958, as the swirling flows of paint were being driven into still more intensely dimensional physicality, Ossorio began to stud the surface with a variety of found objects, making more literal the transformation of the physical that is, and always has been, painting's primary mandate. At first discreetly and then, by 1959, more and more indiscreetly, shells, fake jewels, a rope, a belt, crockery shards, and the like bubbled up out of the plaster (and sometimes sand) that now leavened the oil. These objects seem to have grown like molds out of painting's fermentation. By 1960, the medium of oil paint that Ossorio had rejected throughout most of his previous career because of his associating it with the tradition of Western mimeticism, and that he had only employed for eight years starting in 1951, was once again rejected. The objects themselves now became the primary medium, and a still more astounding profusion of them swarmed across the entire surface like mutant solidifications of paint's liquidity. Like the flows of paint they developed out of, these objects congeal into a homogeneous image. Unlike the flows of paint, each object maintains its individual identity and physical profile.

The teeming proliferation of predominantly hard, shiny, and reflective surfaces of the objects, both organic and artificial, that Ossorio merged with the plane of the support, extended the pulsing currents of Abstract Expressionism's fluidity into a startlingly intensified materiality. The hothouse chroma and unexpected juxtaposing of the various shards of plastic and crockery, pieces of costume jewelry, congealed pours of pigmented plastic, gilded driftwood, shells, bone, a variety of glistening metal objects, etc., transformed the mundane into a savage phantasmagoria—a kind of vernacular sublime.

In their emotional intensity that is at once terrible and ecstatic, in their flamboyant palette, and in the molecular chainlike interdependence of their components, Ossorio's assemblages are very different from the more disjunctive and/or hierarchical structures created

Alfonso Ossorio, *Self-Portrait Balanced Head*, 1968

by most of the other contemporary assemblage artists, such as Robert Rauschenberg, Jean Tinguely, Arman, H. C. Westermann, and Edward Kienholz, who came to the fore in the mid-1950s and early 60s.

"Assemblage" was coined by Dubuffet in 1953 to differentiate the new manifestations of collage from those that had earlier developed out of Picasso's first papier collé in 1912. Although many of them remained indebted to the cut-and-paste aesthetic of Picasso and Kurt Schwitters, these younger artists tended to revel in the sooty distress of the urban and industrial detritus that configured their work. Dada ironies, disillusion with industrialization, and a desire to further decrease the distance between their art and the viewer's environment were endemic to most of these artists. Some, like Rauschenberg, Allan Kaprow, and Claes Oldenburg, extended their work into performances ("happenings") that made moot traditional distinctions between the viewer's and the performer's space. Ossorio, like John Chamberlain, eschewed neo-Dada and Pop disjunctions in favor of an organic wholeness and uncustomary fanfares of color found within the materials employed. Both Ossorio and Chamberlain, so different in most respects, made unique contributions to the art of assemblage that were so critical to modernism's jousts with the plane of painting and with traditional techniques.

Ossorio titled one of his assemblages in 1965 *Congregation* in order to emphasize the multiplicity of unique entities within the unity of the whole. And "congregations" is what Ossorio's assemblages subsequently were called. The term is, of course, freighted with ecclesiastical referentiality, and that was hardly coincidental. In the Congregations, Ossorio's deep scholarly and spiritual engagement with Catholicism and early liturgical art was finally and fully subsumed into a multivalent spirituality and polymorphous referentiality that were more in tune with his own contemporary culture. In many respects, the Congregations represent Ossorio's artistic fulfillment of his 1938 art history thesis at Harvard University, "Spiritual Influences on the Visual Images of Christ," in which he charted the changes in Christian art and iconography with the concurrent changes in social and intellectual life, from earliest Christianity to the Romanesque era.

Indeed, we can view the Congregations as reliquaries for the post-nuclear age. Though no less sumptuous in their multifarious excess, the Congregations are inversions of the savage extravagance of precious jewelry that the renowned Abbot Suger of St. Denis had encrusted upon his church's altar and various holy relics (between 1122 and 1151), so that their material beauty might induce a trancelike passage toward spiritual beatitude. Not unlike Suger, Ossorio found "God present in everything...a little waste piece of plastic or a bone is just as much alive as the abstract concept of

God, which is meaningless unless it is incarnated."[1] Ossorio's concept of God was very different from Suger's, but for both, materiality was not opposed to spirituality. Rather, it embodied the spiritual. The artist's role was to make this embodiment visually manifest and compelling.

In 1950, Ossorio created both a grand summation of his medieval art-influenced beginnings as well as some three hundred small ink, wax, and watercolor works in which he fully assimilated the lessons of Pollock and Jean Dubuffet. In these smaller works, the nature of the medium and the process of its manipulation would embody the transformations and transmutations that were more purely pictorially rendered in the concurrent mural and in Ossorio's earlier work. Henceforth, the metaphor would become more fully incarnated in the making. Ossorio's art, his diary, and his reading of the year 1950 are critical to our understanding of his Congregations.

At the beginning of 1950, Ossorio had returned to his native Philippines, where he spent eight months painting a mural in the Chapel of St. Joseph the Workmen on the island of Negros, where his family refined sugar. The island had been ravaged in the wake of the Second World War; the chapel was a memorial commissioned by Ossorio's family. There he set about creating a vast Last Judgment scene. With its hieratic fury-eyed Christ and patterned wave after patterned wave of linear organic geometries, this mural openly looks back to Ossorio's medieval art–history studies at Harvard (1934–38) and to his summer vacations spent in Sussex, England, at the workshop of the Arts and Crafts movement–inspired Eric Gill. Renowned as a stone cutter and wood engraver, Gill had been strongly influenced by such early Christian illuminated manuscripts as the Book of Kells and the Lindisfarne Gospels. In the Philippine mural, the decorative, interlocking arabesques of figures and swaying tendrils earlier found in Ossorio's Gill-influenced wood engravings (mid-1930s) swelled into a monumental and portentous dynamism.

Not all the references and influences found in the mural were inspired by the medieval, nor was its actual execution. At least some of the bold frontality and blunt stylization of the figures is beholden to Philippine folk art. Ossorio's palette and iconographical inventions bear no relation to the conventions of liturgical imagery of the Romanesque era and reflect his struggle to urge his Catholic-based spirituality into a contemporary visuality. The Philippine climate ruled out fresco, and Ossorio turned instead to the plastic-based medium of ethyl silicate, the hard and shiny surface of which is at a far remove from the softer suffusions generally emanating from fresco's plaster. Plastic, too, is the palette, with its torrid reds and oranges—colors also common to the hard, waxy, seemingly artificial flora, such as anthuriums and bromeliads, indigenous to tropical climes. And a plastic fantastic would erupt not only in the popular culture of the 1960s but in Ossorio's Congregations as well.

On the beams and ceiling above the chapel's main mural, apparitions that look very much like Northwest coast Amerindian masks tumble in and out of a camouflaging flow of ambiguously shaped organisms. "Mix our legends…Jonah in the lion's den…Joseph and Jupiter," Ossorio wrote in his Philippine diary.[2] And he imagines a "Guardian Angel totem pole."[3] Elsewhere in the diary he wrote of this "Chapel of the Holy Blood (like warrior or a wound), heart-fire-rose-vaginal wound."[4] While the giant flaming heart emblazoned on Christ's chest in the actual mural is indeed rose-like, it is surprising mainly in its exaggerated scale. But what of the wounds on Christ's overscaled, outstretched hands that can so readily be seen as vaginal? As Amerindian spirits become Catholic angels, Christ's wounds seem to stigmatize him with a second sex.

For Ossorio, wounds were not just symbols of Christ's suffering for humankind, but for humanity's and the world's constantly mutating incompletion. Wounds, isolated organs, a panoply of deformities, bones, and skulls are all prominent in the surrealist-related drawings he did in the mid-1940s that were partially influenced by the detailed medical drawings he was assigned to produce during his military stint at Camp Ellis, Illinois. "Prenatal existence" (page 55), "amniotic fluid…the waters of life" (68), "missing limbs (and organs) supplied by partner, the only way one can become a whole?" (68), the equating of the circulation of blood with devotion to the Sacred Heart (57), Freud, Jung, Siamese quadruplets—these are but some of the staccato thoughts, phrases, and names that churn through the Philippine diary together with simple recipes for art making. This tumult of fact and fantasy is introduced by a poem written in the third person bemoaning "the necessity for childhood/as lonely as his," "being an Eurasian discriminated against," and the "necessity of being a HS or BS" (homosexual or bisexual).[5]

The vaginal wounds, the streams of ovoids that might be tears or spermatozoa or ovaries found in the mural, as well as the diary's wide-ranging references to Jupiter, Freud, and prenatal fluid, give visual and literary voice to Ossorio's efforts to endow spirituality with an ecumenism that could embrace science and myth as well as his homosexuality and the varying genders and races of the world he found himself in. The Catholicism he was born into and that was so much a part of his childhood education had been tested in adulthood and at least partially cast into doubt. His articulation of a turbulently fluid pantheism driven by the sustaining force of God found support in a book important to Ossorio at this time. Nandor Fodor's *The Search for the Beloved, A Clinical Investigation of the Trauma of Birth and Pre-Natal Conditioning*—with its Jungian emphasis on universal symbols, the importance of the androgynous prenatal state, and the fundamental bisexuality of man, out of which he posited homosexuality as the drive to join the ultimate and completing Beloved—found a more than sympathetic reader in Ossorio. In Ossorio's art and in his life, scholarly knowledge and spiritual turbulence were inextricably bound.

The spiritual quest, the interest in primal beginnings, the conflation of science and myth, as well as the feelings of disenfranchisement constantly alluded to in the diary are very much a part of the deeply subjective flight from rationality and belief in industrialized progress that were so typical of the anguished responses to the Holocaust and the atomic bombing of the Second World War, and so perceptible in the art and in the culture at large of the 1950s. The Abstract Expressionists' search for the sublime and their belief in the primacy of a collective unconscious were close to Ossorio's own convictions, but they, unlike him, shed the pronounced eroticism that was so much a part of the Surrealism they all developed out of. Many of these concerns were mirrored in the culture's obsession with paleoanthropology's search for the origins of humanity as well as in the growing importance of Freud and, to a lesser extent, Jung. The alienated hero and heroine were not exclusive to the world of visual art but battled through philosophy, literature, music, and Hollywood, from Jean-Paul Sartre to William Burroughs to Billie Holiday and Charlie Parker to Marlon Brando's and James Dean's nihilistic glamour. Ossorio's Christ, dubbed the "angry Christ" by the island's inhabitants, has his place among these protagonists so precariously formed by isolation.

The mural, some thirty feet long, is, surprisingly, Ossorio's first creation not made on paper or (very rarely) on small canvases painted with tempera, which seldom exceeded thirty inches in length. Working on the cement surface with a plastic-based paint triggered thoughts that prefigure the Congregations of a decade later: "Cement wall…worked wet…insertions on the cement (rocks, plastic, glass, etc.)…eyes of glass studding Argos,"[6] and "a selection of large and precious scraps, male, female, hermaphroditic, fetal, Trinitarian, Unitarian."[7]

The "eyes of glass studding Argos" would be seen in a Congregation ten years hence. Indeed, from the beginning of Ossorio's art making, eyes had often been emphatically enlarged or isolated, and eyes, mostly prosthetic ones, would become the monograms of Ossorio's Congregations. The eyes depicted in the two unrelated bewitchment-eyed giants, the one-eyed Cyclops and the one hundred–eyed Argos, would become materially real eyes rolling through the more abstract but compositionally related delirium of three "Cyclops and Argos" Congregations created between 1960 and 1965. An eye is also, quite literally, Ossorio's written monogram. His initial "A" encircled by "O" that is his art's most frequent signature was modeled after Albrecht Durer's "D"-enwrapped "A"; but Ossorio's monogram also looks very much like the trinitarian symbol of a triangle enclosing an eye in a circle. This symbol, employed by the secret fraternity of Freemasons and found on the U.S. dollar bill, is the center of a deranged watercolor (*Black Sun, Shell and Hourglass*, 1944), where it is surrounded by a group of maimed and deformed, enwombed figures; it looms large on a beam over the main section of the Philippine mural to subject the parishioners to "perpetual Last Judgment."[8] The eye of destruction, the eye of creation, the eye of Judgment—all are one. "A and O. Alpha and Omega, if you wish."[9]

The eye of Ossorio the artist was not conditioned by oil painting but rather by sculpture, architecture, and most importantly, perhaps, book illumination and wood engraving. Nonetheless, it would be the physical painterliness and spirit of Abstract Expressionism and Dubuffet's painting that would help catalyze the material incarnations of the apocalyptic ecumenism alluded to in the Philippine diary. The medieval art that Ossorio had such full art-historical knowledge of, and for which he had such profound love, was part of what he referred to as the "other tradition" that preceded the mimeticism ruling post-Renaissance art up to the advent of modernism in the West. Like many of his peers in the 1950s, he often invoked and interchanged cultures then referred to as "primitive" and "archaic." It was not the differences but rather the parallels between prehistoric cave paintings, Amerindian art, and pre-Renaissance Christian art that would make it possible for Ossorio to state, "Pollock was carrying on exactly in the tradition I was interested in…like Celtic illumination."[10] Ossorio saw beyond the different mediums and contexts of Pollock's painting and the Book of Kells to the core of the driven, intertwining lines of spirit consuming both. In Pollock, Still, and Dubuffet, he found "the density, unexpectedness, and immediate splendor" he sought for his own art.[11]

In 1947, the mutating organic states that had been so precisely delineated began to shift in more allusive opticality as Ossorio added wax to his watercolor and ink to create a layered viscous opacity. By 1949, the discrete profiles of the figures and organic fragments were further dissolved in layers of linear arabesques that reflect the impact of the painting of Ossorio's new friend Pollock. The transformative states and mutations now began to be drawn from the medium and the making themselves: the medium catalyzed and nurtured the forming. The process itself could now become the metaphor for the fetal states enveloped in amniotic fluid that so often preoccupied Ossorio.

Urged on by Pollock, Ossorio went to Paris to meet Dubuffet in the fall of 1949, to begin a dialogue that would be critical to both artists. Dubuffet's erudition, his meticulous and inventive craftsmanship, as well as his championing and collecting of the art of the insane, the criminal, and the culturally isolated (Art Brut)—all were compatible with Ossorio's persona and art. Both he and Dubuffet came from wealthy backgrounds, and both were compulsive collectors. Like Ossorio, Dubuffet was committed to a non-mimetic figuration and rejected the conventions of painting in oil. Dubuffet had a strong commitment to materiality and extruded his figures from its nature. Since 1946, he had worked with a mortarlike conglomerate of paint, sand, and tar, in which a carnivalesque cast of characters were flayed more than drawn with a trowel, a soupspoon, a wire brush, and/or his fingers. Dubuffet preferred a limited palette of earth-related tones that reflected the nature and texture of his materials and generally pinioned isolated figures to his bristling grounds. Ossorio, on the other hand, was prone to more liquid states and to aqueous dissolution of his figures. His more sumptuous palette might as readily relate to viscera as to coral reefs or tropical vegetation, or all together. In the course of his life, Ossorio was seldom far from water; he was born on an island in Manila Bay and, after 1952, spent the remainder of his life overlooking Georgica Pond and the Atlantic Ocean beyond, in East Hampton.

Throughout his career, Ossorio was an excessive worker, and in Negros, whenever he wasn't busy with his mural, he made more intimate and ambiguously figured works on small sheets of paper with ink, wax, and watercolor. In them the lessons of Pollock's gestural linearity and Dubuffet's grotesque figuration merged with his concurrent preoccupation with a kind of mythic and amorphous marine genesis. Bulbous female figures and infants (*Crowded Mother, First Suckling Baby in the Dark, Purple Family,* etc., all 1950) combined references to Mother Church, the Virgin Mary, bloated prehistoric fertility goddesses, and, undoubtedly, his own mother and family. All are in convulsive, multiple states of simultaneous formation and deformation, writhing throughout the plane. Some of these works were cut out of the rectangular plane of the paper to become free-floating organisms, much like the shaped images found on medieval illuminated manuscript pages or in the books illustrated with wood engravings made by Gill and Ossorio himself.

Ossorio's writerly, mythic forming not only looks to Pollock and Dubuffet but also marks the beginning of his liberation from pictorial descriptiveness. This new figuration precedes by a year related efforts made by Pollock. Ossorio's constantly vacillating, fragmented profiles are in a far more tenuous state than Dubuffet's isolated and hieratic figures. Dubuffet's figures are like implosions, Ossorio's like eruptions; both transformed beauties into beasts and vice versa. Ossorio's new quest to make metamorphosis viscerally visual would find its consummate embodiment in the Congregations.

Ossorio continued making these small paintings through 1952, often meeting with Dubuffet, who was working on his Corps de Dame paintings. In 1951, while Ossorio and his partner Ted Dragon stayed with Dubuffet and his wife Lili, Dubuffet wrote "Les Peintures Initiatiques d'Alfonso Ossorio," acutely and vividly praising Ossorio's "dancing cosmogony" and his ardent attempts to restore an unexpurgated universe to a rigidly academicized culture. When he and Dragon moved into the Creeks in East Hampton in 1952, Ossorio set about housing Dubuffet's Art Brut collection, which he had first seen on his second trip to Paris, in 1950.

With their visionary, often hallucinogenic, intensity, rhythmic repetitiveness, sense of exorcism, and frequent incorporation of found materials, the Art Brut works were an inspiration to Ossorio as they were to Dubuffet—whether Pascal-Désir Maisonneuve's found shell faces, Heinrich Anton Müller's "personnages" that preceded Dubuffet's, Miguel Hernandez's figures of swirling paint, or Adolf Wölfli's obsessively labyrinthine illustrations accompanying his twenty-five-thousand page autobiography. For both artists, the unselfconscious primal power and freedom with materials so visible in these works had a direct effect on their own work. Dubuffet's incorporation, in his art, of such unorthodox materials as bark, branches, shells, sponges, and butterfly wings, between 1953 and 1955, and Ossorio's subsequent, more sustained, and astoundingly variegated accumulations of previously seldom-employed objects were surely indebted to Art Brut.

The diverse materiality and cosmology Ossorio had alluded to in the Philippine diary could not be supported by paper; now he turned to the medium of oil, which he had for so long avoided. In 1953, he began a group of paintings that combined the clearly defined and thinly painted mazelike configuring of the Book of Kells with the arcing linearity of Pollock's purely painterly endeavor. By 1955, he loosened and thickened the broth of his paint; now the work of Still made its mark on the painting.

Pollock introduced Ossorio to Still in 1952, and a lengthy correspondence ensued. In 1953 and 1955, Still spent time at the Creeks in East Hampton. His paintings created between 1947 and the mid-1950s were animated by spiky, ambiguous vestiges of figures and mountains and a thick, agitated surface that congealed in a brooding messianism flooded with lunar light. Still's visionary darkness is closer in feeling to Ossorio's vision than is Pollock's more lyrical openness or Dubuffet's frenetic grotesquerie, and his impact is noticeable on the paintings Ossorio created between 1955 and 1958. Here we are brought back to the beginning point of this essay and the end of the long incubation of the Congregations that began in the Philippines.

Still and Pollock, like Mark Rothko and Barnett Newman, sought a physical unity of surface and image that incarnated a radiant, homogenous sublime. Ossorio, too, sought a physically united, all-over surface but needed to incorporate the vast disparities he saw within that unity. Multifariousness had always been key to his visionary ethos. If the Abstract Expressionists helped guide him away from more literal descriptiveness toward a visceral physicality, it was Dubuffet, Art Brut, and Ossorio's engagement with medieval art that helped point the way toward an animate multiplicity that was literally and physically metaphorical.

The pulsing profusion of objects incorporated in the first Congregations tend to be related in size, and almost all have a hard, glistening permeability that either physically is or visually appears to be one of a multitude of radically varying states of coagulated liquidity. Each object is like an individual brushstroke of an interior complexity, density, dimensionality, transparency, and unique identity that an actual brush might only be capable of imagining. The promiscuous nearness of object to object and their related scale and surface, as well as the viscous slipperiness of the plastic adhesive visible in the cramped interstices, propel the objects into a delirious tide of polymorphously perverse intercourse. Impossible relationships writhe hallucinogenically in and out of focus, as each object asserts, then yields its identity to unexpected assignations with its neighbors. The vulgar, the tawdry, the discarded, the organic, the artificial, the beautifully formed, the ridiculously fragmented, the common, the exotic, the repellent, the erotic, the hermaphroditic, the trinitarian, the unitarian, are all joined in a seamless and lavish tide of terrible beauty that simply won't stop metamorphosing.

The desire to transform painting into a palpably physical and luminous body interacting with the viewer's space and place was made stunningly literal by Ossorio, as were the multiple interchanges of the literal and the figurative. Now the spontaneity and courtship of chance that were so much a part of Abstract Expressionist intentions and the immersion of these intentions in oil paint's liquidity were no longer part of Ossorio's own intentions. He carefully deliberated the minutest detail. The preparation and gathering of materials could consume up to several months. Sketches were made of the support and configuration, then the materials would be laid down on the support, removed to a table while the ground and adhesive were prepared, and finally set permanently in place, with only occasional changes and adjustments being made.

Ossorio's skilled crafting calls back to his love of medieval art and to the precise carving of wood engraving that marked his first making. The irregularly curved and scrolling supports, so often employed by Ossorio, recall the free-floating shapes likewise seemingly distended by their interior imagery that are in the Book of Kells and other illuminated manuscripts; they recall as well the irregular shapes of the block of wood employed for an engraving and the cut-out shapes of some of the Philippine works on paper. The pre-planned interior horizontals and diagonals that pull the seething flow back from the edges of chaos are reminiscent of but much more open than the geometric compartmentalization containing the arabesquing linearity in the Book of Kells. So, too, is the intertwining swirl of figurative fabulism and the more abstract, multi-hued arterial flow not unlike that to be found in the Book of Kells.

Nevertheless, Ossorio's iconography and referential multivalence are at a far remove from medieval art's conventions. The precision of patterned arabesques composing botanical and human forms in his wood engraving *Sidrach, Misach, and Abdenago* (1933–34) has been subsumed into the more amorphous and allusive currents of the various shells, starfish, and other bobbing protrusions found in the 1962 Congregation of the same subject. As the individual objects in a Congregation resolve and dissolve their identity in a variety of mutations dependent upon their shifting alliances, so too does Ossorio's iconography. A crosslike form can as readily be loosened from Christian specificity into a flower as into a spermatozoa.

And eyes are not just in the head, they are rolling around everywhere, animating the surface and the previously not-thought-to-be-seeing objects. The unforeseen, the seen, the judging, and the judged unite in liquid symbiosis, sucking vision into the visionary, eyes witnessing as they are being witnessed, judging as they are being judged.

Eyes, shells, and, in the mid-1960s, a growing array of horns, antlers, and bones give visceral body to the flow and are joined by Buddha hands, artificial flowers, cut-up photographs of human figures, marbles, teeth, nails, handcuffs, chains, household hardware, crockery shards, and more, much more. Ossorio haunted hardware stores and junk shops in lower Manhattan, broke dishes at home, and ordered horns and bones by the dozens. His vast studio looked like a cross between a taxidermist's workshop and Merlin's laboratory.

The objects were not just passively affixed to their ground but rather incited into an increasingly dynamic interaction with its hosting liquidity, so that their forms seem to ooze and mutate out of its culture. Ossorio constantly subjected his grounds to new processes, sometimes adding hair to the surface, sometimes pouring matte medium over parts of a wooden ground and then torching the untreated wood while the medium-coated areas resisted the flame, sometimes making marbleized pours of acrylic that were then pulled up and glued to the ground with the backside up; by the mid-1960s, he began to more actively draw into the congealing ground with the objects that were now often fully in the round. He was as restlessly inventive as he was technically knowledgeable. The Congregations' kaleidoscopic liquidity is as visually compelling from afar as it is at close scrutiny. Again and again, the viewer's eye is shocked into contemplativeness.

All the Congregations have a brutal beauty fraught with ambiguity; but they can range from the stiller, Buddhist mandala-like *Circled Head* (1963) to the claustrophobically humorous abundance of *Unsuccessful Tow* (1961–71) to the aggressive phallic fury of the multi-horned *Full Circle* (1968). The Christian symbolism and iconography first more conventionally adhered to, later subjected to precisely defined surrealist disjunctions, and then more wholly reconfigured in Ossorio's monumental Philippine mural, are now at last submerged in a completely personal and universal sea of referentiality. In *Resurrect II* (1965), Christ has been defigured and refigured in a swarm of disparities, at once gruesome and majestic. His wholeness is atomized across the plane that vibrates with some fifty varieties of symbiotic objects; his barely identifiable head is a piece of broken bone crowned by shards of glass. His apostles are absurdly smiling little teddy-bear heads, and shells, and syringes, and glass carrots, and countless bejeweled encrustations. The figure of Christ, like the artist, is at once creator and the victim of the vanity of trying to be a creator. His eyes, one glaring out, one rolling helplessly up, are simultaneously judging and recoiling from judgment, simultaneously witnessing forming and deforming, beauty and the wounding of beauty. "Religion must aim to inspire awe, to awe man with the splendor of existence," Ossorio said. "By a set of unexpected juxtapositions, it must put you in a state of realization of how splendid things can be, even if they are horrible."[12]

It is time for Ossorio's Congregations to find the wider recognition they so richly deserve. His art, so often considered purely idiosyncratic in the past, now can better be understood when seen in the context of the art of a younger generation that has turned to a re-exploration of the often repressed excesses of the subjective and the spiritual—whether Cindy Sherman's grotesquely gorgeous photographic unmasking of the multiplicity of roles played by the ego and the id, or the vulgar glories and secretions of Carroll Dunham's cavalcade of glandular mutations, or Pepón Osorio's compulsively arranged and deranged installations of charged domestic objects, or the painful jubilations of Kiki Smith's explorations of mortality and the multi-sexuality of spirituality, or Frank Moore's hyper-detailed allegories, so humorously and furiously fueled by the desire for relief and redemption from the AIDS pandemic. Ossorio's Congregations will perhaps be seen to be as universal as they are unique, as beautiful as they are repellent, as true as they are.

1. In Forrest Selvig, transcript of a tape-recorded interview with Alfonso Ossorio, November 19, 1968, 14, in the Oral History Archive, Archives of American Art, Smithsonian Institution, Washington D.C.

2. Alfonso Ossorio's Philippine diary, 1950, 17. This diary, together with many of Ossorio's others, is in the archives of the Ossorio Foundation, Southampton, New York.

3. Ibid., 68.

4. Ibid., 83.

5. Ibid., 2.

6. Ibid., 49.

7. Ibid., 59.

8. Judith Wolfe, "Interview with Alfonso Ossorio, May, June, 1980," *Ossorio, 1940–1980* (East Hampton, NY: Guild Hall Museum, 1980), 16.

9. Ibid., 16.

10. Ibid., 14.

11. Francine du Plessix, "Ossorio the Magnificent," *Art in America*, vol. 55, no. 2 (March–April 1967): 60.

12. Ibid., 62.

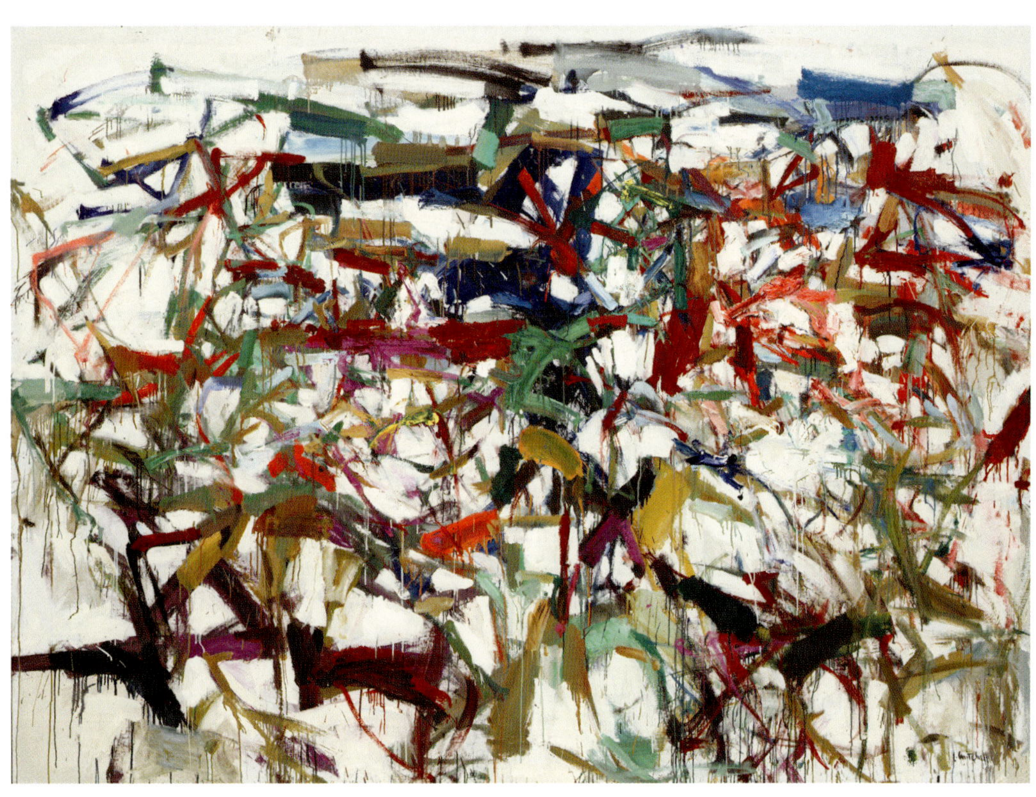

Joan Mitchell, *Ladybug*, 1957

Joan Mitchell

Storms of Paint

The arching calligraphic linearity and paint's more nearly total engulfing of the canvas plane in the paintings Joan Mitchell created in the last half of the 1950s bear a superficial resemblance to Jackson Pollock's drip paintings; however, their making and meaning are quite different from Pollock's. Although he regularly reworked his paintings, they have the rolling seamlessness and variations of a continuously choreographed movement that breaks like a wave across the canvas. Mitchell's more isolated strokes and counterstrokes, in contrast, have the driven grace and give and take of the tennis matches that she would later avidly watch on television. The downward drips and splashes and centralizing arching of her strokes have an in-and-out dynamic that is unlike Pollock's more lateral thrust of paint flung with the canvas on the floor. Pollock's paintings are more all-engulfing; his "I am nature" is very different from Mitchell's being with nature in memory. Pollock is more a shaman, Mitchell more a lover. But both share with Vincent Van Gogh a highly tuned, visceral sensitivity to movement. And both share the quality that Frank O'Hara so aptly attributed to Pollock's paintings: "lyrical desperation."

Mitchell and O'Hara included each other in their work, and O'Hara's irreverently acute manifesto, "Personism" of 1959, as well as his poems reflect the influence of his painter friends. In "Personism," he declared of poetry that "one of its minimal aspects is to address itself to one person (other than the poet himself), thus evoking overtones of love without destroying love's life-giving vulgarity, and sustaining the poet's feeling toward the poem while preventing love from distracting him into feeling about the person." If we substitute the art of painting for that of poetry, this is close to Mitchell's way of working out of the extreme one-to-oneness between viewer and painting that had been made possible by the insistent physical presence of Abstract Expressionist painting (so very different from the generalized relation to the viewer, as part of a larger community, that is implicit in perspective-dependent painting). O'Hara, like Mitchell, replaced the metaphysical heat of Pollock with the heat of "overtones of love."

O'Hara's charismatic presence, sensual charm, and restlessness seem to be part of one of the more joyously frantic paintings Mitchell created at this time. The title, *Evenings on Seventy-Third Street*, refers to the dinners, replete with painters' and poets' swirling egos, at the apartment of the director of the Stable Gallery, Hal Fondren, who had been O'Hara's roommate at Harvard and would remain a lifelong friend of Mitchell's. The pleasurable havoc of darting strokes of red, blue, green, and ocher seen in this painting takes on a new, dire import in *To the Harbormaster* of 1957. Inspired by O'Hara's poem of the same name, this is a rare case of a title preceding, and to some degree predicting, the content and making of a painting by Mitchell. O'Hara's agitated mingling of water and emotion with fraught arrivals that become departures in "To the Harbormaster" does, of course, closely relate to Mitchell's favored themes, and she turned her painting into an epic wail. Broad strokes of harsh red and orange wave like flags of distress over a rage of blues and greens, all gathering into a dark, ominous center. Greater risk of chaos, more variety of mark making, and a more complex weave of light flashing and flickering across the surface—all hold the canvas and won't let go. What structure appears must be intuited and seems to have been created out of exposed nerves.

A fuller aeration of white and a lush congregation of horizontally inclined strokes—from soft green to deep blue to ruby red turning brown to a florid mauve accent that will henceforth recur again and again—make *Ladybug* of 1957 a ravishingly temperamental painting, as stormy as, but far less distraught than, *To the Harbormaster.* If you stand willingly aligned with the center of either of these two works, where the strokes writhingly converge in arrivals and departures, the paintings become viscerally and emotionally wrenching. These are big, deep, and beautiful paintings for which the word masterpiece might well be risked. Matisse's flow of color as light and the stunning circularity of his two versions of *Dance* of 1909–10 and Van Gogh's bristling strokes cum units of nature's driving forces are not directly visible on Mitchell's surface, but the experience of them lies somewhere below.

Mitchell's mastery was taking full flight into the eclipse of gestural painting. Her work was receiving support that was hardly inconsequential, but the art public's gaze was more and more shifting elsewhere. Pollock had died in 1956, still pursuing new ways of painting that many had perceived as sheer decline. The openness and greater accessibility to nature with which Willem de Kooning began infusing his paintings in 1957 was seen as too soft by some of his supporters. Mitchell could hardly have been overjoyed by her inclusion in a 1957 *Life* magazine article devoted to "five of the outstanding young women painters in the U.S.," including the "most celebrated" Grace Hartigan, along with Helen Frankenthaler, Nell Blaine, and Jane Wilson. On the other hand, she would have been furious at being excluded. The same year, the most stolid of Abstract Expressionism's chroniclers, Irving Sandler, wrote "Mitchell Paints a Picture" as part of *Art News*'s series on artists in their studios. The text is remarkable for Mitchell's unconcerned willingness to reject, in mid-article, the painting that she was being photographed working on, and for first quoting her epigrammatic remark, "I carry my landscape around with me." And, also in 1957, she was included in the exhibition *Artists of the New York School: Second Generation,* the subtitle of which would shortly become a term of opprobrium haunting Mitchell and some of her peers. Though Jasper Johns and Robert Rauschenberg were included in this exhibition at

New York's Jewish Museum, they would not subsequently be stigmatized with the label of "Second Generation." Both would become part of the gallery that was to be one of the epicenters of the new, opened in 1957 by Leo Castelli.

In 1955, when her turbulent self-knowledge was blossoming into a fully painted beauty, Mitchell began to spend part of each year in Paris. In so doing, she removed herself from the growing doubts and challenges circling Abstract Expressionism and the very physical painterliness to which she herself was just beginning to give such vibrant life, while artists such as Johns, Rauschenberg, and Kenneth Noland variously sought to move beyond gestural abstraction. Mitchell's life in Paris was connected with no identifiable group and probably continued to free her from the doubts about Abstract Expressionism's validity that followed in the wake of new movements alien to her way of painting. Like her, her lover Jean-Paul Riopelle had been strongly affected by de Kooning and Franz Kline, but, unlike her, he remained uncritically worshipful of them. Deeply resentful of his exclusion from American accounts of Abstract Expressionism, Riopelle was, however, highly regarded in Canada and France. (He too was a heavy drinker, and his and Mitchell's relationship became increasingly fractious and dysfunctional; both had affairs, often within their circle of friends.)

Mitchell's most remarkable friendship was with Samuel Beckett, whom she met through Barney Rosset in 1956. Twenty years her senior, Beckett joined Mitchell in strong mutual admiration and perhaps more. He loved art, she loved writing; both drank heavily, both disliked explaining their work, and both were obsessed with the subjects of loneliness and death. Mitchell, Beckett, his artist friend Bram van Velde, Riopelle, and Alberto Giacometti often drank together at the Dôme, and Mitchell's conversations with Beckett were capable of reducing the others to onlookers. Beckett spent hours in Mitchell's studio, and they frequently met in out-of-the-way bistros and bars. According to Beckett's biographer, "her friendship became a crutch he leaned on heavily."

Mitchell and Beckett discussed her creating visual accompaniment to the published version of his radio play *Embers* (written and published in 1959). The themes of the sea, light, memory, transience, and death that converge in *Embers* were hardly unfamiliar to Mitchell's work. She embarked on a series of watercolors (now lost) before deciding that the play was perfectly colored on its own. While Mitchell's painting is more openly turbulent than Beckett's searingly becalmed and darkly humorous prose, both were equipped with a harrowing accuracy and directness; both imbued a seemingly uncomplicated vocabulary with deep nuances. Neither one permitted the flabbiness of self-pity or self-indulgence. In the course of the 1960s, illness and death rose more emphatically to the surface of Mitchell's paintings, as they would again in the mid-1980s, and heightened the parallels between her work and Beckett's. If the word "stroke" were to join "syllable," Beckett's "every syllable is a second gained" might be his and Mitchell's duet.

The move to France became permanent in 1959. Mitchell took a studio at 10, rue Frémicourt in Paris but still kept her place on St. Mark's Place in New York. And now her paintings begin to surge with a violence that threatens the plane. But, just in time, each seething web of warring brushstrokes diffuses into a hiss and reluctantly subsides into the ambient whiteness, where the marks start to bend their trajectories into greater conformity with the rectangular shape of the support. No less furious is the polyphony of color, as changing hues race across the surface. That this high voltage doesn't short-circuit the light, but rather projects it radiantly forth, bespeaks the power of Mitchell's control.

In 1960, storm clouds of paint begin to gather toward the center, gradually assuming configurations similar to those of the early 1950s. In *Skyes* of 1960–61, the sweeping strokes and pulsing hues of the immediately preceding paintings have been forcefully subdued, as though, all of a sudden, paint and canvas were resisting each other. There are more stops and starts as painted strokes, varying greatly in size, scale, shape, trajectory, and pressure, struggle vainly to gather into a fist of paint and pull out of the atmospheric disturbance of the surrounding smudges and smears. This painting establishes a lexicon of the shifting stages of anger and determination in terms of paint's liquidity. In *Grandes Carrières* of 1961–62, the paint gathers into a still more concentrated distress, as roseate red, cerulean blue, and flashes of bright green seem to be sucked into the central darkness that threatens to engulf the entire plane. Mitchell was probing a beauty that is the beginning of terror.

Mitchell's willingness to risk a mess (quite literally) and then, at the last minute, dare murkiness into clarity is in some ways parallel to the concurrent paintings of Cy Twombly, such as *Empire of Flora* and *The First Part of the Return from Parnassus*, both of 1961, with their scatological denotations of mark making and their seeming utter disregard for completion. While Twombly's offhand elegance and writerly discursiveness are at a far remove from Mitchell's excoriated landscape of memories and denser physicality, both share a deep joy in the ability of the acts of the hand to unite the flow of paint with that of thought. Both continued to draw inspiration from the gestural painterliness of their elders. In their work, both had an excellent year in 1961.

In 1961, Andy Warhol made a thirty-two–panel painting, each panel meticulously reproducing a Campbell's soup can with a different flavor of soup. The same year, Roy Lichtenstein startlingly turned his compositional skill to enlarged comic-book simulations. And Claes Oldenburg created *The Store* in a temporarily rented space he filled with slapdash and wonderfully slapstick plaster reliefs and replicas of supermarket products, splattering them with paint in a way that literally and figuratively "commodified" Abstract Expressionist gesture. The mass media and the arts began to mirror each other. The literal and impassive repetitiveness of Warhol's work found parallels in the objectively systematized abstraction of Frank Stella, which would soon lead into a movement that became known as Minimalism. On almost all new art fronts, the hand was being withdrawn from action, and the subjective and unique were being imagined away. The influence of Barnett Newman and Ad Reinhardt replaced that of Pollock and de Kooning. Undeterred, Mitchell continued on her chosen path.

Most of the 1960s would prove to be a personally troubling time for Mitchell. Her mother began a long struggle with cancer in 1960; Kline died in 1962; and, in 1965, Mitchell's father died. This heavy dose of mortality immediately preceded and catalyzed what Mitchell called "my black paintings—although there's no black in any of them." In these grave and unsparing paintings made in 1964, strokes, smears, and wipes (brush, hands, and rags were all probably employed) are pulled into a shuddering, centralized mass with predominant greens and blues urged toward an ominous darkness—as though sight were being pushed into a sightless zone. The centralized grouping of strokes is too open and amorphous to become a shape. It is rather a gathering of forces; they simultaneously emerge from and submerge into the surrounding dense and deathly fog of white, which vacillates with vagrant traces of blurred color and drifting strokes. In this smooth atmosphere, color and movement struggle for resolution where none seems to be available.

The tarnished green in *Calvi* and *First Cypress* is like that of early autumn foliage, still green but gradually being drained of light by a waning sun. In *Blue Tree*, a cold, winter white begins to roil a constellation dominated by blue; and, in *Chicago*, this white confronts a cold, nighttime blue. These paintings are not a sublimation of pain but a revelation of it; the forces of nature become a metaphor for the trials of life. Yet these works are neither autobiographical nor mimetic; their somber climate is utterly specific to the paint it emerges from. The sizes and massing of strokes are scaled to the size of the canvas and conditioned by its rectangular shape. Again, the strokes respect, and to some extent approach, a rectangularity impossible to their liquid nature.

This group of paintings marks a more emphatic shift toward allusions drawn purely from nature and away from the traces of the urban that were mixed into the earlier paintings. They also give blue a new prominence. If Mitchell had had to choose but one color out of which to make a rainbow, it would certainly have been blue. Whether the blue that makes darkness visible, the blue of water, the blues in Cézanne, Van Gogh, and Matisse, the blue of morning glories or delphiniums, or "the blues" of jazz and sadness, blue was critical to the life of Mitchell's painting.

In the group of "black" paintings are two triptychs. The polyptych format would become more and more prominent in Mitchell's subsequent work. The multiple panels serve the practical purpose of making larger paintings easier to move. At the same time, the interior edges emphasize the physicality of the surface and make possible a more complex dialogue between the illusiveness of paint and the canvas's materiality. The multiple physical panels can be seen as forming both one simultaneous unit and a sequence observed in the real time of the viewer, as the moving eye seems to shift the individual planes into and out of order.

The sense of a somber, nature-bound aloneness in these and many other of Mitchell's paintings strikes a deep chord in an American tradition that includes the paintings of Albert Pinkham Ryder, Marsden Hartley, Clyfford Still, and Pollock. Mitchell's aloneness with her memories of nature, particularly those of the American Midwest, was at its most fraught and compressed at this moment. And the turbulence in her life went on. Her relationship with Riopelle grew more troubled, and their battles included the slashing of each other's paintings. O'Hara—whose role at the Museum of Modern Art had made him a public champion of Abstract Expressionism and its heirs, including Mitchell, and whose poetry, correspondence, and friendship were an irreplaceable asset to her—died in 1966, after being run over by a vehicle on the beach in Fire Island. And in 1967, Mitchell's mother died from cancer. Cancer would henceforth cast a pall over her life.

Although she was never politically active, Mitchell's glum view of the world took cognizance of current events. Her own neighborhood in Paris was made dangerous by the spillover of Algerian hostilities into France. And in her native America, after the great promise of the early 1960s—starting with the election of John F. Kennedy, and including the growing Civil Rights movement and the jubilant rebellion against the repression of the 1950s—came a wave of assassinations, from J.F.K. in 1963 and Malcolm X in 1965, to Dr. Martin Luther King Jr. and Robert Kennedy in 1968, together with the growing American presence in Vietnam and race riots at home. Near anarchy and calls for new order vied with each other, as both America and France were buffeted by growing student protests late in the decade.

Artists in the United States were becoming more politically active, but this was nowhere visible as such on the surfaces of their works. Most abstraction was ruled by the cool, analytical side of consciousness, and the insistence on self-contained objecthood, drained of outside reference, brought new prominence to sculpture. Among abstract painters, Brice Marden and Agnes Martin were almost alone in their desire to imbue paint with emotional resonance, but their rigorous reductiveness and emphatic structural clarity drew the praise of the Minimalist fold and led to their inclusion in it. The ambiguities of Marden's monochrome paintings, begun in 1965, suggest a certain kinship with Mitchell's "black" paintings. He was one of the few artists still looking to de Kooning and Kline, but he introverted the surface emotionality of their work with spartan disciplines that left only vestigial evidence of his hand. In time, when he would actively start to return drawing to the surface of his painting, he would become a strong Mitchell enthusiast.

Mitchell's painting did not simply become the passive reflection of her emotional landscape but made its own demands on that landscape. And now, her painting seemed to call for a brighter nature and a return to the coloristic brio that had emboldened her paintings late in the 1950s. At the height of Mitchell's moroseness, in 1966, her painting began slowly to call to clearer hues and light. Although hardly jubilant, the triptych *Chicago* of 1966–67 is lighter in touch and in its massing of strokes, with more nourishing light and the occasional emergence of the greens that come with spring. The title, given after the painting's completion, was intended to honor her dead mother.

For some time, Mitchell had wanted to leave Paris and move to the country. With the trust fund from her grandfather that she received after her mother's death, Mitchell in 1967 bought, almost on the spur of the moment, an imposing stone house in Vétheuil, some thirty miles northwest of Paris. The house, with a separate studio in back, crowns a hill overlooking the Seine; an ancient linden tree dominates the courtyard entrance, and a lower garden is found to the side. The view from the property includes fertile countryside, much of it cultivated, rows of poplars, and the Gothic church in Vétheuil. Monet had painted in this lush yet ordered landscape from 1878 through 1881; he lies buried in the church cemetery. His small house is at the bottom of Mitchell's property, and the avenue that leads to her entranceway bears his name.

The Seine, the linden tree, the flowers, and the fields now became part of Mitchell's landscape—one that was richer, and had more history, than the landscape outside of Chicago but which was related to it in its ordering. As Pollock had responded to the vastness of the American West, its endless horizon and plains, and to the related vastness of the ceaselessly rolling ocean near his studio on Long Island, Mitchell responded to the more contained landscape of the American Midwest and Vétheuil. Indeed, Vétheuil itself became part of Mitchell's culture more than Monet would. Though Mitchell and Monet shared its landscape, Monet's paintings are more about capturing that landscape and its changing light than are Mitchell's. Instead, her Vétheuil was merged with her Illinois. And her often wildly bristling strokes, and the concurrent need for the discipline of the canvas's grid, are in fact closer to Van Gogh and Cézanne than to the structural looseness of Monet. It was the rise in

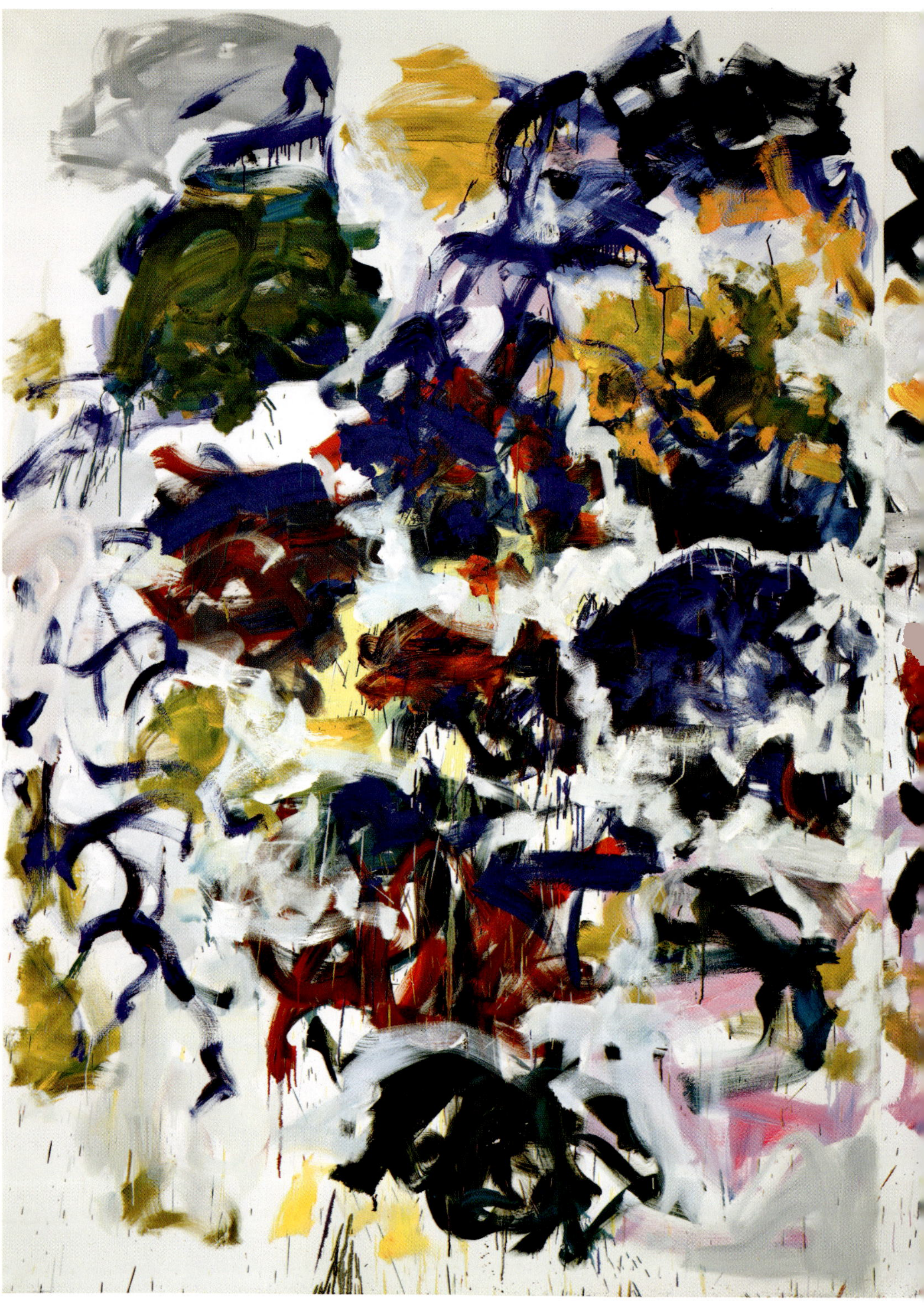

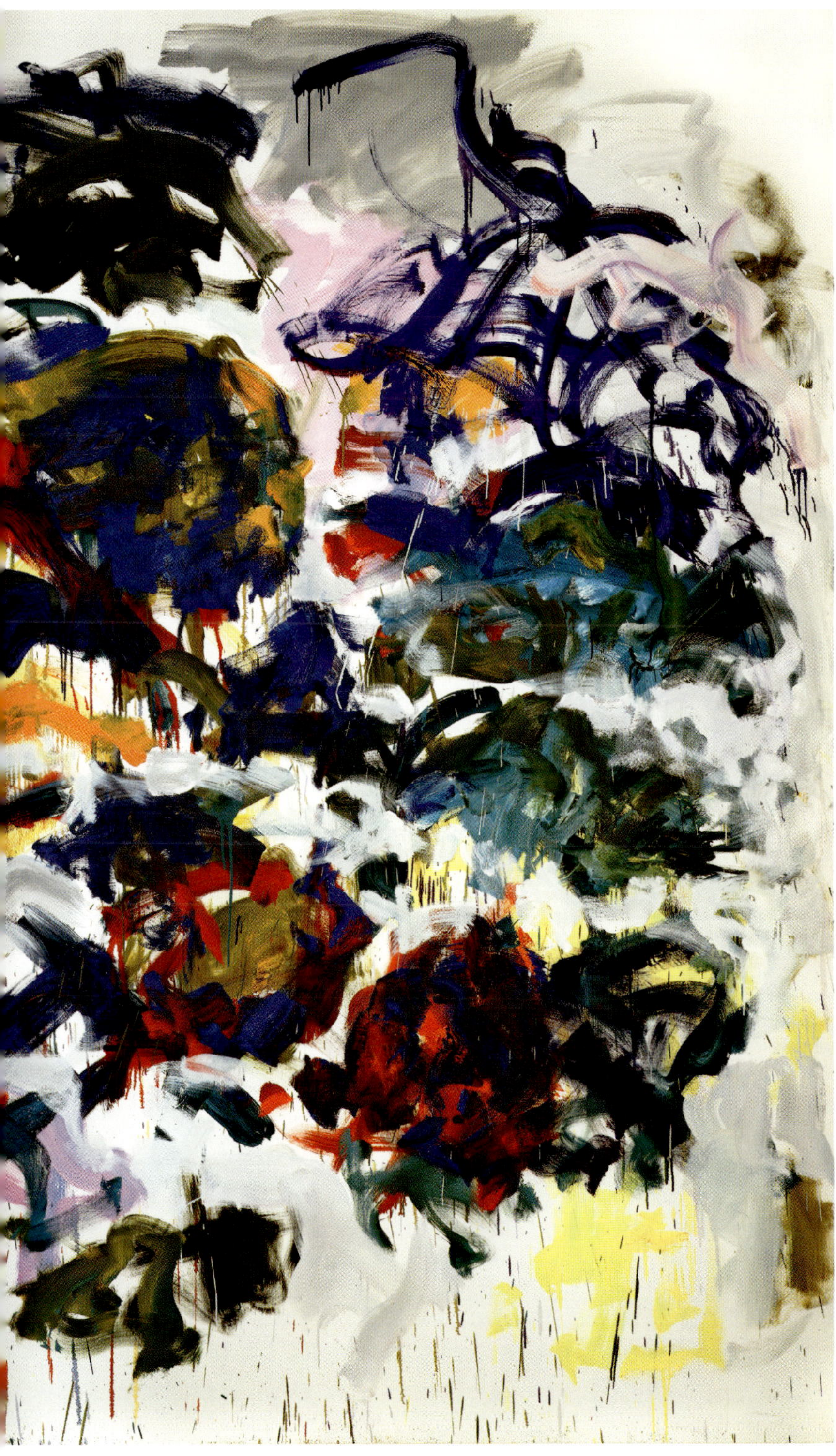

Joan Mitchell,
Sunflowers, 1990–91

Monet's stature among contemporary artists in New York in the 1950s, based on his previously little-known late paintings, together with the location of Mitchell's house that led to numerous comparisons with Monet and speculations about his paintings' influence on hers. Mitchell correctly, but perhaps too defensively, renounced these conjectures.

Mitchell was happy in her relative isolation in Vétheuil. Except for her own art, and that which she haphazardly collected or traded, hanging on the walls, the house, for as long as she was to live, looked like she was still moving in. Her love of dogs led her to give her four Skye terriers the run of the house; other dogs would follow. (Dogs were an important part of her life and often her only companions.) Though Riopelle had an immense studio nearby, where he also kept a sizable collection of cars, he seldom spent the night in Mitchell's house, often leaving after a fight. There were friends like Hal Fondren, who usually visited twice yearly, and the poet J. J. Mitchell (no relation), who would stay a week or more; and there would be a variety of younger artists, often ones influenced by her, who would also be invited. And, of course, there were Paris and New York. But mostly Mitchell was alone in Vétheuil with her dogs and her painting.

From 1967 through 1975, the less pained and more bucolic side of Mitchell's memory dominated her painting. The aloneness and precarious new independence that inevitably came with the death of her second parent, along with the concurrent move to the country, seem to have played a part in Mitchell's need to stabilize her paintings with a strong emphasis on structuring. In the intense, organic struggle between chaos and order, it was now order that came into more visible prominence on the surface of the painting. Mitchell's need for a new order reflected her need to reorganize her life, after the harsh losses of the 1960s, as much as it did her effort to establish control over the ambitious size and scale she was undertaking in her work.

Even before her complete move from Paris, Mitchell had given herself over more totally to nature. Now, all traces of urban grittiness were dissolved as she reclaimed a landscape. The Vétheuil she took as her own was at once similar to the landscape of her childhood and a completely new landscape free of familial references. *My Landscape, La Seine, Vétheuil* her titles quite simply proclaim. And for a while, the immediate presence of Vétheuil dominated.

The Cézannesque, geometrized organicism that marked Mitchell's first mature works, early in the 1950s, returns in *My Landscape II* of 1967 with a new amplitude that shows her mastery of paint's allusive liquidity. The upturned reflection of sky and landscape rematerialized in *La Seine II* of 1967 embodies a "sea change" of paint at a far remove from the churning discord of *To the Harbormaster* of 1957. In *La Seine*, the triptych's contrapuntal play of vertical and horizontal—downward dripping paint and vertical interior edges, against the horizontal (and vertical) flows of paint and the overall horizontality of the canvas support—keeps the surface taut and shuffles a simple sequential reading into shifting layers of time, space, and place.

Although hardly representational, these paintings are more closely bound to nature than are Mitchell's earlier works and seem less acculturated with her past. The buoyant, podlike blue and green configurations in *Vétheuil* of 1967–68 take a pleasure from being in, and with, nature that is very different from the internalization of the forces of nature found, for instance, in the clenched massing of the "black" paintings. This less fettered joy in nature, in concert with a greater obedience to the dictates of the support's rectangularity, dominated Mitchell's paintings until 1975. Now, instead of the lugubrious light of fall and winter, the brighter light of late spring and summer controls the paintings' climate. The work of this time is often parallel in feeling, while radically different in execution and configuration, to de Kooning's nature-bound, all-over abstractions created between 1972 and 1979 in the Springs, in East Hampton, where he had moved permanently in 1965.

Mitchell's momentarily undisturbed happiness in nature was vividly embodied in a new inspiration. She planted sunflowers in her garden; they would remain her favorite flower, and become a recurrent theme in her art until the end. Van Gogh's 1888 *Sunflowers* was intended by him to be part of a series decorating his room in Arles and was among his most openly joyous paintings; his bunches of impacted strokes became an ode to light and growth. In a group of large vertical paintings from 1969 and 1970, Mitchell took up this subject, and it was to both Van Gogh and nature that her passion turned. From a vibrant ground of white flickering with yellow and green reflections, she extruded single or multiple rounded clusters of intense yellow-orange, offset by vermilion, mauve, and blue. Like Van Gogh, she was seeking to make light's life-giving radiance material.

It is not only the blossom's intense yellows, which make it an exemplary manifestation of nurturing light, that suggest the sunflower as a metaphor for painting. The oil extracted from its seeds can be used for cooking—but also for making paint. Moreover, a yellow dye can be made from its petals and paper from its stems. Thus the sunflower has the potential of being the subject, object, and medium of painting. And for Mitchell, the visibly spiraling, tubular florets of its central disc recalled her frequent, earlier preference for an energized circularity.

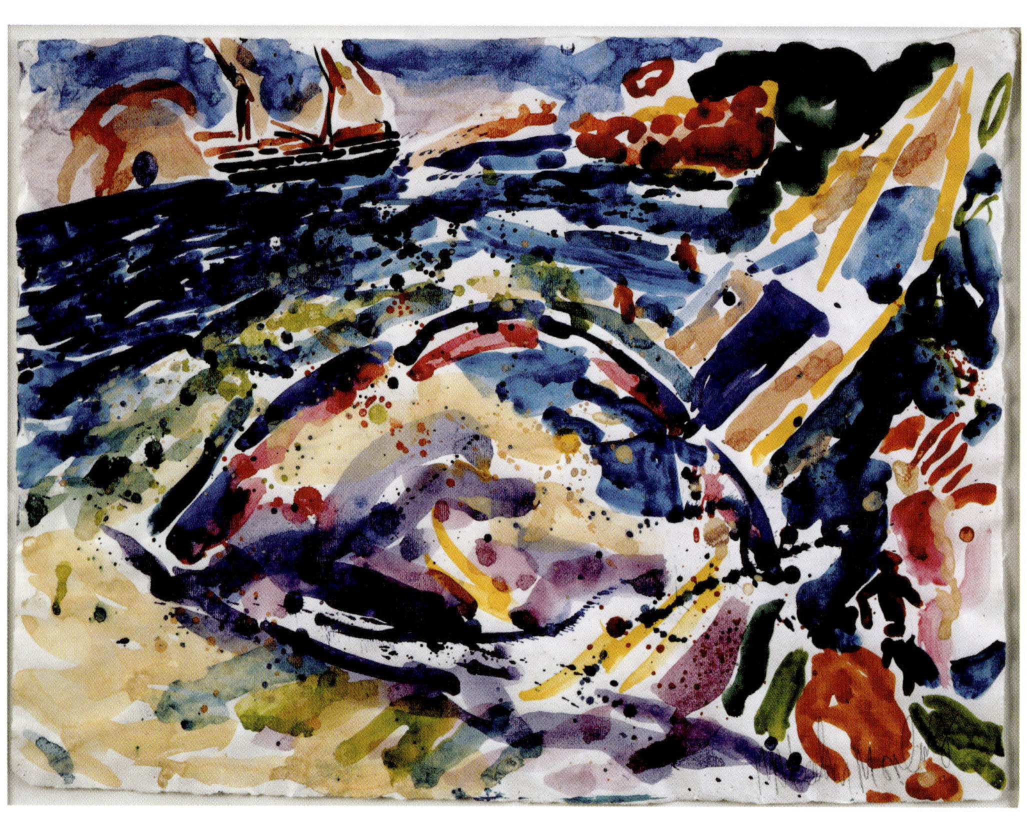

Malcolm Morley, *Windsurfer in Antigua*, 1987

Malcolm Morley

Seeing Is Imagining

"It was kind of like sailing—an adventure," Malcolm Morley responded when asked how he could paint on such a large sheet (thirty-two by forty inches) at the beach. Indeed, like a seasoned sailor, Morley knows just how to draw on, with, and against the wind. In his watercolor, *Kite on Gibson Beach* (1984), the washes, splashes, and dashes propelled by the shifting pressures of his brush do not so much describe as they become the will of the wind. The watercolor and its paper support conjoin as a pneumatic two-dimensional vessel that contains and shapes perception. Morley's art is deeply grounded in and committed to perception, but perception that is comprehended as painting. The procedures of perception must metamorphose into the procedures of painting; describing must lose itself in becoming. Writers can only write about the ocean whereas painters can paint like the ocean.

Watercolor? Painting outdoors? It has been some decades since either of these activities has been associated with a major contemporary artist; however, the multifarious virtuosity and vitality that comprise this exhibition [*Malcolm Morley: Watercolors*, Tate, London, 1992] give more than ample proof of watercolor's potential for painterly consequence. It is watercolor that has literally and figuratively generated Morley's art the last ten years or so. But long before that, watercolor had already preoccupied him. Watercolor was actually his first medium. Untrained and untutored in the rituals of modernism, the young Morley joined the ranks of amateurs that still blotted and often blighted the landscape of his native England. Watercolor was largely a British invention (long, long ago) that turned into a veritable flood by the end of the nineteenth century. While the likes of Constable and Turner infused their watercolors with a vision that quickly spread beyond British borders, there were also legions of highly skilled local landscapists who remained just that. Morley admits to a certain admiration for these provincial watercolor painters and a kind of kinship based on his and their shared technical skills. He has even expressed the desire to curate an exhibition of some of their work. Although he is now totally immersed in the medium, when Morley left the ranks of amateurs to go to art school and quickly thereafter to New York (in 1958), he turned to weightier paint. The bourgeois civilities connected with watercolor (some in England even regarded its practice as one of the social graces) were antithetical to the mostly macho competitiveness and intensity of inventiveness that were prerequisites to the success of a Manhattan modernist.

When Morley returned to the medium of watercolor in the mid-1970s, he brought to it the joys and anxieties of a mature artist highly skilled in the arena of late modernism. Watercolor became a major component of the painterly figuration that Morley was so crucial in reinventing and transfusing into painting's mainstream. Watercolor now took its place

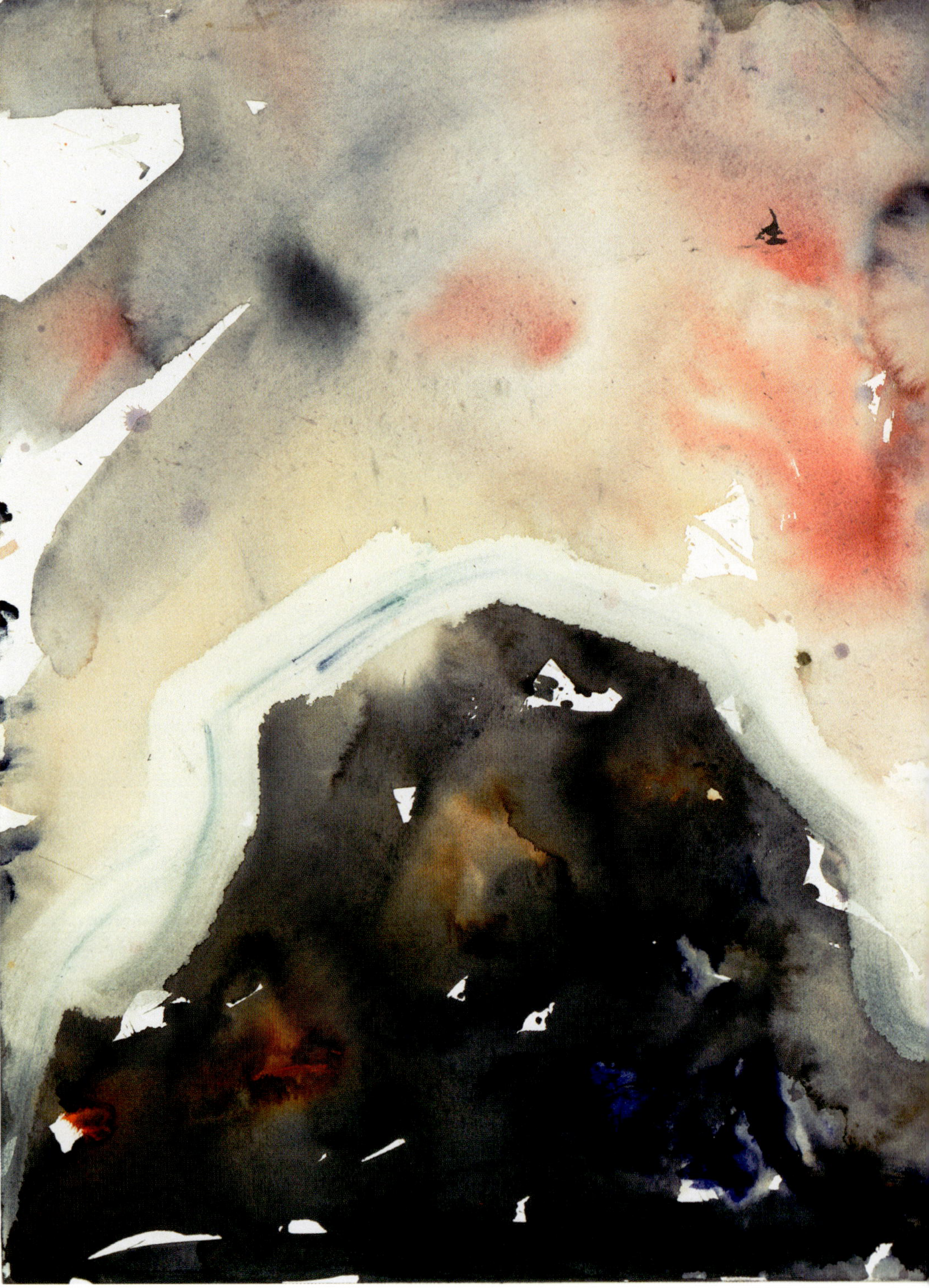

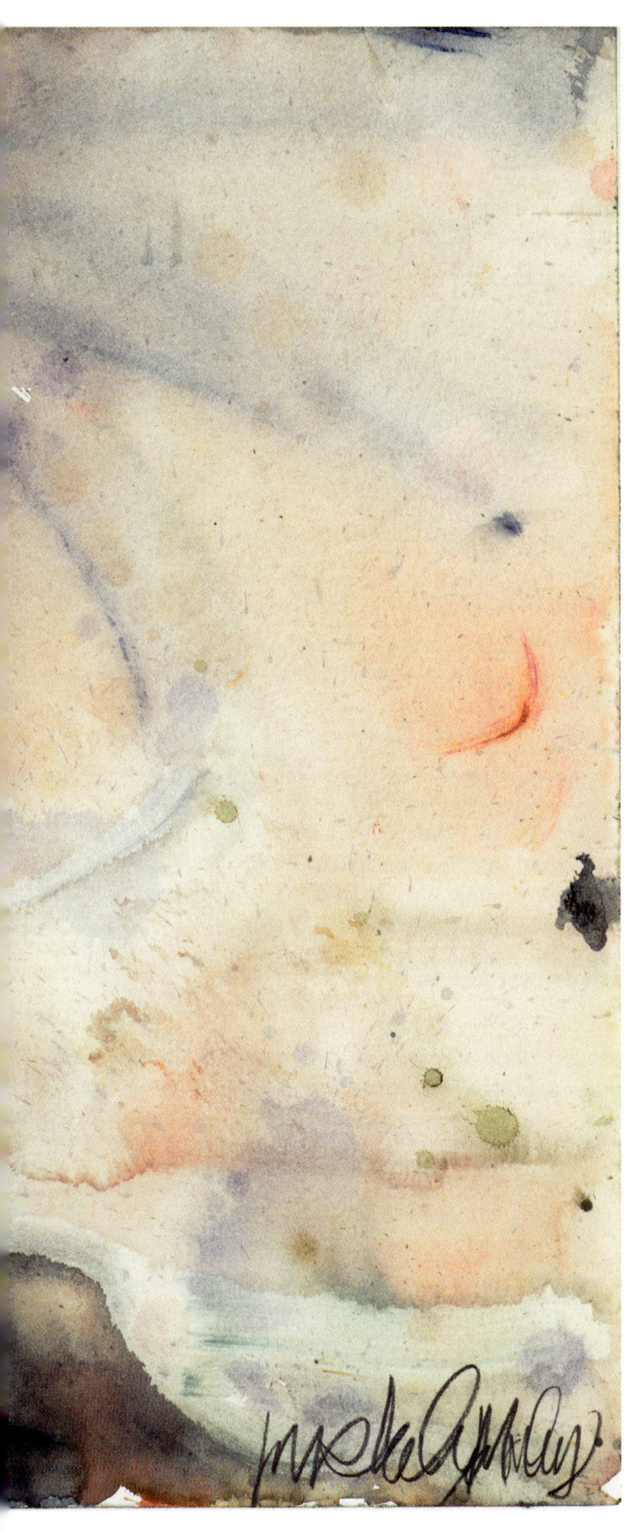

Malcolm Morley,
Landscape, 1983

at the forefront of what Morley refers to as "the Quest." It is the Quest that separates the educated tourist (watercolorist) from the Odyssean voyager trying to come home to the plane of world-sized emotion. Armored with a startling coat woven with threads of bravura and humility, sophistication and yearning for lost innocence, humor and foreboding, Morley pursues his literal and figurative travel—moving through culture, painting styles, geographic states, and emotional states.

At the time when Morley returned to watercolor, it had not so much been rejected by vanguard painting as subsumed into it. For the first two decades of this century, watercolor played a significant role in the development of modernism. Much of German Expressionism, especially the work of Ernst Ludwig Kirchner and Emil Nolde, is unthinkable without the inclusion of their work in this medium, and so too with Paul Klee. Wassily Kandinsky's first abstraction was performed in watercolor—"improvisation," which titled so much of his early work, is one of watercolor's strongest wonts. John Marin, a major messenger of modernism in America, transformed and spread Cubism's lessons with the limpid liquidity of watercolor before giving equal time to oil paint. Charles Demuth and Charles Sheeler followed in Marin's wake. The painterly directness, spontaneity, openness, and economy of means that were central to so much of Abstract Expressionism are, of course, inherent to the medium of watercolor, though the heroic size and scale of Abstract Expressionism are certainly not. While watercolor played but a minor role at best in the first wave of New York's new abstraction, its affinities with the "stain" painting of subsequent abstractionists, such as James Brooks, Morris Louis, and then Jules Olitski, are unmistakable. The transparency, thinness, and amorphous effusiveness they were able to explore with the new water-based paints drew watercolor into painting and seemed to render watercolor itself superfluous. The striving for rigorous anonymity of touch that ruled and repressed the surface of so much of vanguard art of the 1960s (including Morley's own) made watercolor quite unthinkable. The reawakened need for a more vivid and visceral painterliness and the accompanying desire for freer spatial and metaphorical referentiality that Morley as well as the older Philip Guston helped spearhead in the late 1960s and early 70s again made watercolor credible—in Morley's case, incredible.

Morley has been, and continues to be, a painter who requires a model to ground his painting and cue its authenticity. He must first see what he is to imagine as painting; and what he imagines is subjected to the dictates of the support's two-dimensional plane. Morley's oil paintings, as the acrylic paintings before them, are all gridded off and painted module by module, with the area not being painted covered up. In this way, figure and ground are given equal prominence as surface; execution is kept fresh because every module must bear the responsibility of being an individual painting. Grid and paint catalyze a molecular chain of events that congeals simultaneously in viscous flatness and illusion. The ocean-bound cruise ships that were the primary subjects for Morley's painting from 1965 to 1970 were neutralized and mediated by photography (mostly taken from travel posters). Surface execution was variegated, but the pleasures of the hand were strenuously repressed and depersonalized. The seen as photograph, the seen as paint, and paint as the seen are united in contradiction. As Morley began to feel increasingly deprived of the erotic tumult of three-dimensional sight and two-dimensional surface physicality, he first enriched acrylic with encaustic and subsequently turned to oil paint. The growing liberation of touch called for new models that paralleled his more personal engagement with his paint. Photography was replaced by often elaborate tableaux staged by Morley and viewed through a grid as they were painted—Morley himself became a camera. Cruise ships gave way to, among others, model planes and trains and toy soldiers whose layered iconic authority brought Morley back to his childhood. Complex and disjunctive narratives that occasionally included actual objects and frequently focused on surreal disasters and technological breakdowns are painted with a scumbled agitation that often matches the violence of the subject. By the end of the 1970s, the violence began to subside (but certainly not to desist); paint application became less clotted, more open and varied in pressure, shape, and duration. A vibrant clarity began to inhabit the plane. A new means of making a model had taken place: watercolor.

Morley's watercolors exist both as self-sufficient works and as models for his paintings executed in the opaque medium of oil. The watercolors themselves have an astounding range and vitality. Their stylistic variation is not so much dependent upon their linear development in time as upon the constant search to merge the nature of the subject with the nature of the medium. There are few constants, no firm rules. There are the frequently recurring subjects of bodies of water (generally vast), boats, airplanes, animals, bathers, and soldiers—very often subject and paint revel in movement. The subjects can be clearly defined or lapped up in a flood of paint. Aleatory splatter, razor-cut lines, billowing veils of wet on wet paint, dryer and denser pigment pushed into clear contour—all variously dominate or combine in activation of the plane. Some of the watercolors are all but instantaneous reflections of immediate perception; others are built up over months. Sometimes previously painted images are re-created and combined in disjunctive, mythic allegories.

The seen as painted is almost always radically tilted forward in tension with the flatness of the paper plane. Where the horizon is low, the primary subject looms high up on the sheet or the freneticism of sheer paint pulls the painted plane forward again. The eye is not invited or permitted into the scene kinesthetically but more purely optically—bobbing up and down and in and out on the buoyant clarity. Like the painter, the viewer is at once outside of the seen and inside the seen as painting.

Morley's outsideness is made literal by the choice and location of his subjects. From the arid mesas of Arizona to the tropics of Costa Rica, from a parrot habitat in Florida to Caribbean and Hellenic islands, Morley seeks to regenerate his vision in states of relatively untroubled nature—places that hold out the promise of pre-Edenic bliss and/or the innocence of childhood, places where his cultured sophistication makes him a stranger. When technology is seen, it is seen as destructive; where culture is alluded to, it is with the tremors of ambivalence. Urban centers are largely avoided (his rare watercolors of New York enact untroubled vistas generally only seen from touristic observation points). These watercolor travels do not so much seek escape as they seek release—release from cultural and cultured inhibitions into a purer erotics of perception.

The subjects Morley chooses simultaneously pulsate with a psycho-mythic charge and a predisposition to paint. The strokes of a paint-loaded brush easily incline to arabesques, and what better embodies arabesques than the joyous gaudiness of parrots? The simulated jungle that triggered *Parrots III* (1978) turns a yearning for the ever-shrinking exotic turmoil of the primal jungle into a delirium of paintedness, or vice versa. The pleasure in beach-bound bathers has as much to do with the innocent leisure as with the festivities that the colors of bathing apparel's artificial fabrics permit Morley's palette to celebrate. And, of course, the bodies of water that are never far from Morley's sight are the perfect paradigm for paint's liquidity. In *Seastroke* (1986–89), a bristling rock rises like a pending storm from the sea and blots out the horizon with its menacing agitation.

Morley's relationship to the art of the past, like that of so many artists of ambition, is both celebratory and anxiety-ridden. If his forebears are not directly alluded to, their presence is, nonetheless, an integral part of his surfaces. Van Gogh, not nature, brought Morley to paint; he has made a pilgrimage to Arles to pay homage to Cézanne and Cézanne's landscape. The tradition of visceral painterliness, from Rubens and Hals to de Kooning, is part of his optic nerves. Allusion to the work of other artists, whether intended or spontaneously generated by his hand and watercolor's will, ripple through his work. Green staccato strokes falling like and as leaves call to Oskar Kokoschka's watercolors; the Cubistic quirkiness and improvised openness of *Fourth of July* (1986) look to Marin's New York views. The linear frenzy of *Barcelona Cathedral as a Blood Red Orange* (1988) was generated by the near-hysterical sublime of Gaudi's neo-Gothicism but also carries with it echoes of Giacometti's towering, eviscerated personages—and so on. But the very nature of history threatens to clog the arteries of inventiveness. It is the unstable balance between unfettered freshness of perception and processed intelligence that Morley's restlessness is constantly grappling with.

Culture neurosis is made quite specific in some of Morley's more literally narrative and allegorical composite paintings. *American Sailor Looking Back on Greek Antiquity* (1986) is literally and figuratively a portrait of the young artist all but blotted out by the past. The classical torso of the left foreground merges with a vaguer ectoplasmic apparition that resonates both with the sheerest wet-on-wet watercolor virtuosity and with a menacing that pushes the small white-clad sailor into the background. In *Albatross* (1985), a disjunctive composite of previous watercolor images that include sculpture from museums in Greece, mullets swimming in the sea, and the formerly jubilant kite in *Kite on Gibson Beach* is uncomfortably crowded into apocalyptic stillness punctuated by a stream of blood emanating from a Cretan horse's nose into the sea. Have we wounded antiquity or has antiquity encroached upon the freshness of our vision of the sea? Is art burden or inspiration? Where is the border between destruction and creation?

Morley's quest continues. Many of his most recent watercolors have been built more slowly with heavier pigment. They seem engendered as much by their subjects (the rugged sturdiness of Maine's seacoast and its fishing industry) as by the need for new solutions. Spontaneity and floods of wetness do not now threaten the equilibrium of the plane; the more premeditated constructs of composition have, instead, taken over the role of destabilizing the eye's expectations. In *Kristen & Erin* (1988), the reflection of a boat turns out not to be a reflection at all but rather a painted image of a boat turned upside down over a nearly identical painted image of that same boat—the upward pointing trees of one image meet the downward pointing trees of the other, in the center of the plane. So expectant of veristic reflection is the eye that it at first refuses to believe what it is clearly seeing—a reflection of and on painting. Deliberation is here as surprising as improvisation.

There is no end in sight.

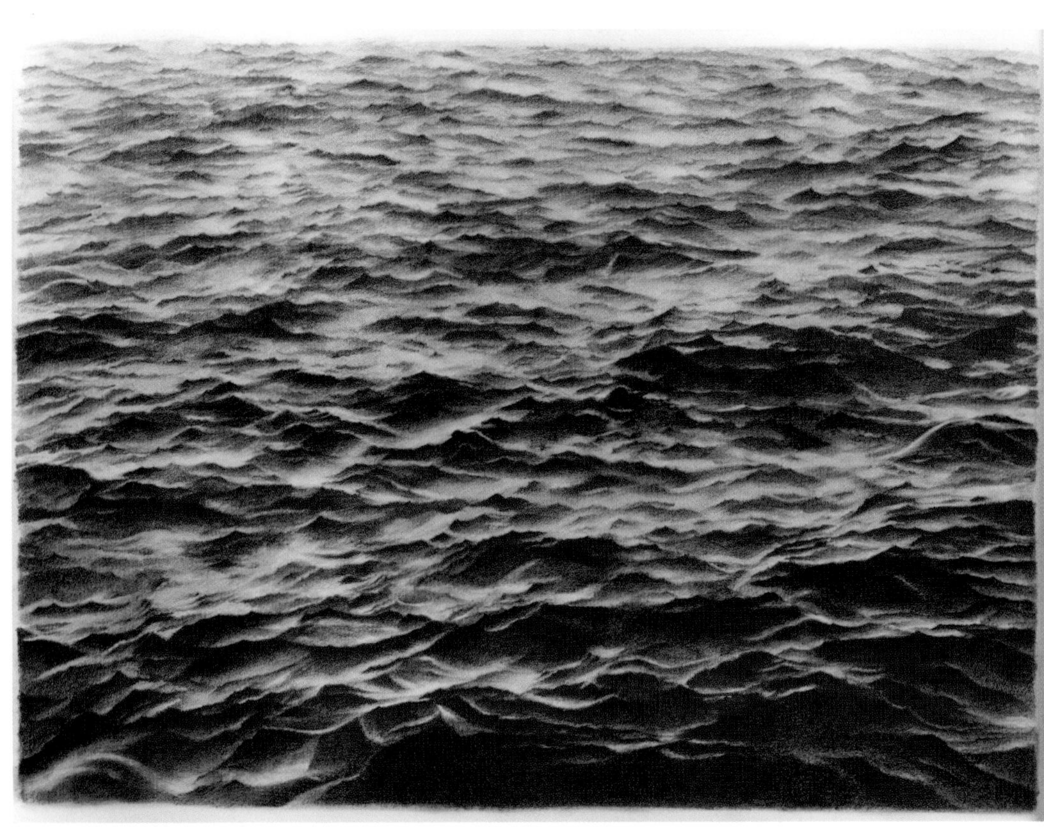

Vija Celmins, *Untitled (Ocean)*, 1969

Vija Celmins

Seeing Stars

Vija Celmins's art has a beauty at once rigorous and sensual, cosmic and intimate, insistent on its flat physicality and endlessly illusive. Simple acts of seeing become layered acts of imagining as Celmins transforms her extreme mental concentration into the extreme concentration of her work. For some twenty-five years, first in graphite drawings, then in oil paintings, Celimins has caused an incalculable number of obsessively disciplined, minuscule marks to congeal into panoramas vast in scale but small in size: panoramas of the ocean, the surfaces of the moon and Mars, the desert floor, the night sky teeming with tiny points of light. From a distance, they seem to mimic the homogeneous shiny surface and landscape phenomena found in the black-and-white photographs they are so often based upon. But, if we step up close, our eyes are invited to explore and be ravished by the microscopically sensual architecture of the plane of her art's making. Then the illusion dissolves into an infinitesimally rich articulation of the surface that reveals the intense energies focused on the lonely but joyous experience of seeing and making.

"Focus" and "distill" are words given great weight as Celmins talks about her old work and gestures to several uncustomary (for her) large canvases on which she is thinking of "opening out" her work to in some way become more physically responsive to her painterly procedures. A year has gone by since her retrospective at the Institute of Contemporary Art in Philadelphia opened in 2002. At the time of this writing, her much-acclaimed show is drawing to a close at New York's Whitney Museum of American Art, and she is worrying about the installation at its final stop: the Museum of Contemporary Art in Los Angeles. Celmins worked in Los Angeles from 1962 to 1981 before moving to New York City. By turns shy and exuberant but always strong-willed, Celmins gently mocks her perfectionism in this period of challenge.

On a windowsill in Celmins's SoHo studio sit a number of rocks that are among the many her visual acquisitiveness has led her, at various times, to pick up from desert floors and elsewhere. From 1977 to 1982, she cast in bronze and painted eleven pairs of duplicate "rocks," displaying them together with their natural models in a mesmerizing piece titled *To Fix the Memory in Image*. The point of this mimetic subterfuge was neither to dazzle us with the relentlessness of her powers nor to ironically fool the viewer but to pull us down into visual intimacy and concentration, and to encourage our deep reflection to mirror Celmins's own. It is this piece that led her back into the greater spatial and physical density and malleability of oil painting after some fifteen years of devoting herself to working with graphite on paper.

"How much lead can the paper hold?" Celmins asked herself as she undertook her 1982 Star Field drawings that are, to date, her last works on paper. Layer upon layer of tightly compressed, shiny black graphite is suffused with myriad shimmering pinpoints of white. Such is Celmins's literal and physical concentration that she could make herself draw around the tiny areas of white that are the actual white of the paper's ground as she built up her layers of lush night. It is this densely wrought and felt compression that takes Celmins's art beyond mere miniaturization and opens the plane out to breathe in glowing light. These drawings carry to an extreme the tense fluctuation between vast and spatial illusion and the near absolute and abstract flatness of the rectangular plane of their making.

A similar subject configures the most recent oil paintings (the Night Sky series) that conclude Celmins's retrospective, and a smaller unfinished version rests on the easel by a window in her studio. Now the points of white are actually painted and each must be covered with a rubber solution before a new layer of black goes down. Then the rubber is removed and more white is painstakingly filled in and brought up to the surface, before the whole process is repeated once again—up to five or six times, Celmins explains, to create an extraordinarily dense and intense surface. Like all of Celmins's subjects since 1968, this painting looks to a vast and almost always horizonless space. But it is less specific than the more recognizable incidents of the ocean's rhythms or the desert's rock-strewn ground that figure in other drawings and paintings. These works render moot all distinctions between representation and abstraction. They subvert recognizable strokes and style while distilling the sensual wonder of our vision.

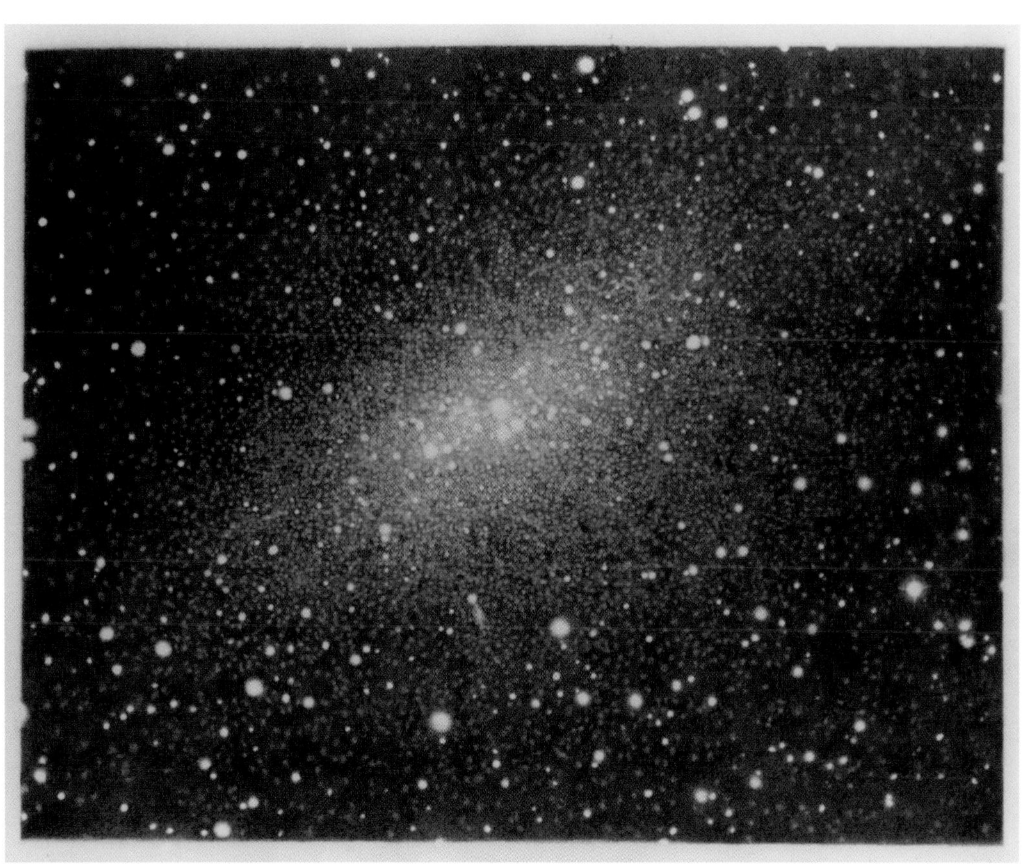

Vija Celmins, *Galaxy (Cassiopeia)*, 1973

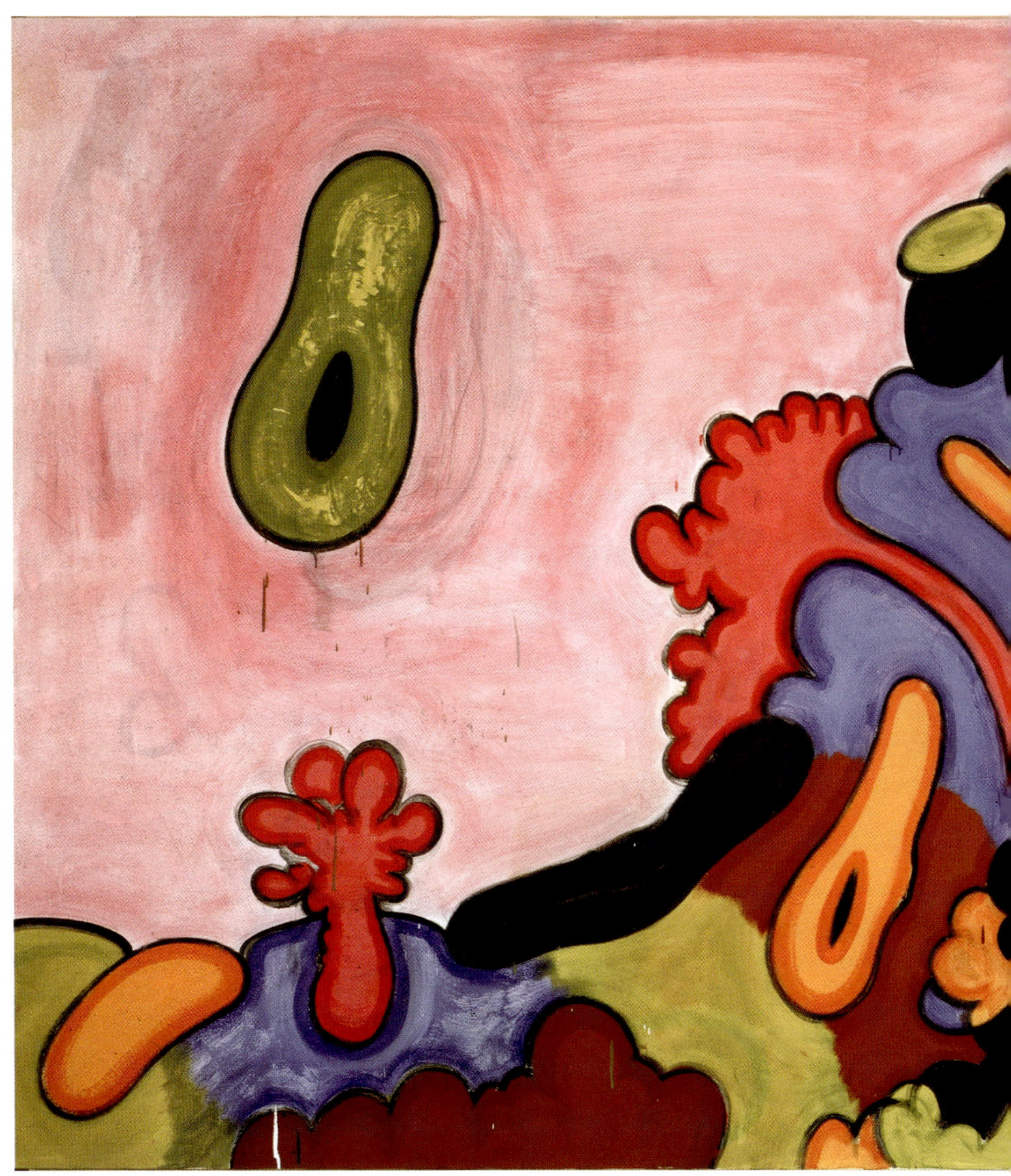

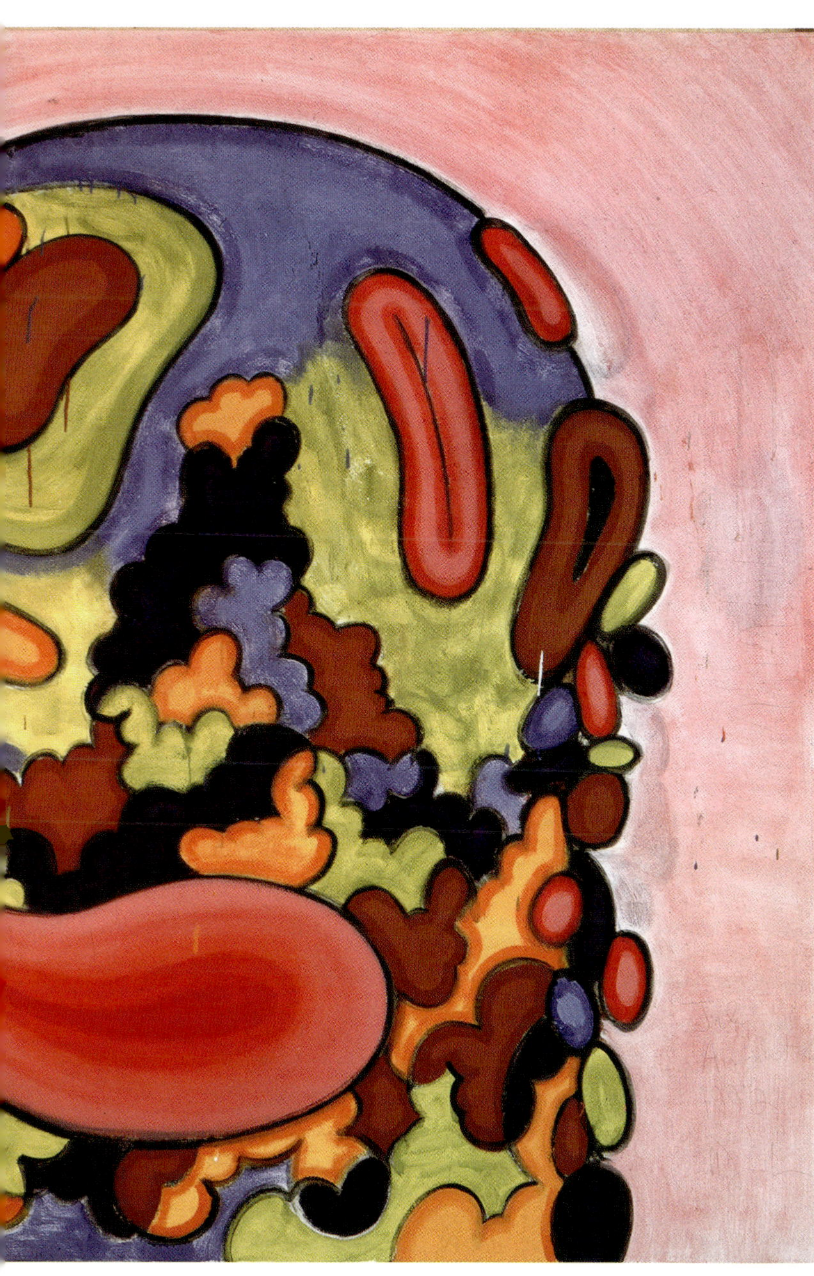

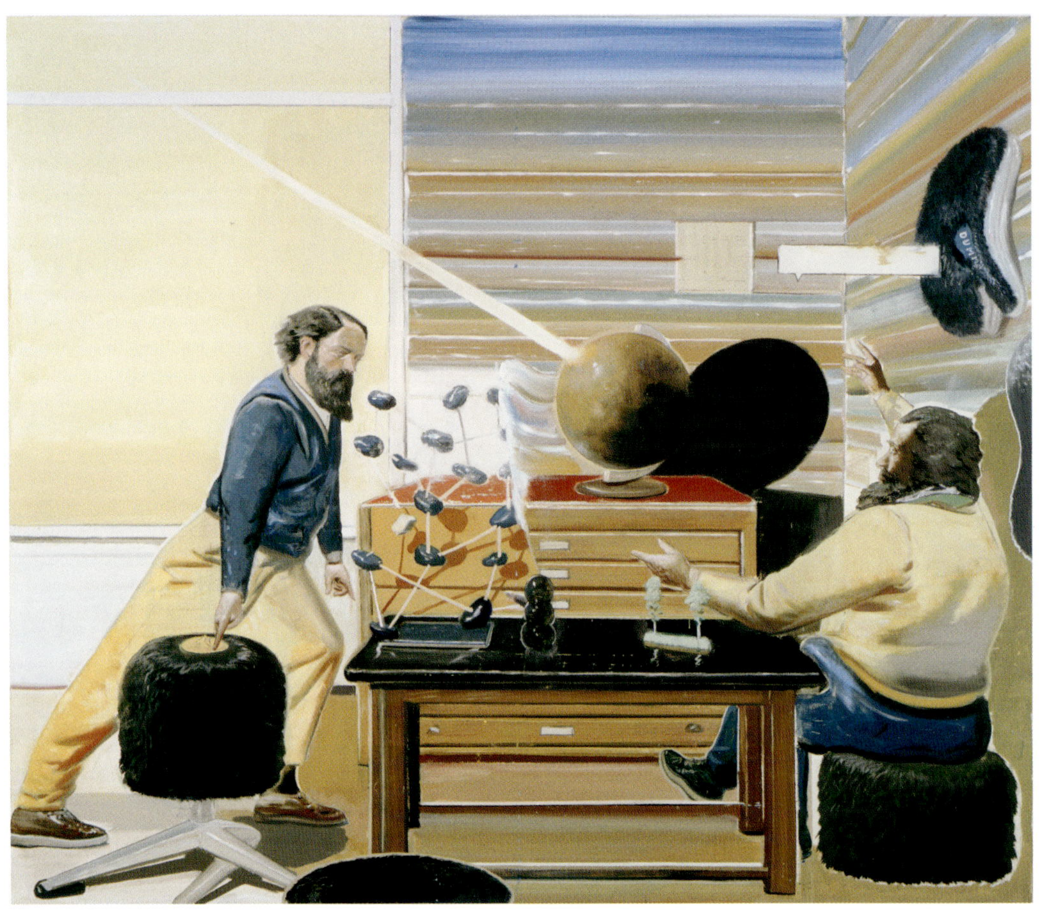

PREVIOUS SPREAD: Carroll Dunham, *Two Things (Mound D)*, 1992
ABOVE: Neo Rauch, *Schöpfer*, 2002

Brushes with Gods, Devils, Demons, Monsters, the Milky Way, and Planck's Constant

In the last decade, growing numbers of artists, in various mediums, have set sail for the further shores of fantasy to once more explore and reinvent myth, allegory, and fable. Not since the psychovisual excesses of Surrealism, as well as those of subsequent individual forebears, including Philip Guston, Peter Saul, and Sigmar Polke, have we been confronted with such fanciful protagonists and iconographic complexity. This exhibition focuses on five of the most noteworthy of these geographers of the imagination: the painters Carroll Dunham, Ellen Gallagher, Chris Ofili, Neo Rauch, and Matthew Ritchie. Unlike the Surrealists, these five neither explore under a single flag nor adhere to a common manifesto, but rather create within the panoply of multiplicity endemic to the contemporary art world. Their individual influences range from scientific theory to Mayan glyphs to hip-hop music, to name but a few; their paintings range from schematic painterliness to lavish icons reveling in craftlike decorativeness and procedures. Nonetheless, common themes and aims exist within this group. This essay points to some of the links that loosely join these artists.

The late modernism practiced in the 1960s and 70s continued to expand the self-containment and visible clarity of the procedures of artmaking initiated by Manet and Cézanne in the late nineteenth century. How to paint remained the paramount concern. The 1980s witnessed the breakdown of and reaction against modernism's historical imperative and ushered in a free-for-all of isms, all jostling for position under the umbrella of post-modernism (as in post-historical). Anything was possible. Modernism became but one of many alternatives; its uniqueness became moot. Sherrie Levine could create a photographic duplicate of a Walker Evans photograph and call it a Sherrie Levine. Gerhard Richter's simultaneous desires to paint like Caspar David Friedrich and to create abstract paintings cued by Jackson Pollock proved more laudable than schizophrenic. What to paint began to acquire some urgency. Quasi-documentary narratives sometimes not averse to agitprop and driven by issues of race, gender, and sexuality claimed increasing space on museum walls and floors by the early 1990s, as new gender-neutral words claimed their place in our vocabulary.

At the same time, numerous artists, also interested in narrative and also anxious to capitalize on the freedoms presented by the collapse of modernism's hegemony, sought to plumb the depths of the vagaries of the everyday world, be they racial, sexual, or scientific, through the invention of imaginary worlds. What to paint now was enfolded in myth, fable, and allegory, mining the depths of ambiguity that could draw the viewers into a mirror of the complexities of their consciousness without paying heed to the academic tenets of political correctness. Simultaneously these artists reinvented how to paint to make it reflect and merge with what they painted. The highly expressive brushstroke, so long considered the hallmark of "serious" painting from Willem de Kooning to Joan Mitchell to Georg Baselitz to Julian Schnabel, was suppressed or rejected in favor of more disciplined procedures, sometimes wildly decorative and obsessively crafted. The artists distanced themselves from their making in order better to serve their subjects, and their subjects often called a new visual originality into play—nowhere more so than in the work of four of the artists represented in Fabulism. The fifth artist, Carroll Dunham, had already begun his imaginary journey a decade or so earlier.

Some ten years or more the senior of the other four, Dunham literally and figuratively drew his way out of the Minimalist and Process art of the 1960s and 70s. Arriving in New York in 1972, he became the studio assistant of Dorothea Rockburne and absorbed the lessons of such artists as Mel Bochner and Barry Le Va. Dunham was strongly attracted to the painting of Brice Marden, Robert Ryman, and Robert Mangold. Slowly he twisted and turned this highly reductive painting, dependent upon the planar architecture of the canvas support, into an unlikely union with Surrealist automatism and dream imagery. Via the psychedelia of his 1960s youth, Dunham developed an interest in the most discredited side of Surrealism, the squirmy illusionism practiced by such artists as Roberto Matta and Yves Tanguy. In the early 1980s, his previously abstract linear doodles began to mime, grow out of, and transform the patterning of the wood veneer he now chose to work on. A kind of psychosexual delirium dependent upon the striations and knots of the wood plane erupted in intestinal, phallic, and vaginal allusions inflamed by a Looney Tunes palette. Like painter peers such as Terry Winters, Bill Jensen, and Philip Taaffe, Dunham was pushing abstraction toward figuration, but with an intensity and comic hilarity both unique and prescient. The queasy alliance his line formed between subjective, organic invention and objective interaction with the rectangularity of his painting plane has activated his work to the present day.

In 1988, Dunham returned to painting on linen, urging a pneumatic libidinal organism to funnel into the plane from the bottom physical edge of the support and surrounding it with vagrant galaxies of graffiti, including various written dates of its making and his signature. From a single color, this shape began to expand like a giant fungus on the linen host and became a raucous Technicolor *Mound* (1991–92). In subsequent works, this form began to mutate more and more toward the figurative, until these quasi-characters turned into a vagina dentata–mouthed demon. By 1997, mobs of glyphic, penis-nosed warriors and multi-breasted amazons battled for territory on the plane and the planet they polluted. With scabrous humor, scruffy paint, and incisive line, Dunham mocked and mimed our culture's mindless pillaging of the planet. Guston's startling turn, in the late 1960s, from Abstract Expressionism to schematic, comics-inspired figuration was crucial in setting the stage for not only Dunham's figuration but that of all the artists represented here, as well as countless others. However, in their flatness and hieratic rectangularity, Dunham's figures call more directly to Mayan wall painting, as well as to comics. No matter how obstreperous his characters become, they always remain creatures of and may even be entrapped by the rectangle they seek to conquer. Victim/victimizer, victor/vanquished.

Since 1997, a single figure, possibly a self-portrait—most often top-hatted, suited and starch-shirted, occasionally armed, penis-nosed when not headless, sometimes called Killer—has laid claim to Dunham's plane. In the last several years, this single figure has required Dunham's exclusive attention and represents him in this exhibition. A derelict painterliness, raw and impoverished of color, roils the Mesokingdom paintings (2001–02)—a painterliness, as in all of Dunham's work, in devotion to the painting's subject. Seen only upwards from shoulders pinioned, from painting to painting, to one or another outer edge of the plane, the figure bleeds in and out of the landscape, his top hat similar to and as disheveled as the shanties that dot the landscape. The trees echo the distressed eroticism of his testicular nostrils. He wears his landscape, or he is worn by the landscape. The prefix "meso" means intermediate; this is the kingdom of the intermediate, a kind of funky purgatory, a purgatory embroiled by a tour-de-farce variety of mark making.

In the more recent *Personal Distance* works (2003), the figure has cleaned up his act (or had it cleaned up) but has hardly improved his condition. Now flatly painted and graphically bordered in black, a still more fragmentary shoulders and/or head have been subjected to cold geometrization, folded and ironed into and out of the plane of their making. Can the subject be as heroic as the scale of these paintings or is he enslaved by the heroics of his making? With hilarious pathos, these works call back to the geometries of the 1960s and early 70s, where Dunham began—and we are still left to ponder the meaning of in between.

Like Dunham, Ellen Gallagher's art is very much drawing-driven, and, like Dunham, she has subsumed elements of late modernism into her painting narrative, most specifically the grid that ruled much of 1960s art. Like so many of those of the 1960s, her grids mirror the rectangle of the painting plane; but unlike the abstract, self-reflexive geometries so previously prevalent, Gallagher's grids serve more allegorical functions—as containers, cells, or stages for clichés of old-time negritude. Quite magically and very quietly, she has turned issues of race into a painting medium.

Agnes Martin, the most subjective of the 1960s geometers, became an early influence on Gallagher. Hardly out of Boston's School of the Museum of Fine Arts, in 1992 she replaced Martin's lyrically hand-executed grids bathed in transparent washes with myriad sheets of mechanically lined penmanship papers pasted onto the surface of the canvas. Onto these sheets she drew countless big lips and/or bulging eyes that were hallmarks of the comic black impersonators performing in the Old South's minstrel shows. The resultant shimmering sea of monogrammatic clichés hovers somewhere between the handwritten and the printed, the visual and the verbal, mark making and writing. The endless repetition of small increments draws the viewer into a slowly shifting meditative riff. The lips can be read as vagina as readily as mouth, maybe even as hot dog in a bun. Something erotic ripples across the plane. The repetitiveness both of the drawn elements and the lined paper might imply we are dealing with craft, craft impersonating painting, or vice versa. A gentle undermining seems to take place, an undermining of black clichés, an undermining of conventional notions of painting. Sometimes blacks took part in minstrel shows and impersonated whites impersonating backs. Nothing is black and white, black or white.

In Gallagher's more recent work, the fragments of clichéd physiognomy that become characters in and activate her paintings perform their ambiguities in spaces vast in scale and size. In *Purgatorium* (2000), an almost infinite repetition of lips is bordered on two sides by a sea-like emptiness, here and there punctuated by amphibious, phallic spouts erupting and ejaculating out of the lined paper. Whether the lips are damned to an eternity of cliché or await a fuller, more individuated identity remains moot. We are enveloped by an epic that is lyrical, intimate, and full of questions.

Earlier in her life, Gallagher spent a summer at sea for a marine biology project, and the sea has played an important part in her life. Rolling umbel fragments of white whale-like forms constructed out of cut-up penmanship paper float across the paper whiteness in *Blubber* (2000) and are accompanied by a tumbling school of flip wigs and eyes. Here, we might have arrived in the environs of *Moby Dick*, that astounding verbal epic admired by Gallagher, whose paintings, like Melville's writing, are made up of countless minuscule details slowly gathering into a monumental wave of ambiguous meaning. And all those bobbing, bewigged heads might call to the souls lost at sea during the days of slave trading.

Black, of course, takes on extra-aesthetic meaning when employed by an artist of color. And, partially in response to critics who have faulted her for not making her content less ambiguous, less fluid, Gallagher has undertaken a number of monumental black paintings. The title *bling bling* (2001) refers to the clattering of excessive amounts of gold and diamond chains and rings associated with many a rap musician. The actual image is of another galaxy of stars, the Milky Way. The painting is obsessively constructed out of layers of penmanship paper, hand-cut pieces of rubber, and black enamel paint, and its reflective blackness makes it almost impossible to see other than as an enveloping wave of amorphous, black evanescence. Only the closest inspection reveals traces of the underlying grid and the repeated scattering of rubber eyeballs and tongues. We are left to ponder what is the identity that can be seen beyond the glittering of bling bling and whether our or anyone else's identity can be identified by its color. As viewers of art, we are given the opportunity to explore and understand our identity as we view ourselves in the ritualized reflections of the artist's consciousness.

Matthew Ritchie also charts epic tales. He has set out to do nothing less than remap the creation and evolution of the universe. With exuberance, humor, and high intelligence, he makes not only figurative but literal painting as the ground for thought. His is a multimedia enterprise, perhaps more installation than painting, that draws on science, religion, alchemy, myth, popular culture, the works.

After graduating from London's Camberwell School of Art in 1986, Ritchie embarked on his slacker years. In 1988, he moved to New York, took a job as a building superintendent, and pondered his options. Joseph Beuys's construction of a personal mythology and interest in art as a didactic tool had impressed him in school, as had the painting of Frank Stella and the enigmatic, alchemical metaphors created by Sigmar Polke. He observed what he thought to be the liberating effects of the breakdown of what he refers to as "the master narrative" (the all-white, mostly male modernist catechism) on artists like Julian Schnabel—anything was possible, any artist or style could be appropriated. In the midst of this heady contextless anarchy, Ritchie felt the need to build a world, to recontextualize art. In short, he needed a new narrative. The art created by two of his peers spurred Ritchie on—the brilliant, acerbic silhouette cutouts that recontextualize tales of Southern whites' marginalization of blacks created by Kara Walker, and Matthew Barney's filmed and sculpted combinations of myth, magic, athletics, 1960s and 70s body art, and more. Both Walker and Barney reinvented the elaborate historical narratives so prevalent in premodernist painting. And so Ritchie began to plot his narrative.

Voraciously curious, Ritchie spent countless hours reading books on science and philosophy that he found discarded in the environs of New York University. He began to see painting as a continuous flux, one that is not a creation of space but rather a concentration of information slowed down, and this flux mimes the continuous flux and upheavals of the universe. He imagined one continuous painting starting with the Big Bang and continuing ever forward into the present. By 1994, the materialization of this process began to crystallize.

With his first exhibition in 1995, Ritchie began to reinvent the grand history painting of premodernism. The number seven looms large in this world. Forty-nine elements divided into seven groups of seven. And each element can mutate into seven different ones, depending upon its interaction with the other elements. The forty-nine elements are characters with precisely defined functions. The plot can vary, characters can be added; all get absorbed into the continuous flux. Seven colors are employed, each corresponding to one of the seven areas of the brain. For instance, green represents the frontal lobe, the character Mulciber, the builder, the sign Mu; black is the occipital lobe, Tamaii, Ta. Seven representational modes are employed in this endeavor: drawing, photography, sculpture, wall painting, painting on canvas, published texts, and digital media.

Quite unbelievably, the information overload called into play by Ritchie is embodied in vibrant clarity and joyousness. The basis of his ongoing project is usually one or more paintings on canvas depicting countless varieties of intertwining, swirling, and twisting waves of his seven unmodulated colors and trailing hundreds of shards and fragments of tumult—a kind of archeology of the tracks of creation and destruction. Emerging from these vectors of energy, almost like fleeting hallucinations, are delicately drawn comic personifications of some of the forty-nine elements, scientific equations, and occasional bits of writing. Extending around the wall from the painting and onto the floor are more diagrammatically constructed whorls of colored waves, either created with paint or a Formica-like substance (Sintra) that draw the viewer into the vortex of Ritchie's world. The written text (often a small published pamphlet) accompanying this visual excess is wonderfully written in old-time whodunit noir, full of intrigue and gambling, and likely to combine a Golem and an astronaut and countless other characters with multiple identities, such as Bubba, who is Beelzebub, the principal of growth, and Planck's constant. And photographs of scientific phenomena, or Miami's Eden Roc Hotel, and tables of Ritchie's elements, and diagrams, and reproductions of limpid watercolors—all adding still more layers to Ritchie's narrative. So, too, does his interactive website, where the player can test his or her wits with one or more element/character. Einstein meets Japanese anime meets the Old Testament meets pulp fiction meets William of Ockham meets Frank Stella, and on and on and on.

The viewer is free to interact with as much or as little of this concentration of information as he or she chooses. The more we study, the richer the world becomes. In the free-floating multiplicity of the world without a dominant narrative, in which we find ourselves, we tend to not know the iconography of medieval European and Italian Renaissance painting much better than we know the continuously morphing gods of Hindu art. With inquiry and study, visual beauty is likely to accumulate more profound density, whether facing the monkey god Hanuman leading his simian warriors on a relief at Angkor Wat or Ritchie' s churning universe. His characters' polymorphously shifting identity is not dissimilar to the multiple identities made possible by the internet. His startling conjunctions of different systems of information are not dissimilar to the seemingly discontinuous overload of information we are confronted with when flipping channels on the television remote or paging through the newspaper. Ritchie embraces this incredibly complicated world and urges us into his fluid narrative.

Like Ritchie's macrocosmic creation as metaphor for the artist's microcosmic creation, Neo Rauch's paintings might be read as metaphors for making. However, "might" is the operative word here. More inscrutable and more opaquely painted, Rauch's world is frozen in incompletion and filled with troubling disruptions and pauses. Hypnotically his figures move; enigmatically they construct. Born into the slow death throes of East Germany's socialism in 1960, Rauch has, among much else, turned the promise of Socialist Realism upside down. However, his figures are not localized but enact more universal, allegorical disjunctions. Rauch is drawn to such conjurers of disturbed entrancement as Max Beckmann, Balthus, Francis Bacon, and Georg Baselitz.

Rauch's early work includes a number of large (some ten feet in diameter), irregular tondos sparsely composed in quadrants of distressed, faded color, fragmented space inhabited by one or two puppet-like gnomes performing odd acts of devotion and/or something torturous, and one or more words in block letters that may or may not be germane to the activity represented. The paint has physically troubled the paper surface with wrinkles, lumps, and creases. In 1995, this dark world moved into more ample, detailed landscape spaces often disrupted by and disrupting fragmentary, obsolete factory buildings and machinery, and just as often disrupting and disrupted by somnambulistic, mostly male laborers wielding improbable tools (sabers, something like hockey sticks, unwieldy lengths of poles, etc.) and performing improbable tasks forever doomed to incompletion. Rauch's manner of painting is the most conventionally figurative of Fabulism's participants: clear, spare execution with short, assured strokes; no more paint than necessary for the representation of the subject; even light; complexity of composition as assured and clear as the handling of paint. He is a brilliant painter. Most of the figures he paints are sturdy Nordic males who would easily be capable of performing Socialist Realistic tasks of stalwart work and goodness. One of the males frequently recurring in Rauch's paintings may or may not be himself. All of the males perform dysfunctionally. The quandary of their movements and surroundings suggest something far more than the breakdown of socialism that took place during Rauch's youth.

As precise as Rauch's conundrums appear, they are not predetermined. He starts with tiny preliminary sketches, then outlines the basics of his initial creation, compositional thoughts on the canvas, and begins to dream his way into the painting, urging the painting to dream on into an organic totality, not entirely knowing until after that totality has been achieved what he has painted. Although slower, more painstaking, and less revelatory of the process of making than Dunham often is, Rauch, like Dunham, submits to the climate of his intuition. He paints from the inside out. Inside becomes outside and vice versa. The low-lying landscape seen in many of Rauch's paintings is drawn from the familiar surroundings of his native Leipzig into the unfamiliar, as is the disheveled architecture. The faded pastels so often pervading his palette are based on colors remembered from childhood.

In a painting created in 1999, the title, *Neid*, hovers in the empty fireplace of the interior, depicted on the right-hand side. The word is a protagonist as hard to explain as the giant fungi beneath it and those growing from the large timbers on either side of the fireplace, and as hard to explain as the dark sod or moss hanging from the ceiling. A tense, electric light fills the room and the mirror over the fireplace with pallid green. The two male occupants seem trapped in the overbearing rectilinearity of their interior, taking no note of the erosion of that interior inflicted by fungi and moss. And on the left side of the canvas invades an inexplicable cascade of planes, maybe shelf-like, maybe referring to an obsolete industrial process, maybe to 1960s monochromatic painting or an exploding Donald Judd sculpture. As mutely frozen as the painting seems, the eye is drawn in and around over and over again, constantly trying to construct a narrative, to make connections, to understand the meaning of a previously unseen detail, maybe getting jealous of the certainty of the word that means "jealousy" in German.

But there are other words in other paintings hovering just as certainly and ultimately having their meaning questioned by their surroundings. In many ways the viewer reenacts the subject's striving for coherence in a world that has none, seeking meaning, floating on the edge of comprehension, bemoaning the loss of modernist utopianism, performing acts that no longer can be productive but must be enacted nonetheless. Seeking comprehension, while knowing none can be found. Like Max Beckmann's spiky toxic beauty, Rauch's viral stillness silently guides our quest.

Occasionally, landscape alone embodies Rauch's dreaming. As in most of his paintings, *Acker* (2002) provides no kinesthetic entrance for the viewer's body but only space for the eye to roam. The swath of mining-wounded land at the bottom of the canvas blocks the imaginary entrance of the viewer's body and leaves the eye to seek its own path. The painting becomes a stage performed upon by the artist's conscious/unconscious will and the viewer's eye's mind. One must struggle like the starved weeds straining to grow out of the disruption of the ground. Seldom has a landscape been so still and so fraught. In *Haus des Lehrers* (2003), more expansive in scale, space, palette, and troubling depth, we witness the commingling of landscape, architecture, and figures that more frequently enact Rauch's puzzles. Strange bacterial growths envelop scattered household furnishings and tree stumps, swallowing books of learning as two male figures look on in stunned silence. Has learning infected nature, we might wonder, or could the painting be an oracle from which we have not yet learned to ask the right question?

The vivid exuberance of Chris Ofili's paintings might at first convince us that he, unlike Rauch, is dealing with more certainty. However, the only thing that might be said unequivocally about his work is its joyous embrace of beauty. Like Ellen Gallagher, his subjects deal with clichés of blackness, and, like her meticulous collaging and cutting, Ofili's multiplicity of obsessively repetitive and precisely placed collage elements approaches craft—as does his excessive decorativeness. Ofili, however, is as brashly direct as Gallagher is cryptic. His choice of subject matter has turned to the gaudier side of how blacks are perceived by others and themselves. However, he undermines the very clichés he celebrates. The rhythmic thumping, exaggerated sexualization, lavish sparkling, and hyper-artificiality that swirl so precisely through his paintings call to the hip-hop musicians like Lil' Kim, Foxy Brown, and Wu-Tang Clan he adores and occasionally iconicizes, and to the pimp and gangster paradise of 1970s blaxploitation movies. But this same artist grew up a Catholic, was once an altar boy, and seems to believe in the possibility of a hip-hop heaven. The visionary William Blake resides in Ofili's pantheon, as do Guston, Francis Picabia, Polke, and Ofili's jazz-obsessed predecessor, Jean-Michel Basquiat. This artist who so gleefully turns his back on the pieties of political correctness is Bible-knowledgeable, and was inspired by Blake to create one of his first figurative paintings, *Satan* (1995). Irony and sincerity, religion and pornography, seduction and irritation, abstraction and figuration are collaged into his work.

In 1992, while still at the Royal College of Art in London, Ofili traveled to Africa—a trip that fertilized his beginnings not only with elephant dung but also with the repetitive patterns of dots he saw in the cave paintings in the Matopos Hills of Zimbabwe and with many things that have no physical form. Africa is, of course, where humans first evolved, made marks that had no practical function, and developed language. Upon his return to London, inspired both by his African sojourn and by the brilliant American trickster David Hammons, who in 1978 had made a sculpture of a three-wheeled mound of elephant dung and in 1983 had set up a stall selling snowballs, Ofili set up a stall on the streets for the exhibit of elephant dung, placed an "Elephant Shit" ad in the art magazine *Frieze*, and made a sculpture out of a dung ball and his own hair. While this dada voodoo phase was short lived, this conflation of new Afro and traditional tribal African creating would be absorbed in Ofili's subsequent work.

Like Dunham, Ofili's first mature paintings are abstract, amongst them *Painting with Shit on It* (1993). Pulsing with thousands of tiny, dimensional, oil-painted dots in whorls of concentric circles intertwining with transparent rectangles, studded with a resin-dripping dung ball, and propped on the floor on two more dung balls, the super-obsessive, ritualized beauty of this painting serves as the door into Ofili's world. By 1995, his paintings propped up on dung began to take a more figurative turn that turned into full-frontal figuration with his now infamous *The Holy Virgin Mary* (1996) and the first of the Captain Shit and the Legend of the Black Stars paintings. Captain Shit is the swaggering superhero inspired by the 1970s blaxploitation films that have so heavily impacted hiphopdom; by various black and white comic book heroes, including Spiderman, Black Panther, and Black Lightning; and by Andy Warhol's Elvis (who was, in turn, inspired by swiveling black musicians). This imposing figure is surrounded by black stars and partially encircled by dung balls (four, each with a white star, and one with the monogram BS that forms the Captain's belt buckle) and, of course, is endowed with a mythic penis. The pale, creamy ground has been painted with phosphorescent paint; when the lights go out, Captain Shit fades into the background and is all but obliterated by the black stars. The macho star is vaporized and recedes into an insubstantial illusion. The cliché is celebrated, questioned, then dissolved in light. First impressions are deceiving.

A group of Ofili's paintings, begun in 1999 and continuing through 2002, celebrates a kind of monkey king and ends with a glowing chapel-like installation of twelve paintings of individual monkeys that are the participants in the Last Supper. Ofili is entranced by light and sparkle (bling bling, again) and his paintings can be as opulent as a bejeweled Gothic reliquary, but his sparkling, jeweled excess is fabricated from the shine of the dots of oil paint, glitter, map pins, and resin. The models for these paintings are Rhesus Macaque monkeys, known to be loud and active pranksters with highly developed dexterity. For the purpose of research, these monkeys were introduced into an island off Puerto Rico, now known as Monkey Island, and there they enchanted Ofili. Does the prankster monkey's dexterity suggest a surrogate for the artist, or does the prankster play with another cliché of blackness? There is no proper end here.

All five of these artists are somewhere in mid-career. Already they have added new chapters to art's most malleable medium, perhaps the medium capable of greatest depth. They are here not to give us answers, but to make us wonder as they create wonders.

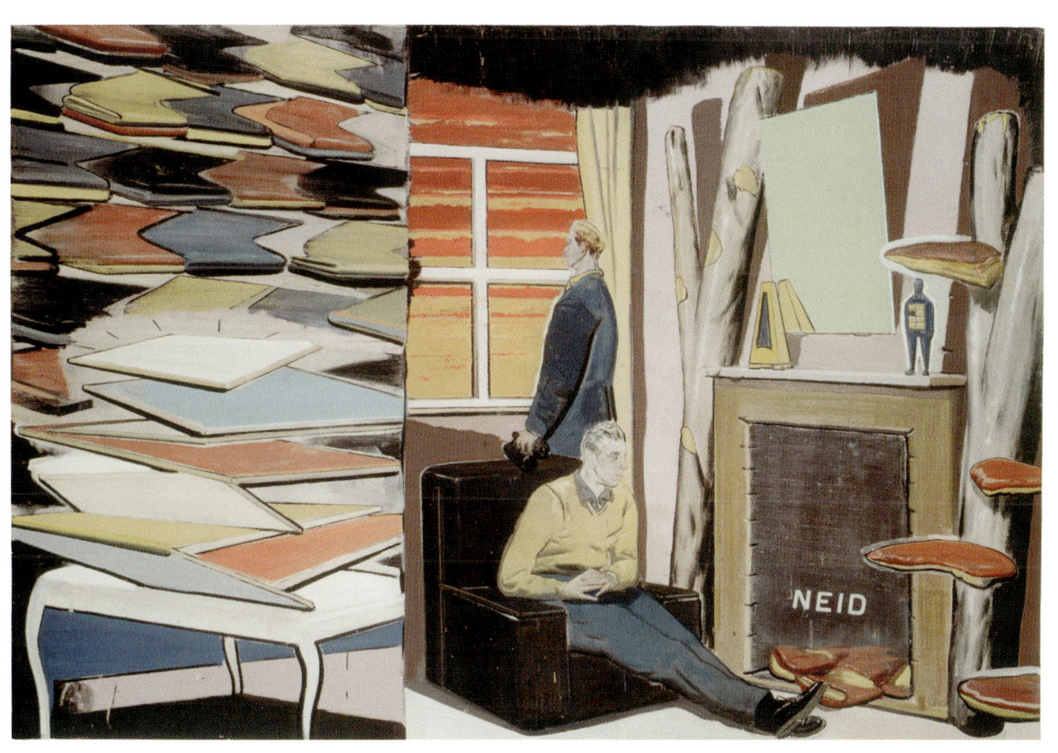

Neo Rauch, *Neid*, 1999

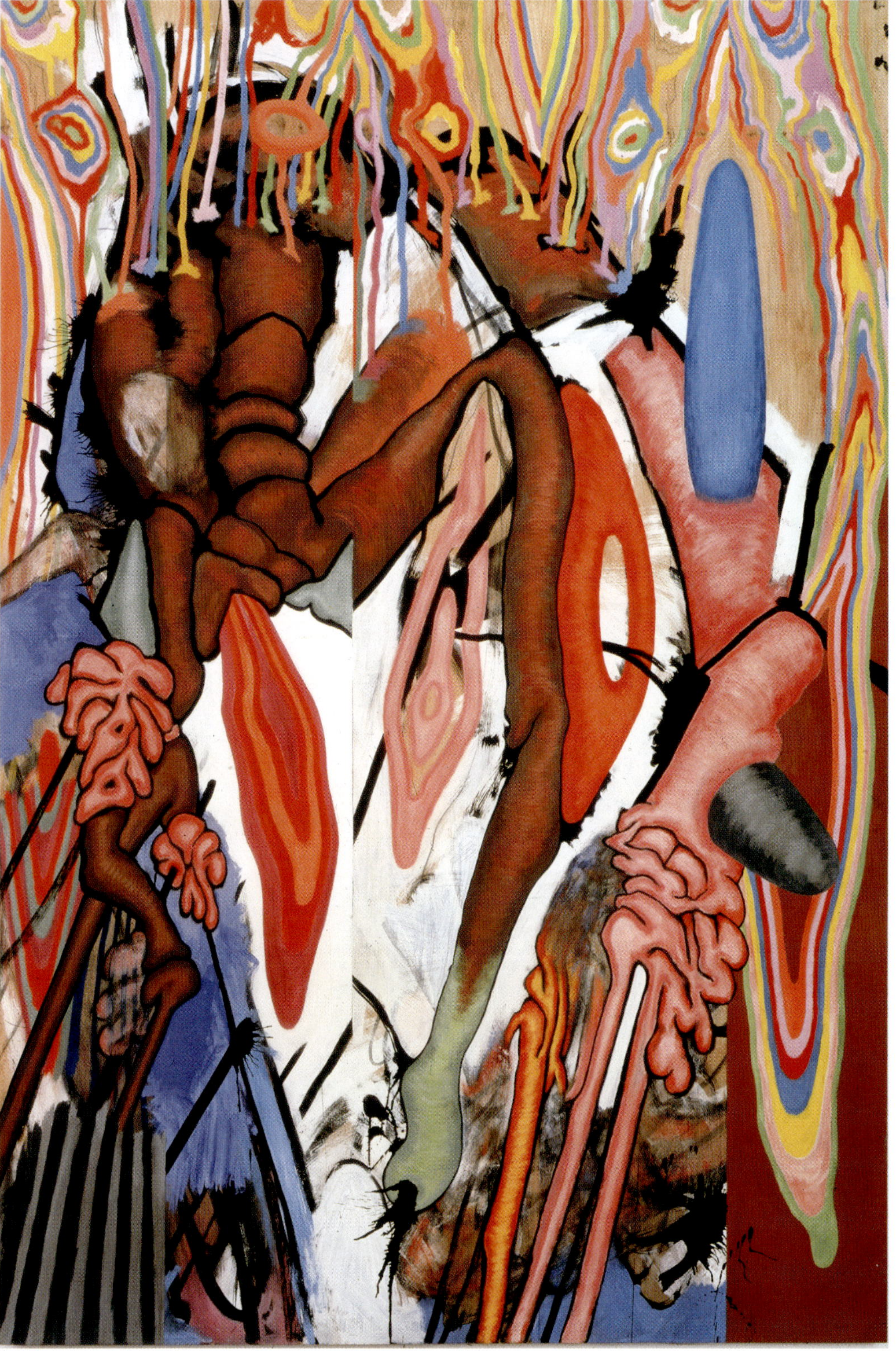

Carroll Dunham

Drawn into Consciousness

Drawing is the literal and figurative lifeline of Carroll Dunham's art. For him, imagining drawing and drawing imagination cannot be separated, nor can formal deliberation and spontaneous invention. More emphatically than any of his generational peers, Dunham renounced the bans on the subjective acts of the hand imposed by Pop and Minimal artists in the 1960s. With lyric vengeance he has reinstated the erotics of art.

Line has led Dunham through gastrointestinal deliriums that he refers to as "sensual galaxies," to landscape accretions mutating into animate and animated mounds, to animated mounds mutating into glyphic figures of penis- and vagina-encrusted demons of Mayan Disney descent, to swarms of penis-nosed warriors and vagina dentata–headed Amazons pissing, posturing, and polluting, to a porkpie-hatted, penis-pistolled, nattily suited cartoon of a noir mobster who may or may not be the artist's portrait of himself.

The line triggering Dunham's excesses of picturing is as varied as the pictured. The pictured and the picturing revel in interdependence. Indeed the pictured can be seen as an embodiment of the picturing. When the hand is left to drift and doodle, following its natural inclinations into and out of curves, something like the coupling of two wriggling, prehistorically large caterpillar-like shapes might be aroused to claim the rectangular plane, as in *Shape with Puddle* (1999). Exerting a little more control might yield a more concentrated tumescence such as *Mound* (1992). Exerting extreme control might result in a pointed, razor sharp, rectilinear rigidity that readily articulates the cold determination of a killer, as it does in the headless personification of a half-swastika titled *Invisible Killer* (2000). Incarnations, not illustrations.

Interdependence, too, defines the relationship of Dunham's mutating shapes to their rectangular support. The tutti-frutti barnacle-and-orifice-encrusted shapes Dunham painted in the early 1990s ooze out from one or another "physical" edge of their support; the shape expands into the rectangular plane, its organic curvature inclining to that plane's rectilinearity—its size, shape, and scale adjusting to the geometric nutrients of the ground it emerges from. So, too, the demons that followed, with their beings seemingly arising out of the rectangulated hallucination of the plane of their making. And those raucous, boxy warrior glyphs from the dickhead gang are battling for supremacy of their homeland plane. Among much else, they are metaphorical personifications of the artist perpetrating the victimless crimes and various misdemeanors necessary to claim art territory and to make a mark on the world. What is the Invisible Killer if not a plane folded and honed into a weapon? What is the relationship between art and power?

Carroll Dunham, *Fourth Birch*, 1983

Rude, sometimes lurid, often grotesquely humorous in a Boschian Garden of Earthly Delights kind of way, and rich in metaphor, this art's squirmy psychosexuality is embraced by visual, formal acuity. Indeed, Dunham's visual intelligence and procedural clarities owe much to his immersion in Minimalism and so-called Process art, some thirty years ago.

While still in college, in 1970, Dunham spent a semester in New York City as Dorothea Rockburne's studio assistant. When he moved to New York in 1972, he again worked for Rockburne and became acquainted with some of her peers, such as Mel Bochner and Barry Le Va. He helped install Rockburne and Le Va exhibitions at the Bykert Gallery, which I ran. He acquired a clear understanding of their procedures. When I was unable to follow Le Va's installation directions for a piece to be included in an exhibition I was co-curating at the Yale University Art Gallery, I called on Dunham for assistance.

Dunham was particularly drawn to the fleshy dignities of Brice Marden's oil and wax paintings, as well as to the paintings of Robert Mangold and Robert Ryman, and he could very well articulate his understanding of their work. But he revealed nothing about what he himself might be doing, other than saying it was no longer possible to make work related to the painters he so admired; he showed no inclination to invite me to his studio. In point of fact, little if anything was being made by him. No rush, he was percolating.

Sometime in 1976 or 1977, I was finally asked to the studio. I encountered line, gently doodling and looping against a modulated one-color ground on paper or Masonite —somewhere between Mangold's delicate linear outlining of irregular geometries attuned to the shape of their support and Cy Twombly's more writerly exuberance. Modestly, with a kind of self-effacing conviction, Dunham was nudging and being nudged by drawing's more wayward inclinations. Slowly, over the next five years, his line gained more painterly body, then began to loop in and out of scrolling figuration and multiple exchanges of figure and ground. The work felt intimate, personal, and intelligent; but line's lapsed urges and deeper desires still lurked somewhere beneath the surface. Then, quite suddenly, later in 1981, line took a sudden turn for the visceral.

The verbal, narrative sequencing conventionally expected of a writer proves ill equipped to handle this moment of Dunham's development. The following are simultaneities (not progressions) that occurred with varying frequency and frequencies: his articulate composure could only superficially shield Dunham's struggle with line—and with drugs and alcohol. A painted wood surface hazily appeared in a dream and occasionally shadowed Dunham's waking hours. He was grasping for some new solution. Not only the paintings of Hieronymus Bosch and Dirk Bouts but Dunham's proclivities for Surrealism surfaced, seemingly at odds with the intentions of the artists he respected and with his Connecticut

Yankee restraint. He was enticed by the most discredited side of Surrealism—the close-toned, slippery pictorial extravaganzas staged in gaseous representational spaces by Roberto Matta and Yves Tanguy. He wasn't embarrassed to admit having been attracted to Salvador Dali's lurid painting of the Crucifixion at the Metropolitan Museum of Art. The vivid graphic histrionics of the drug culture's posters and paraphernalia, ever present in the 1960s as his adolescence unfolded, somewhere buzzed anew in his head. Twombly's bacchanalian linearity and Mangold's plane-geometry–embracing linearity continued to assert their presence. This lumpy paragraph brings us somewhat closer to the astonishing brew of organic implausibilities that was to erupt on Dunham's plane.

Dunham grasped for wood and began to paint. Painting like the grain, against the grain, with the grain, turning the wood into an illusion of itself, turning knots into nipples and vice versa. First probing cautiously, then by 1982, exuberantly. By so literally and figuratively embedding his drawing/painting in the plane of his making, Dunham could free his curving and doodling line to spill its guts out into lurid glandular deliriums. The shapes' reliance on and generation out of the given configurations of the wood surface, as well as their lack of closure and rolling interchanges of figure and ground, are certainly compatible with late modernist emphasis on procedural clarities and planar rigors; how-ever, the heated organic referentiality, erotic and otherwise, the disjunctive and abundant variety of mark making, and the flabbergasted palette were discharged from another zone. Dunham had liberated his imagination and grounded it in a visually self-evident and plane-dependent process of making.

Like all compelling art, these paintings bristle with inevitability and, in retrospect, seem to make perfect "sense"—as in, "he donned his Mangolden lenses and looked through Twombly to Surrealism." This makes critical sense (I myself have previously proposed it in writing about Dunham's early work) but tends to deny the nonverbal disjunctive vagaries that, oblivious to our conscious aims, course through our brain, whether in dreams or wakefulness. Dunham's dream about painted wood didn't constitute a startling epiphany but rather an event on the periphery that slowly and not entirely explicably drew itself into the foreground of his consciousness. He let himself be drawn. He is more than an artful strategist, although he is that too. Dunham's receptivity, his willingness to be led into his drawing, has catalyzed the startling mutations his art has undergone—mutations that we mustn't too easily turn into evolutionary sense. His grounding in and associative collaboration with the configuring of the wood surface gave his art access to his other side. Having gained that access, he could ground his art more figuratively in the blankness of the canvas plane's structure.

Visible Language titles a 1994 painting in which a murky, rectangular blob dripping phallic protuberances and punctured by a variety of orifices trails and/or excretes a recti-linearly chopped-into rectangle that buzzes with a green ovoid pattern against an orange ground—afloat in a cloying mauve field. This flat glyphic shape looks like a jocular tropical fish and acts, at least for the duration of this paragraph, like an allegory of art. The central blob endowed with a plurality of genitalia is hermaphroditic; it reflects the androgyny of the state of art and, more figuratively still, the state of the artist while making. Like some tropical fish, and like many orchids, the blob seems capable of self-procreation, as we can see in the wood grain—reminiscent ordering of the orange and blue patterning emerging from the blob. And its growth is related to and in dialogue with the field of its making—a purely visual alliteration on rectangularity, a visible language.

This blob glyph, as well as its more anthropomorphized demon peers and descendants, has often been written about in relation to the raucous cosmicomics of Philip Guston's late paintings. As critical as Guston is as a precursor, Dunham's forming is visually more related to pre-Columbian glyphs and relief sculpture. His shapes are more rectangulated and flatter than Guston's inclinations to round volume, and his line spikier. Guston's figures have eyes or slits in hoods implying eyes beneath; like glyphs, Dunham's figures have no eyes. But unlike glyphs, Dunham's figures have no designated verbal analogue. Seen, not heard, not seeing.

The creature's blindness denies them an extra-visual dialogue with the viewer. Like rudimentarily sighted moles and blind voles, they are built to burrow in the ground. They are creatures of the plane. Their shaping, not their seeing, expresses their purpose. Their impurities are purely visual. As they have become more turbulent, they have become more gender-specific. Whether their maleness has been generated out of the urge to self-portraiture or out of the fact that most violence is male-created or both remains moot. What remains certain is that Dunham has found and continues to find a visible language that accommodates the world's mess—and the rectangle.

Matthew Ritchie

Painting as Information Jazz

Even before entering *Universal Adversary*, Matthew Ritchie's exhibition at Andrea Rosen Gallery in New York in 2006, I was confronted by a text on the building's facade that forewarned me of the apocalyptic storming within.

> "Their appearance and their work was as if a wheel within a wheel; as for their rings, they were so high they were dreadful and their rings were full of eyes, round about them four. And when the living creatures went, the wheels went with them for the spirit of the living creature was in the wheels."
> — Ezekiel I: XVI–XX

Ezekiel's words still ringing in my ears, I walk into the main room of the gallery to be engulfed by Ritchie's light-suffused paintings and a black, folded latticework sky suspended above me. A painting on the end wall seethes with the gushing surge of a crackling brown network of sharp lines and shapes interspersed with whiplash spirals of white and pointy shards of rust raining down on a hapless, possibly sinking ship. Paint as rage, rage precisely calculated, engulfs the plane. *We Leave Today,* this expanse of almost twelve feet is titled. "Too late," I think, as I'm drawn evermore into this cruel beauty. Three more sagas of liquid violence roil the long side wall of the gallery. *God of Catastrophe* pulses with circular detonations, the largest of which has sucked a boat out of the waters below; one can see a ring of eyelike shapes that recall Ezekiel's prophecy as well as the rings of eyes found in William Blake's similarly themed *The Whirlwind: Ezekiel's Vision of the Cherubim and Eyed Wheels* (1803–05). The other two paintings in the exhibition, *We Will Not Be the Last* and *Personal Virtue,* are no less enflamed with apocalyptic skies wreaking havoc on the waters below.

A steep ladder, like one that might be found in a large ocean-going vessel, led me up to a platform in the latticework sky, where I could look into an oculus which featured a projection titled *Ezekiel I;* a not-quite film of a not-quite possible future, quite dire, flickered, while an ominous voice uttered cryptic warnings. Connecting the two levels was an illuminated, double-story lightbox with images of slender figures drifting and floating in a landscape awash in soothing luminosity. The scene called either to the possibility of a future healed earth or to the myth of the Edenic garden wiped out by the Deluge. If a promise, it is as slender and fragile as the figures it contained, perhaps just a taunting mirage.

Ritchie named this remarkable installation *Universal Adversary* after the collective title given by the United States government in 2005 to the fifteen scenarios classified as major threats to the U.S. population (none of which included income disparity, pandemic disease, resource depletion, or radical climate change). The opening quote from the book of Ezekiel was probably written about 500 B.C. during the exile of the southern Israelite kingdom in Babylon. Ezekiel was a giver of oracles and warned of the destruction of Jerusalem because of the Israelites' misdeeds. Ezekiel's dreadful rings full of eyes are the Ophanim, angelic forces integrated into the throne of Yahweh, which is the physical manifestation of the universe. Some commentators believe the text, which includes the famous "valley of dry bones," describes the end of Israel as a political force and its rebirth as a spiritual nation. Others have seen in Ezekiel's texts the symptoms of schizophrenic hallucinations. Not by coincidence, Babylon's ancient ruins exist today some fifty-five miles south of Baghdad and suffered further damages by U.S. forces invading Iraq in 2003. The explanation of the title's meaning, like the contextual information for most of Ritchie's exhibitions, was readily available to all viewers and serves, like the others, as cues to the visual. The title of the installation and the quote from Ezekiel I that Ritchie chose to appear at the entry of his show framed the works between the sixth century B.C. and 2005–06, and layer Ezekiel's prophecies with the violent reckoning being enacted by global warming and terrorism in our present time.

Long before Ritchie's invocation of Ezekiel's prophesies in his work, William Blake had looked to Ezekiel as his own spiritual ancestor. Ezekiel became the inspiration for Blake's unfinished major work begun in 1797, *The Four Zoas*, which traced the fall of Albion (the oldest name for Great Britain). While Ritchie has not localized his apocalyptic visions, he has long admired his British predecessor's visionary art and verse.

Ezekiel, Blake, and Ritchie may seem a rather mismatched trio, but on further reflection I realized what they shared; they are all visionaries and givers of oracles, and does not many an artist, including my present subject, aspire to giving oracles? Further, Ritchie, following contemporary scholarship, understands the bearers of Ezekiel's "wheels"—a lion, a bull, an eagle, and a man—to be not only the first representations of the four evangelists but also the four cardinal signs Leo, Taurus, Scorpio (frequently seen in early esoteric texts as an eagle), and Aquarius. Ritchie interprets Ezekiel's wheels as depicting the solar system, beloved predictive tool of the Babylonians, and so finds in Ezekiel's visionary science a parallel to contemporary visionary cosmology, such as string theory, which purports to be a final unification of the four forces that constitute the universe.

All three—Ezekiel, Blake, and Ritchie—favor seeing with the imaginative eye. And, as much science continues to move ever further from the physically observable into the speculative and the imagined, scientists have increasingly become visionary prophets.

The visual and narrative clarity and drama so apparent in Ritchie's *Universal Adversary* installation were not yet apparent when I viewed his first one-person exhibition in 1995. The show was titled *Working Model* and a sheaf of explanatory notes, in the form of a press

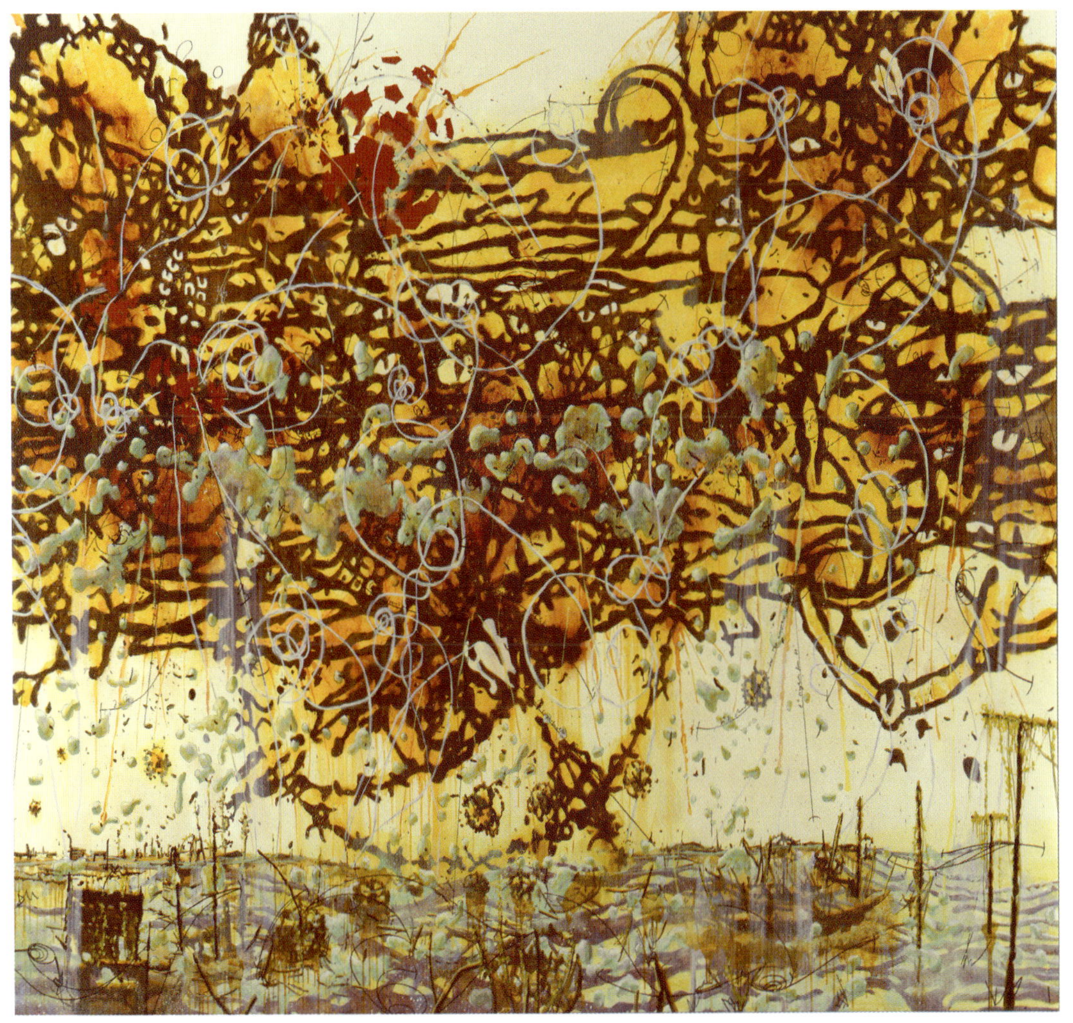

Matthew Ritchie, *We Will Not Be the Last*, 2006

release, as well as charts and graphs painted directly on the wall or presented as painting, conspired to make me spend more time reading than viewing. The simple geometric forms and bright clear colors seemed to have turned the space into a kind of 1960s Minimalist playroom. And where would I begin? I was annoyed and a bit disoriented; I wasn't sure I wanted to play in this room. I remember a pedestal from which emerged seven rods each holding three or more round or nipple-like shapes in varying colors. They looked vaguely like the dreidls Jewish children play games of chance with at Chanukah.

On the wall behind them was a chart with a vertical row of seven colors, each followed by seven sets of attributes, symbols, and signs; they included "Lucifer," "free will," and "p," for example. Across the top of the chart ran a horizontal row of shapes—the same shapes seen in various colors and combinations rising from the pedestal. Ritchie titled the table *The God Game.*

What Ritchie had created in 1995 was a kind of game board, the eponymous working model that encouraged the free association and combinative play so crucial to the creative process—whether in the creation of a painting, a sonata, or a scientific theory. For *Working Model,* Ritchie had made a grid of forty-nine elements that interested him, ranging from DNA to solitude. Each of the forty-nine elements was represented on the grid in seven ways, through scientific symbols, laws, colors, shapes, emotions, characters from esoteric traditions, and narrative functions. The grid could be used as a map, the map turned into a story, the story turned into a game—a kind of universal game of multi-dimensional Scrabble played with a set of colored shapes with multiple potential meanings. Ritchie had inverted the systemic graphs and grids endemic to the visual and mathematical certainties of so much painting and sculpture of the 1960s and early 70s into a grid warped by unseen, often unknowable complexity and freely associated. Some time was necessary for me to understand that this working model was for the formation of a wholly new, personal, and hopefully universal mythology. More like an index of artistic possibilities than a painting exhibition, this undertaking announced the arrival of an artist not unwilling to admit to playing the God game—and in his game, the stakes would be very high. In an interview from that same year, Ritchie stated he was seeking a symbolic language "as pure form in itself and as a bridge between various pre-existing symbolic vocabularies."[1]

A look back to Ritchie's beginnings will help fill in the aesthetic distance between the eleven years that separate these two installations. At the beginning of his artistic maturity, Ritchie wanted to build a universally dechiperable visual language comprised of configurations, symbols, and equations potentially accessible to a vast and varied audience. In order to achieve that, he first had to build a universe. With cavalier disregard for historical cohesion, he commenced to mix, match, and fuse myth, religion, science, pop culture, and art. The as yet empirically unknowable theories of visionary science, such as string theory, and the empirically unknowable visual hallucinations found in visionary art such as that created by Blake, and the visionary theology of the Bible's book of Ezekiel are but a few of the resources Ritchie has mined. And as he married disparate traditions and bodies of knowledge, the artist's sense of humor and play remained ever-present.

Ritchie was not alone in his construction of new mythologies. While in London's Camberwell School of Art (from 1983 to 1986), he had been duly impressed by Joseph Beuys's self-mythologizing metaphors of survival based on his World War II experiences, as well as his interest in art as a political and didactic tool. Sigmar Polke's often gleefully mysterious forays into metaphors of alchemical transformation also impacted Ritchie's art ponderings. When he moved from London to New York in 1987, Ritchie continued his education, though in decidedly less formal circumstances. These first ten years in New York—when he took a job as a building super-intendent in SoHo, a time he often refers to as his "rebuilding" years—began a remarkable period of self-education abetted by the many textbooks he found discarded by students in the environs of New York University. He may not have been making art, but he did become the custodian of a remarkable body of knowledge that included science, religion, mythology, and history.

It was also during the 1980s that Ritchie witnessed the free-for-all of new liberties being taken in the wake of the erosion of modernism's hegemony that had started in the late 1970s—ranging from Julian Schnabel's jubilant portraits created with smashed crockery as surrogate brushstrokes to Susan Rothenberg's figuration brimming with a reinvigoration of drawing as painting to Carroll Dunham's retrieval of Surrealist psychosexuality found in the paintings of Roberto Matta, Yves Tanguy, and Salvador Dalí, so long suppressed by late mod-ernism's disdain for subjective imaginings. And, in the realm of photography, Sherrie Levine's appropriations questioned the value of uniqueness so endemic to modernism. Historical artworks re-entered contemporary dialogue, and imagination reclaimed lost territory.

The return of self-contained historical narratives—now wildly and willfully fabricated—would mark the beginning of the 1990s and inspire Ritchie to begin writing art criticism, and he was invited by Francesco Bonami to write regularly for *Flash Art*. He was strongly impressed by Kara Walker's intensely acerbic and uproariously ribald re-viewing of the ante-bellum South's racism, surprisingly rendered in her retrieval of the genteel art of the cutout silhouette. And he was similarly impressed by Matthew Barney's brilliant mythology—a hybrid of football lore, Harry Houdini, reproductive biology, classical mythology, tabloid serial killers, and more, much more—realized in film and sculptural installations most often featuring Barney as one or another of his protagonists.

By 1995, Ritchie was prepared to step into this arena as an artist—his concerns cosmological, his context and material the information age; his aim was to make paintings that are "pictures of thinking."[2] Of course, all paintings that lay claim to success are pictures of thinking, but the self-enclosed narratives of Barney's, Walker's, and Ritchie's art look back to and reinvent the grand historical narratives that preoccupied so many artists from antiquity well into the nineteenth century. While the meaning of Barney's fabulist narratives are not always immediately evident, both his and Walker's works unfold in clear narrative sequence, whereas Ritchie's tales are derailed, layered, and frequently rife with nonsequiturs resulting from spontaneous interruptions, games of chance, and combinative play.

As his project continued to develop, Ritchie favored a kind of multimedia Gesamtkunstwerk evolving around several paintings. He regarded painting not so much as a construction of space but as a continuous flow of slowed-down information—multiple strands of overlapping information that might readily interrupt and/or threaten to cancel each other out. These overlapping, intertwining strands of flow mimic the flow and upheavals of the universe and as readily mimic the countless trails of neurons racing through the human brain—not to mention the stops, starts, and false starts twisting through the process of a painting.

The Big Bang is a continuous subject of Ritchie's art; indeed, in his imagination, he sees one continuous painting bringing the Big Bang, or moment of genesis, into the present moment. The paintings of this writhing knot of currents and countercurrents of energy, painted in the seven colors presented in the chart seen in *Working Model,* have frequently been the centers of Ritchie's installations. He has, on occasion, also created paintings of luminous and vaporous invented landscapes more conventionally configured with ground and horizon, as well as paintings that combine both this mode and the swirling knots. Some works are painted directly on the wall; in addition, he has created mosaic-like wall- and/or floor-bound accumulations of shapes cut from the soft plastic material Sintra.

Until now, most of the writing charting Ritchie's quest for a universal language of painting has focused on the vast body of knowledge that informs his work, rather than the actual work itself. Ritchie himself has added—and one might say interpolated—this writing with his own occasional printing of pamphlets to accompany exhibitions that present neo-noir tales shuffling time, plot, and characters with both humor and literate dexterity.

For this essay I have chosen instead to focus on the visual embodiment of Ritchie's ideas. His visual repertoire is large and varied. I will examine the affinities of Ritchie's work with the history paintings created by J. M. W. Turner as well as with Jackson Pollock's flung and dripped painting and the illuminated manuscript pages of the Book of Kells. This inquiry is undertaken as much to make clear the similarities as to highlight the quite radical differences. The concept of affinities more than that of direct influences is stressed here. And the journey will zigzag through Ritchie's recent installations—a landscape tour, landscape as information.

I will begin with Turner. The nineteenth century, in both Europe and America, witnessed an astounding outburst of landscape painting growing out of and extending many of the conventions of Dutch landscape painting of the seventeenth century. While that tradition was marked by secularity and largely created for middle-class burghers, some nineteenth-century painters, such as the German Caspar David Friedrich, sought to imbue landscape with a pantheistic sublime. In the United States, some painters depicted the still vast stretches of virgin landscape as the new Eden. Among these painters, Thomas Cole was perhaps the most avidly in pursuit of suffusing landscape with religiosity, as can best be seen in his four paintings depicting the *Voyage of Life* (1839–40), in which tiny figures are dwarfed by virgin landscape as they are guided through Childhood, Youth, Manhood, and Old Age by an angel. Friedrich, Cole, and his American peers were all heirs to and continued a traditional European realism. Turner's work, however, marked a radical shift in landscape painting, and in his hands it metamorphosed into history painting. The drama of urging light into darkness and vice versa that took place in a stormy diaphanous vortex configured many of Turner's paintings; he had a particular predilection for storms at sea, frequently incorporating "deluge" in the title. One such painting, *Light and Colour (Goethe's Theory)–The Morning After the Deluge Moses Writing the Book of Genesis* (1843) finds the spectral figure of the seated Moses emerging from a whirlpool of color and light. Beneath him hovers the coiled snake on a staff (a prefiguration of the Crucifixion) found by Moses in the wilderness in the book of Exodus. Still lower and still more fugitive churn bodies washed up in the Deluge.

Something akin to the Deluge was also found on the wall when I entered Ritchie's installation *Universal Adversary*. Stormy, watery, indeterminate, and threatening, shattered imagery enveloped in shifting light and dark, Ritchie's tonalities of cataclysm are not unrelated to Turner's. Growing up in London, Ritchie was intimately familiar with Turner's remarkable paintings, but when chroniclers of modernism counted Turner's directness of execution and pursuit of light as color as a precursor of Impressionism, thereby assigning his achievement solely to the domain of formal issues, they suppressed his overarching intent of painting history into the landscape. Aesthetic similarities aside, Ritchie would be more in tune with Turner's larger purpose. Further, Turner's conflation of biblical events—both recorded (the Deluge) and imagined (Moses writing the book of

Genesis)—with contemporary scientific theory (Goethe's theory of color) set a precedent for Ritchie's habitual, willful conflation of events. Though it must be noted that Turner was more likely to depict events in sequential time, whether historical or contemporary, his radical transformation of landscape into history painting, with its consequent downplaying of the figure, finds a contemporary parallel in Ritchie's painting. And, like Turner, Ritchie views painting not so much as a personal expression but as part of a public discourse.

I will now discuss the development of what might most readily be referred to as Ritchie's unraveling knots of information. The knot paintings comprise Ritchie's most radical invention. Some strands of these knots seem to provoke the rage in the sky of the seascapes discussed above. They began toward the turn of the century, when he urged his paint to congeal into precisely rendered open knots—something like writhing orgies of octopods—that often spill out onto the floor and/or surrounding wall and ceiling, as could be seen in his installation *The Fast Set* for North Miami's Museum of Contemporary Art in 2000. Interspersed in the tangle of tentacles frequently are found scientific equations and symbols related to the subjects of thermodynamics, the science of change, as well as eyes, tiny figures, and written words and phrases that often invoke games of chance, such as betting odds. This tangle is like the visual embodiment of the outrageously layered and tangled, fragmented narrative that motivates the installation. In *The Fast Set*, a large amorphous blue-and-gray shape is identified as *The Swimmer*, which is the headless corpse of Lucifer now become Infinity and cloaked in yellow to become the visible universe in a story line that "encapsulates the history of thermodynamics as seen through Gnostic mythology."[3] And that's a radical abbreviation of what ensues.

In his even more elaborate installation *Proposition Player* (2003) exhibited at the Contemporary Arts Museum, Houston, eleven variants of these raveling and unraveling—even reveling—paintings of knots were included in the large exhibition space. Now denser, richer, and visually more complex than those in *The Fast Set*, these writhing serpentine members/feelers/forces/sensors hover in a kind of nowhere space, neither deep, nor flat, nor grounded with one exception: in *The First Sea* (2003) the knot seems to rise out of the sea at the bottom edge of the canvas. In *Snake Eyes* (2003), the churning knots seem to be self-propelled and self-sustaining phenomena: at once vast and flat, dense and transparent high-voltage tangles of energy often, as here, with eyes bobbing in the wild profusion of tendrils. Occasionally miniature simian figures and scientific equations emerge from the twisting snarl of linearity.

Also revealed in *Proposition Player* is the relooping of narrative progression found in comics, articulated in the work's reversible narratives that unfold across several panels and in the interchangeable and mercurial natures of their protagonists. "Snake eyes" refers to the throw of dice resulting in one pip per die, the lowest possible roll in many a game of chance—seemingly unpredictable chance, bad luck, and loser. Snake Eyes is also the name of one of the ninja-powerful heroes fighting in Vietnam featured in the G.I. Joe comic book series. The graphic directness and clarity, as well as the propensity for explosiveness, regularly found in adventure comic books, whether Japanese anime or American Marvel, are also an integral part of Ritchie's visual vocabulary—a visual vocabulary seeking a clarity and directness found in many a comic book.

Chance plays a significant role in *Proposition Player*. Ritchie wanted to collapse all stories, categories, and characters from his previous works into one moment—"a moment where the viewer can enter or begin to play the game him or herself."[4] And so each viewer was given a card from a deck including Ritchie's forty-nine original characters; the cards are divided into four suits representing the four basic forces of the universe (more on this below). The card was given to a "dealer" at a gaming table who then "handed" the viewer digital dice cast from prehistoric elk bones in the Museum of Natural History (meant to simulate the first dice ever made and remind us of the origin of the "throwing of the bones"). As a game of craps was played by the viewer, sensors in the dice registered the cast and triggered an animation on the surface of the table; these images evolved through more throws to progressively recapitulate all the paintings in the exhibition.

Winding through the exhibition space was a raised, flat black powder-coated aluminum, perforated fretwork with rods topped by something cubistically headlike rising through some of the interstices called *The Fine Constant*. Each one of these heads was based on a sculpture made by young students in Houston who participated in a workshop with Ritchie. Each head was scanned in 3-D, decimated by 95 percent because "we can only see 5 percent of the universe. We've called another 25 percent 'dark energy' and the remaining 70 percent 'dark matter'."[5] In spite of this reduction, they were still recognizable as heads. And so one learned how little we can actually see of the universe and how even that 5 percent is loaded with sufficient information to negotiate our lives. The painter Alex Ross, a mutual friend of both Ritchie and myself, refers to this kind of metaphorical play so typical of Ritchie's work as "information jazz," and I have appropriated it as an apt title for this text.

Ritchie is a fan of certain forms of jazz, especially the melding of the twin meteors of bebop and cool jazz in Miles Davis's electric *On the Corner* (1972), which uses a form of polyphony that has both flatness (cool jazz) and superheated knots passing through, under and around each other—knots as jazz. It has both an underlying hard structure and a looping, sprawling circularity.

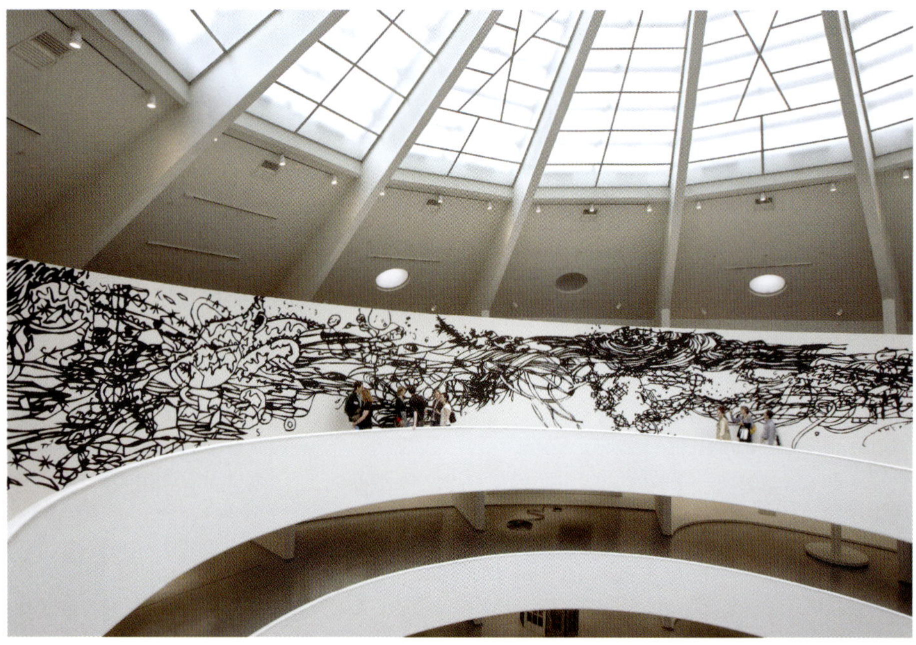

The Fine Constant became a physical embodiment of the The Hierarchy Problem, a vast black arabesquing linearity painted on the wall that seemed to grow out of and extend and interconnect the paintings of the swirling knots. On the floor under the fretwork was placed an undulating mat of rubber and Tyvek configured in a kind of psychedelically colored reprise to the aluminum fretwork called The God Impersonator. All resulted in a lyric opera of painterliness transforming wall and floor into profoundly complex and pleasurable visuality. A new form of landscape painting; a new form of history painting.

The pale backgrounds and yellows and blues that predominate in the knot paintings for Proposition Player, as well as their relatively open configurations, contribute to the lightness and playfulness of the installation's festive casino mood. However, the four knot paintings that constitute The Measures (2005) from four years later, together with the central fretwork cupola-like structure The Universal Cell and the black mark making that extends from the paintings onto the wall each is centered upon, are endowed with a sterner bearing. Many of the serpentine linear contortions now have a metallic, somewhat foreboding appearance; other arabesquing swirls are a brackish brown, prickly and thorny. A large human skeleton head emerges from the lower right side of the twisted layering in The Measures I and a smaller skeleton rises to the top of the knotting/unknotting of The Measures IV. The bobbing eyes in all four of the paintings now seem likely to be involved with surveillance. A harsh beauty, vivid and dynamic, rules these tense paintings that, for me, count as some of Ritchie's most compelling works.

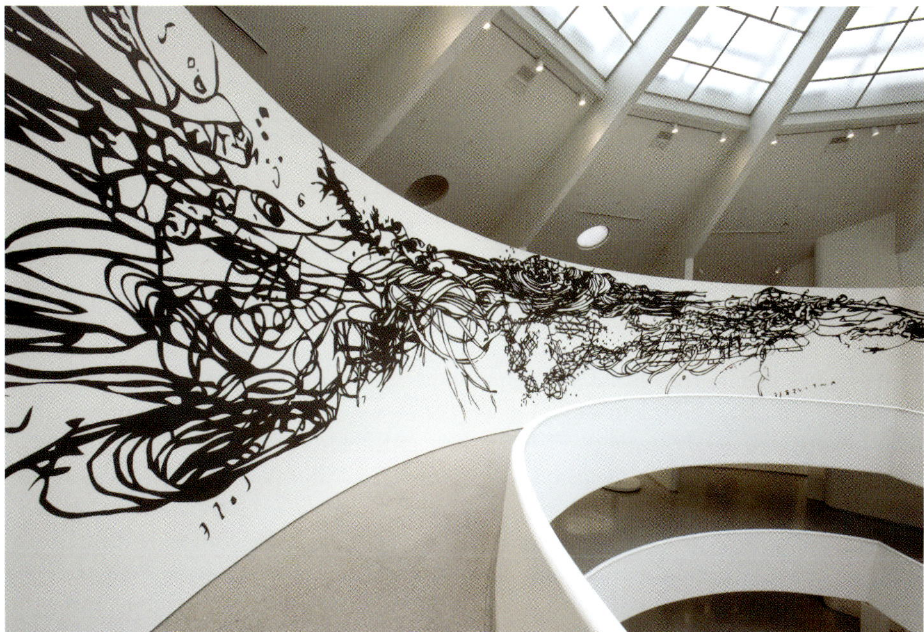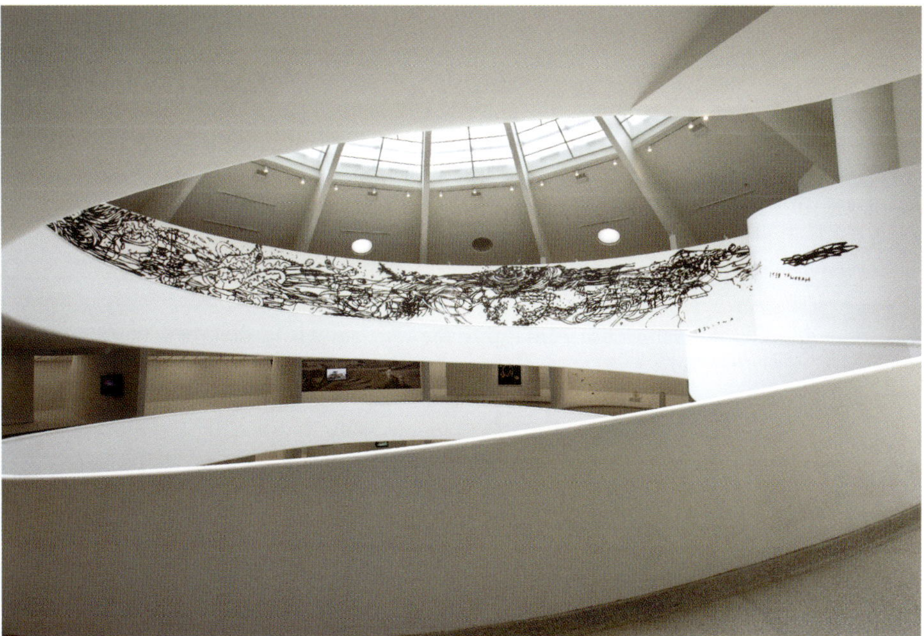

Matthew Ritchie, installation views of a work created for *The Shapes of Space*, a group exhibition at the Solomon R. Guggenheim Museum, New York, 2007

"What are *The Measures*?" I inquired of the artist, a question to which I received a lengthy reply. They are "the four universal constants of free space—the speed of light, the gravitational constant, the Planck limit, and the force constant which are carried by the four aces in *Proposition Player*…*The Measures* also refer to the punishments of the four half-divine traitors of Tartarus painted in the Titian cycle *The Damned*."[6]

From this truncated version of Ritchie's explanation, it is obvious that *The Measures* are not, cannot be literal representations of *The Damned* or those scientific phenomena known as the universal constants. They are leaps of Ritchie's imagination, just as Blake's rendering of Ezekiel's wheel within a wheel required a leap of his imagination. Ritchie created visual realizations of these scientific phenomena—*The Measures* might be seen as the Four Apostles of Modern Science. They are far more unlikely to be rendered "accurately" than, for example, the Four Apostles of the New Testament, whose immediately recognizable symbols and masculine gender identify their varying incarnations through the ages. When I saw these paintings in Ritchie's studio, he was going through the final throes of revision—re-vision—that depended upon his visual intelligence fueled by his scientific knowledge but not beholden to it, or else how could Tartarus have entered the fray of the paintings?

In conversation, I mentioned to Ritchie that the meticulously detailed and rendered layered arabesquing linearity of the knot paintings looked not unlike a digitalized version of Jackson Pollock's flung and dripped, layered whiplashes of paint, seen in his works between 1947 and 1951, that, while courting accident, never eluded Pollock's magnificent control. However, Pollock's (in)famous proclamation "I am nature" subsumes the universal into the personal, whereas Ritchie seeks to build the opposite. He proposed the Book of Kells as a parallel comparison.

The illuminated manuscript containing the four gospels in Latin was created some time around 800 A.D. by Celtic monks. Its illustrations pulse with staggering intricacy and precision of layered, often foliate spirals and curling arabesques intertwined with dragons, cats, birds, etc. The illustrations were probably drawn with a quill, and their making would likely have been aided by rulers, set squares, compasses, and possibly a French curve, but without benefit of magnifying glasses. The minute and elaborate process defies imagination.

Although rooted in Judeo-Christian myth, Ritchie identifies Celtic culture and its legacy in European culture as another significant element in his own history. He has said: "The Celts, the first transnational European culture, were shape-shifters, speakers of tongues…I grew up with their stories of endless change: the wounded king and his wasted land, the green man and the severed head…They called it 'tuirgin,' the transmigratory cycle of investigative experience."[7] Ritchie was deeply influenced by the Celtic "belief that the world is derived from experience, not rationalization," as the competing Greco-Roman culture believed.[8]

Empiricism, of course, does not rule out imagination, even leaps of the imagination, in art or in science. Dark matter, for instance, is of unknown substance that does not emit or reflect sufficient electromagnetic radiation to be observed directly; however, its presence has been inferred, by knowing scientists, from the gravitational effects on visible matter. A leap of scientific imagination brought the unknowable within the realm of the understanding. The unthinkable can be thought. For Ritchie, dark matter becomes a metaphor for the unknowable, the visibly absent; his quest is to imagine the unknowable into painting thought. Ritchie's Celtic-description continues: "Their sign was the unraveled knot that twists into a labyrinth, that grows into a serpent, that consumes itself. DNA, the coiled dimensional instruction book that can build a living world from dust and as easily dissolve it back again."[9]

The references are clear: the severed head, a frequent symbol in Ritchie's work, was used by the Celts as an oracle. The wasted land and the green man are symbiotic, as seen in *The Measures* and the landscapes. The serpent could be Jörmungandr, or Ourobouros, as the Romans called him, the circular archetypal image of eternity.

Pollock's line, drawn from the same Jungian depths, is a lyrical layering in the terms of knot theory, the mathematical branch of topology that studies knots; but it is not a knot. Although Ritchie certainly wouldn't contest Pollock's astounding achievement and though he frequently cites *Number 1, 1950* as the greatest picture of the twentieth century, Ritchie's particular interest in lines and knots has more to do with what can be woven together, what knots can bind.

This is an issue with special relevance for Ritchie's now frequent collaborations with architects, scientists, and institutions, where his approach must adapt to the information that comes with each new project. An example of this is his recent commission to create work for the Wayne Lyman Morse U.S. Courthouse in Eugene, Oregon, designed by Thom Mayne and Morphosis.

Unlike a gallery or museum installation, Ritchie was required to deal with the constraints inherent to a specifically themed government commission. He was initially presented with a laundry list of points to be dealt with, as well as with a presiding judge/patron considerably more conservative than himself. In the end, the tree of justice blossomed. "What does justice look like?" Ritchie asked a group of young local students in

Eugene. A dog, a monkey, an eagle, and a crown (echoes of Ezekiel) were some of the figures the students responded with. Using techniques similar to the ones described earlier in *The Fine Constant*, the heads of the figures made by the students were rendered and placed on top of pylons that held up a black-powdered aluminum drawing that Ritchie created on the terrace of the third floor, where the building's six courtrooms are located. This drawing, again like *The Fine Constant*, is a raised undulating fretwork that incorporates multiple strands of information. The sculpture is titled *Stare Decisis*, a Latin legal term meaning "to stand by that which is decided" and the foundational principal of constitutional jurisprudence. It loosely maps the Willamette River system that runs through Eugene and includes abstracted fragments of text citing the precedents for the United States Constitution and gyroscopically turning rings equal in number to the articles and amendments of the Constitution. The river becomes a metaphor for a legal system at once established in the past and fluid in its responses to the continuous changes wrought on its terrain. The idea of fluidity parallels the courthouse itself. Completed in December of 2006, the courthouse is composed of stately but embracing curves. The septet of curves configuring the aerial view of the building is meant to represent the seven articles of the federal Constitution. The configuration's accuracy of profile notwithstanding, Ritchie's map with its tangle of curves disrupts any single reading.

A small circular section of Ritchie's map even flows through the glass windows onto a bench into the curving interior lobby, where Ritchie created three large lightbox murals called *Life, Liberty,* and *Pursuit.* The images were printed on film and mounted on lenticular prismatic acrylic panels creating two shifting views as the viewer passes: the landscape of Oregon facing the actual landscape of the state seen through the windows of the lobby, and a more abstract landscape inscribed with names and landmark cases from the evolution of law over the last four thousand years or so. The murals' shifting views vibrate with a lyric lightness of touch; they become literal and figurative reflections on landscape. They also raise enticing questions about the relationship of climate and topography to the evolution of law.

The local response to a building, certainly unconventional as courthouses go, was overwhelmingly positive judging by the jubilant opening-day celebrations. Local officials were imagining the building as their Bilbao, expecting a revival of downtown Eugene and a new influx of tourists. The complex narrative—the story of law—told by the works had been seamlessly integrated into the project. The "site-specific" information Ritchie was asked to represent in collaboration with architect Thom Mayne translated into the visual vocabulary he had independently developed, absorbing the information and re-rendering it into his own language in an architectural context. The entire history of law was now included in Ritchie's system and would immediately be put to use in *Ezekiel I*, the projection in *Universal Adversary* mentioned at the beginning of this essay.

This universally inclusive property distinguishes his narrative strategies from many of his peers and runs deep in his other collaborative projects such as *Games of Chance and Skill* at MIT (2001), *We Want to See Some Light* (2006) at Portikus, and *The Morning Line*, a new structure unveiled at the Venice Architecture Biennale in 2008, which is a traveling performance space that contains countless layers of structure. It will intertwine Milton's *Paradise Lost* with the most recent advances in physics and cosmology through scores played and sung by rock gods, modernist composers, and you and me, if we are fortunate enough to be in Venice, Seville, or London.

In all of these projects, and indeed his entire body of work, Ritchie has created a visual vocabulary that binds a variety of subjects with visual tropes that have proven to be remarkably versatile in his quest for the universal, or semasiographic, painting system he has been developing for the past decade, where the parts can not only be intertranslated between works but also adapted to absorb any form of content.

He has achieved this without sacrificing visual pleasure or visual variety. And his vaulting ambition is tempered by his deep intelligence, his humor, and his willingness to play. And it's just the beginning.

1. Owen Drolet, "Matthew Ritchie Interview," *Urban Desires: A Magazine of Metropolitan Passions* (March/April 1995).

2. Thyrza Nichols Goodeve, "Reflections on an Omnivorous Visualization System: An Interview with Matthew Ritchie," in *Matthew Ritchie: Proposition Player* (Ostfildern, Germany: Hatje Cantz; and Houston: Contemporary Arts Museum Houston, 2003).

3. Ibid., 98.

4. Ibid., 44.

5. Ibid., 46.

6. Email from the artist to the author, January 3, 2008.

7. Email from the artist to the author, December 19, 2007.

8. Ibid.

9. Ibid.

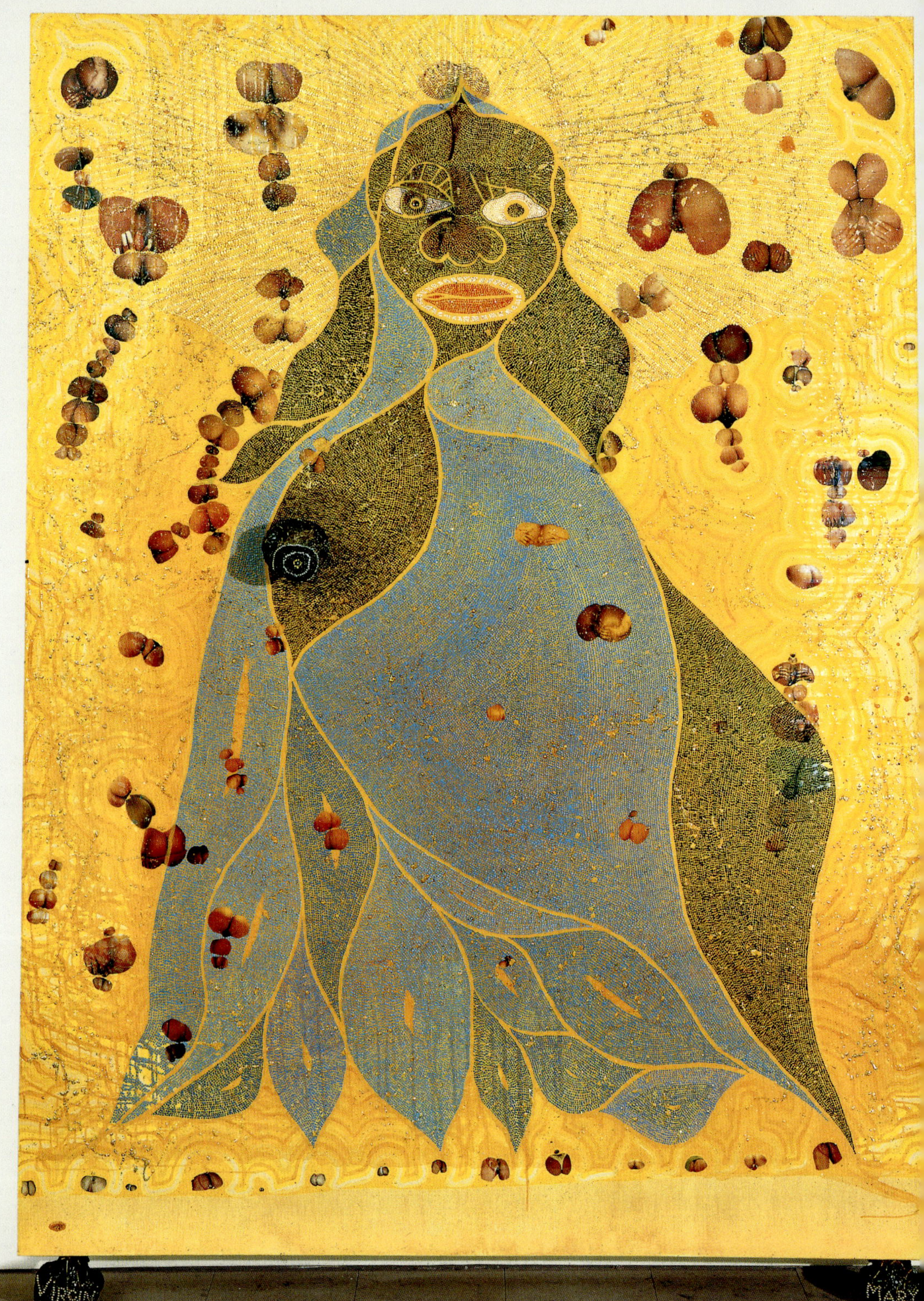
VIRGIN
MARY

Chris Ofili

Just Desserts

> *"time has come for most of us*
> *2 choose in which god we trust"*
> — D'Angelo, *Devil's Pie*

Caribbean tourist destination or Garden of Eden, rape or ecstatic communication, hip-hop queen or Virgin Mary, monkey business or Last Supper—Chris Ofili's beauties are fraught with challenging ambiguities, visual and iconographic. His deep involvement with the process of creating often enmeshes beauty in a surprising symbiosis of disparate cultures and religious practices that cultivate a constantly shifting referentiality. He seeks to restore spirituality to the body. Ofili has recontextualized the Catholicism he grew up with, imbuing Christian iconography with radically new pomp and circumstance while imbuing the figure, in three dimensions and two, with a vivid new life. He renders holy sexy and vice versa. Ofili provides aesthetic pleasure in generous portions but intends that pleasure to draw the viewer in to question and/or reconsider conventional beliefs.

Ofili had begun painting, as a student, in the late 1980s; in 1993 it became his primary pursuit. Brilliantly—literally and figuratively—he transformed the flat rectangle of canvas into a bejeweled, shimmering, obsessively decorative reliquary, now abstract, now embodying a hip-hop commando, now the Virgin Mary. Not with precious jewels but with acrylic, oil, resin, glitter, map pins, and elephant dung did he achieve his iconic luminosity. In 2005, for an exhibition titled *The Blue Rider* in Berlin, Ofili added sculpture in the round to his making and seems to have foresworn glitter and map pins in his two-dimensional work. Amongst the sculptures he created is a standing couple, embraced in a kiss and entwined by a snakelike coil. One exemplar of this work was cast in blue-patinated bronze, another in nickel silver; each stands some twenty-two inches high. *Bound* and *Gagged* they are titled. A kiss is not just a kiss. This couple is the precursor for two different versions of the Annunciation created in 2006, together with other sculptures of biblical figures.

Ofili had been thinking about a work based on the Annunciation and was finally inspired to do one after seeing several versions of that subject in the Fra Angelico exhibition at the Metropolitan Museum of Art in the fall of 2005. Ofili's paintings share with many of Fra Angelico's a high degree of detailed decorativeness, combined with a sleekly pared-down formal language. However, the sexualized, possibly predatory tension of Ofili's two sculpted works is at a far remove from the reserve of Fra Angelico's paintings.

Chris Ofili, *The Holy Virgin Mary*, 1996

Only the wonderfully detailed construction of the wings of the Annunciatory angels created by each artist might allude to some connection.

I was stunned by the bristling physicality of Ofili's two sculptures of the *Annunciation* (2006), as he and I viewed them at a foundry in upstate New York. In both of his versions, the black-patinated angel is presented potbellied and Afroed, with a long, pointed, phallic beard, rather than the young androgynous angel so often encountered in this subject. In the first of these sculptures, the exaggerated curves of the Virgin Annunciate's glisteningly smooth body yield a cross between a Brancusi sculpture and a blow-up sex doll. Her bent legs have literally melted into the thighs and out of the knees of the angel, as his almost hidden from view, prodigious announcing member thrusts toward her. Angel and Virgin are held in tense, precarious balance—his potbelly with her bubble butt, her arm bent in an angle over her head with his pointed wing, his rough blackness with her highly polished smoothness. She holds on actively; he does not. Whether their conjunction is voluntary or involuntary remains moot. Her distended, slithery arms guided my eyes around the sculpture—her left arm pulled me up and over, her right arm pulled me around to and down the angel's back, as it disappeared into his ass.

The taut in-the-roundness of the sculpture presents a sharp contrast to the vividly detailed, hieratic flatness of Ofili's paintings. In answer to my "how" question, Ofili explained that he worked as though creating simultaneous drawings, as he moved around the armature. He worked at or very near full scale, piling and molding clay onto the armature, moving into the round, section by section—often dragging clay off the armature and starting a section afresh. Instead of the out-of-scale peaks and valleys that often occur when a hand-modeled figure is vastly pointed up and a thumb mark becomes a giant ditch, we are confronted with a cast of the actual comings and goings of Ofili's fingers imparting molded life to the angel's flesh—in stark contrast to the seemingly untouched flawlessness of the Virgin's flesh. Material contrast and tension conjoin with psychological contrast and tension.

The second Annunciation is still more fraught. The angel is kneeling—almost levitating—with one knee off the ground, the tips of his wings barely balancing him on the ground. Once more the Virgin is furiously embracing him. This time her right breast is buried in his chest, and her arms are distended into curving serpentine arcs. Her hair is swept wildly back, as though she had just leaped onto the angel. Is the Virgin aroused by the angel or enraged by her parthenogenetic fate? Should a hard-on be the annunciatory agent? How does the childbearing seed enter the Virgin's womb? Could the child possibly be carried in the angel's pot belly? And what of the Virgin's hand disappearing into the angel's ass?

A digression is called for—not perhaps to fully answer the above questions, but at least to give them a context. In his remarkable book, *The Sexuality of Christ in Renaissance*

Art and in Modern Oblivion, renowned art historian Leo Steinberg explores the sexuality of Christ as depicted in Italian and Northern European Renaissance art between 1400 and the middle of the sixteenth century. Citing sermons and providing abundant illustrations of the Christ child's penis being revealed, touched, and/or fondled by the Virgin Mary and/or St. Catherine and intensely stared and marveled at by the adoring Magi, Steinberg explicates the making visible of Christ's penis as the proof of God's making him human (he employs the term "humanation"). Christ is clearly sexed. During his adult life, because of his choosing chastity, his penis is not visible in most paintings or sculptures of his deeds. Only in death did Christ's penis become once more visible and/or implied—whether in the depiction of Christ's hand over his penis in many representations of the Lamentation, or in his frequently swollen (with an apparent erection) loincloth. Indeed, Christ's post-mortem revival was symbolized by an erection. Steinberg illustrates with a Jacques Bellange print of the Pietà (ca. 1615), in which Christ's slipping loincloth could hardly be held up by anything other than an erection, and several Man of Sorrows paintings by Maerten van Heemskerck with swollen loincloths. After the sixteenth century, the Christ child's penis, in earlier depictions, was regularly subjected to suppression by the addition of a veiling loincloth—accompanying what Steinberg refers to as a "massive historic retreat from the mythical grounds of Christianity."

Ofili was unfamiliar with Steinberg's book, when I mentioned it. However, in his sculpture and his painting, it could be maintained that Ofili has, in his very personal way, set out to remythologize Christianity and to retrieve the physicality and sexuality so often purposefully drained from biblical subjects—whether fertilizing his painting with the addition of elephant dung, or endowing the Annunciatory Angel with a penis, or turning to mass imagery such as blaxploitation films, travel posters, or hip-hop stars' promotional images to vividly, even luridly, impart a new immediacy to his subjects. Ofili continues to probe and provoke questions about the relationship of the body's physicality and sexuality to spirituality, as he forges his symbiosis of the vulgar with the sublime, the profane, and the sacred. Just as one doesn't have to be a devout Catholic to be drawn into the highly eroticized ecstasy of Bernini's Saint Teresa, one needn't be a believer to be swept up by Ofili's visually psycho-sexualized drama of the traditionally demure subject of the Annunciation.

Mary Magdalene, often associated with sins of the flesh and occasionally thought to have been Jesus's wife, has provided many an artist with the opportunity to create a Christian, female nude—Titian, for instance, in 1533. She is still more exhilarated than the Virgin. The idea for the sculpture *Mary Magdalene (Infinity)* came from a watercolor

Ofili had created of a kneeling nude with both her arms sharply bent over her head. "The working title for that sculpture was *Infinity* because of the never-ending line that is traced by her arms and legs," which seem to follow the path of the symbol for infinity. Looking at the watercolor, one can readily imagine Ofili's explanation of proceeding as though giving three-dimensional body to a drawing. A seated Buddha, a whirling dervish, a pulp-magazine pinup, this sculpture is as liquid as mercury, sensuous and wildly enigmatic. Mary Magdalene's slippery legs disappear into her ass to create, if not exactly infinity, endless revolutions of visual arousal.

Dung has played a role in Ofili's work since his art's beginnings. In 1992 while still a student, having returned from a trip to Africa, Ofili set up a stall in London to exhibit elephant dung, placed an ad for "elephant shit" in *Frieze*, and made a sculpture out of a dung ball and his own hair. These works were inspired both by those ritual African sculptures that incorporate human blood, shit, and more, and by David Hammons's *Blizz-aard Ball Sale* at Cooper Square in New York City in 1983. One of Ofili's first paintings was titled *Painting with Shit on It* (1993); for the next twelve years, all of Ofili's paintings would be propped up on two lacquered and decorated balls of elephant dung. His 2005 *Blue Rider* exhibition included sculptures, both male and female, based on a popular Catalan Nativity figure called Caganer ("defecator" in Catalan), whose visible defecation is regarded as beneficial fertilizer. Both the male (*Blue Moon* in blue-patinated bronze) and female (*Silver Moon* in nickel silver) have squatted, bared their rears (mooned), and defecated a serpent-like coil. And now here is the Virgin, uniting herself with the announcing angel not only by her legs melting into his but also her hand disappearing into his ass, while both feet of the Magdalene are sucked into her own ass.

All these anal events seem to imply the possibility of forming a verbal conclusion about creation—especially with the obvious analogy between dung and clay. However, if a conclusion is to be drawn, it is left to the viewer to formulate. Ofili refuses to attempt to bond his work to a verbal explanation beyond revealing some of its sources and inspirations. Like many artists, once he has started a work, he often finds it taking him over and leading him to an unpremeditated end. Even the process he employs for the creation of his sculpture permits substantial opportunity for intuitive, ad hoc moves. He is extremely bible-literate, and his Catholic upbringing and altar-boy experiences remain close to his consciousness. However, Ofili is more prone to layering metaphors and allusions to diverse cultures than adhering to traditional dogma. He welcomes the resultant openness and ambiguity that permit the viewer to enter the work and extend the possibility of self-reflection and self-revelation.

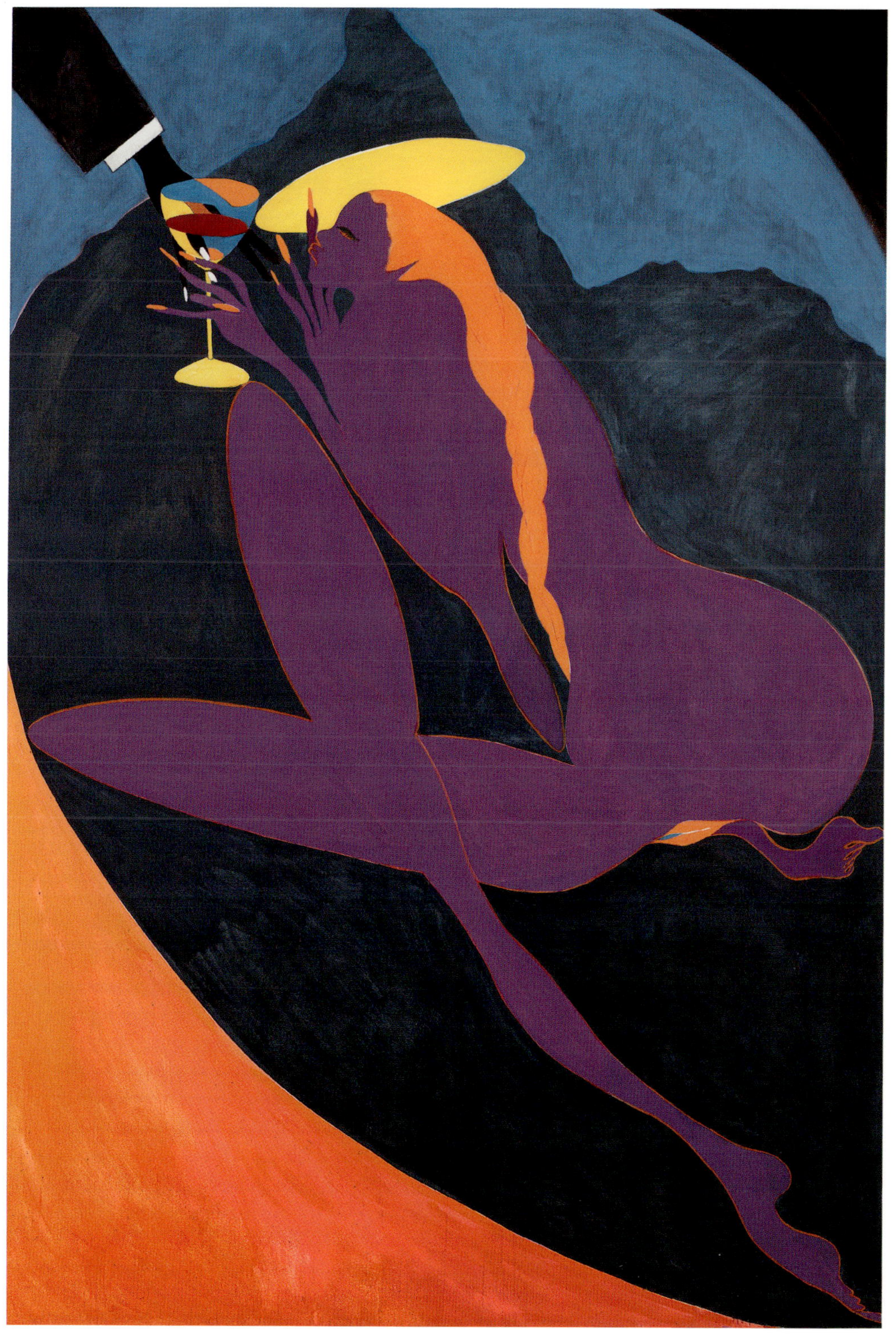

Ofili's *Saint Sebastian* is one of the most literal of his syntheses of aspects of disparate traditions. Sebastian, whom piercing arrows could not kill and whose martyrdom has so frequently been homoeroticized by his portrayers, takes particularly androgynous form in Ofili's hands. Not arrows but countless nails, encouraged to bleed rust onto the bronze, stud the body. Countless nails and more cover the ritual figures called Minkisi Minkondi, created by artists of the Bakongo tribe to help hunt down witches, thieves, adulterers, et al. The nails are driven in to arouse the figure's powers. Unintentionally, the torturing Romans' arrows aroused Sebastian's powers. Dropped to his knees, arms bent in a hopeless attempt at protection, this bereft Sebastian might also call to mind contemporary victims of terrorist nail bombs.

A highly stylized, wall-hung crucifix (*The Almighty Shadow*), several feet in height, provided the conclusion of our viewing at the foundry. The intertwined limbs of Christ and the cross form a chorus of linearity—seemingly one continuous modeled band of bronze. On the train back to New York, I pondered the possibility that the profanity of some of Ofili's forming might be intended to provoke spirit in a manner analogous to that launched by arrows and nails. And I pondered the liquidity of the various arms—grasping, flailing, shielding—as they seemed almost to melt into linearity. Liquid limbs imparting drama to the three-dimensional making. I thought about line, knowing we were on the way to see a set of etchings and a group of drawings at Ofili's gallery in Manhattan.

Grace that yields to the organic inclinations of the drawing hand seems to have taken up permanent residence in Ofili's drawing hand. "They gave me the plates, and I just started to draw," Ofili volunteered, as the eleven etchings comprising *The Agony in the Garden* (2007) were placed in front of me. Taut, delicate, arabesquing line spins the narrative of Judas's betrayal of Christ in the Garden of Gethsemane—each of the eleven etchings representing the view of one of the disciples. The first etching is a garden of mostly curlicues sprouting arching flower stems, or turning into flower petals or meandering into space. This disciple's view of the kiss is obscured by the garden's pirouetting foliage. In the next ten, silken threads of line unfurl the embrace, now in close-up of the two heads, now full figures kissing under a starlit sky, now enrapt in a disciple's cascade of hair, now lost in a naked embrace, and finally ending in an embrace enveloped in something orchidaceous. The flowing curvilinearity of these tensile abbreviated figures call to mind the more graphic drawings and illustrations of the great turn-of-the-century draftsman Aubrey Beardsley, whom Ofili has long admired. In these etchings, the multiples of the tiny encircled Afro head that is so often Ofili's monogram become Jesus's necklace, or border the image, or become stamens, or hover in the air like fireflies.

In seven 2006 drawings, each of a sensuously full-bodied female nude, the freehand graphite lines are transformed into a continuous chain of Afro heads—thus further animating the languid curvilinearity. They are related to the lush creatures that have often filled the plane of Ofili's paintings, such as *Foxy Brown* (1997), and are at once comic and boldly beautiful, reveling in their physicality. And, as though this beauty needed further embellishment, each sheet is strewn with the most delicate of flower blossoms. They are "The Sobbin' Women" found in Stephen Vincent Benet's posthumously published short story, which was based on the tale of the ancient Romans who abducted the Sabine women so that they might propagate a nation and that much later inspired paintings by Nicolas Poussin, Jacques-Louis David, and others. The short story in turn led to the 1954 Hollywood musical *Seven Brides for Seven Brothers*, by Stanley Donen. The cinema sisters, headed by Jane Powell, are a far primmer lot than Ofili's sobbin' women. Each drawing has been titled with the biblical name of her betrothed, as given in the movie, from Adam to Gideon. There existing no male name beginning with "F" in the bible, that sobbin' woman drawing is titled *Frank*, short for Frankincense. The film's lively music and dance found favor with Ofili's wife. And there those gorgeous lines began.

Ofili's painting has always been line driven; but only recently has the amplitude of his line fully risen to the surface. The extravagant mantle of map pins, glitter, etc., that set his surface aglow with shimmering light was shed in 2004 as Ofili sought a more direct mode of painterly presentation. Between 1993 and 1997, he alternated between all-over abstraction and a centralized figure. Not infrequently the figure approached abstraction or the abstraction approached the figurative. The single figure that ruled Ofili's planes from 1997 to 2001 always emerged from an abstract ground. In 2002, a second figure entered the plane and the setting became more specific—generally, a landscape. However, bold simplification, purity of form, and complex but clear composition's respect for and congruence with the flatness of his painting's plane remained.

The twelve *Within Reach* (2002–03) gouache and gold leaf works on paper that continued and accompanied the paradisiacal/touristic paintings of Afro couples—still aglitter with map pins, etc., in the British Pavilion at the 2003 Venice Biennale—begin to look forward to Ofili's more recent tropics-grounded biblical- and secular-themed paintings. The Blue and Silver paintings on paper (2005) included in *The Blue Rider* exhibition move into larger scale and more varied subject matter. Limited to the lunar glow of various shades of blue together with silver or aluminum leaf, these works writhe with snakes, waves, and various humans and creatures of the night. They seem to bespeak, at least partially, a more lived experience of the tropics.

Indeed, they were created in Trinidad, where Ofili moved in 2005 and where he has created most of his paintings since.

In 2007, Ofili's paintings, now on canvas, have effloresced into a fantastical spectrum of color and composition grounded in and responsive to the flat rectangularity of the painting plane, while simultaneously gliding into the hallucinatory. I viewed three of these paintings in New York, two of them depicting Lazarus in the throes of rising from the dead. Ofili, I was told, had based the figure of Lazarus on a photograph he had taken of a man asleep under a palm tree at Blanchisseuse Beach in Trinidad. In each of the two works, Lazarus has begun to rise up out of the bottom edge of the painting and is propped languidly against the lower right edge; his right arm distends radically and stretches up diagonally to merge with and become the trunk of a palm tree with its leaves clinging to the top edge of the painting—quite literally enacting the planar resurrection already forecast by the somnolent figure's erection. In *The Raising of Lazarus*, Ofili drew three successive profiles of Lazarus and ended up retaining all three, so we see successive stages of the resurrection. The lush tropical palette, concise reduction of shape of the figure and the tropical vegetation, as well as the acutely shaped negative spaces, reflect Henri Matisse's treatment of the tropical vegetation seen in the landscapes he created in 1912 and 1913 in Morocco. Both paintings of Lazarus are loosely and economically brushed, giving breath to the reductive flatness without calling undo attention to the strokes.

When I began this essay, Ofili was still completing his final painting for his exhibition in New York, and he was reluctant to have a visitor in his studio. When it was finished, there was just enough time for me to fly to Trinidad before the paintings were crated and shipped. I was spared having to work from printouts. I arrived in the afternoon and shortly thereafter found myself in Ofili's studio perched high up on a hill, called Lady Chancellor Hill, looking down on the capital city Port of Spain and the surrounding hills and mountains. Assuming I would return the following day, I asked few questions and let my eyes do the work. They were seduced.

Trinidad and Tobago was acquired by the British in 1797 and will shortly celebrate its sixtieth year of independence. Of the two islands that form this nation, Trinidad has the richer culture with its mix of races originally from Africa, Asia, and Europe. It provides the United States with much of its natural gas and has little tourist activity. On my second and last day there, Ofili took me on a tour of the northern side of the island—hairpin turns up a steep mountain road along walls of thick juicy vegetation (it was rainy season), some of it now to be found represented in his paintings. Every now and again a mountain vista opened up to us; the air was very clear. Sparsely populated, here and there small cabbage patches had been claimed from the rain forest, but mostly lush, variegated walls of untouched green predominated. Human population is scant; however, Trinidad is the most densely populated island in the world by avian species. We drove down to a popular beach, ate a roti sandwich, and went to two other beaches—one of them the aforementioned Blanchisseuse—before landing in a rain-soaked ditch until a friendly beachgoer towed us out with his truck as I worried about missing my second studio visit.

Ofili seems completely happy in these surroundings. A tropical richness has pulsed through his painting since his beginnings; now he lives in the middle of it. Often Ofili has incorporated direct references to his influences, interests, and surroundings—previously ranging from William Blake to Foxy Brown; now some aspect of Trinidad is frequently drawn into his work.

The second painting of Lazarus, *Lazarus (dream)*, that I had seen in New York contains a bubble suspended from the long, dripping palm leaves to which Lazarus's distended arm/tree trunk is attached. Inside the bubble a couple in modern dress dances with heads delicately touching. The dancers are based on an enchanted young couple captured by the well-known photographer from Mali, Malick Sidibe. The photograph is titled *Christmas Eve*, and Ofili layered the resurrection of Lazarus with the anticipation of Christ's birth that is celebrated on Christmas Eve.

Ofili also reimagined Sidibe's photograph in three large works. The large collage, *Christmas Eve (palms)*, finds the couple at night in a forest against a darkened, coruscated, silver-leaf ground in a seeming trance: dancing but not touching, solemn, as though contemplating the momentous event to occur the following day. They seem oblivious to the menacing palm leaves that fall around them.

This somber beauty is lightened in palette and mood in the other two versions, the latter of which, *Douen's Dance*, finds the couple floating in a reverie at the nexus of the lushly hued tripartite division of the canvas. Disparate, clear pure shapes come together to configure the couple as though they glided together with the turn of a kaleidoscope. With one more turn, they might slide into a fulgent modernist abstraction. Indeed, the buoyant, seeming ease of the convergence of the various interlocking shapes which the painting contains appear as serendipitously achieved as that resulting from the turn of a kaleidoscope—such is Ofili's compositional skill. He did, however, happily admit to the unconsciously achieved play of the interlocking shapes between the two dancers. As these shapes flip from negative to positive, the female acquires a second face, now kissing the male, and the black space closest to the male flows from what might be his beard into the shape of the female figure's breast. Sometimes hand-to-eye dialogue wisely excludes consciousness.

The shape of the aforementioned Lady Chancellor Hill upon which Ofili's studio is perched makes specific the site of *Confession (Lady Chancellor)*. The radically distended right leg of the nude stretches from the bottom almost to the top of the hill, as though turning that hill into her confessional. Her deep orange/red hair, her seated position, and the elliptical yellow aureole on her head might indicate that she is Mary Magdalene, who is most often portrayed with red hair (as she was by Titian)—a hair color frequently associated with female promiscuity. Ofili showed me a page from an early *Playboy* magazine with photographs of this nude's 1950s predecessors. Perhaps the rainbow-colored concoction in the martini glass being handed to her is a celestial cocktail/communion. And the hand reaching down from the heavens to proffer the glass belongs to whom? ("If Jesus ever loved a woman," Johnny Cash sang.)

The locations with which Ofili chooses to ground his subject are as readily taken from an art book as from the experience of his local environment. In *Lover's rock–guilt*, one of two blue paintings that, because of their silver underpainting, shimmer elusively like moonlit reflections on water, Ofili based an awkwardly embracing amorous couple on a gentler and more courtly, erotic Chinese painting. He replaced the rock in the painting with the elongated head of an old bearded man, watching, spooking. The number and variety of reflective blues make it necessary to constantly shift position, now seeing an extended hand, now a hard-on, now a hand squeezing a breast, now the leer of the old man, so that the viewer's eyes shift, and grope, and turn, much as the painting's protagonists do. The blues arouse and seduce en route to metaphor and enigma.

In *Iscariot Blues*, because the figures are more isolated, they reveal themselves more readily—two musicians on a wooden balcony, one playing a banjo-like instrument. This twosome is based on a wooden trompe l'oeil cutout of musicians playing a kind of Portuguese music sung at Christmas time, called Parang, that Ofili encountered on one of his outings in Lopinot, Trinidad. Hanging from the right side of the top edge is Judas, as the Iscariot in the title indicates—blues played for the betrayer painted in blues. Or maybe not a betrayer but, instead, the necessary enactor of God's will. And also hanging from the top edge are the oversized leaves of the rain forest, including the deeply scalloped and beautifully curved monstera leaf so often seen in a Matisse painting: leaves I still remembered from our tour.

At the end of my second and last studio visit, Ofili brought out a number of new drawings. In one pair, both titled *Black Milky Way*, both outlined by those rolling, encircled Afro heads, two couples embrace in joyous coitus, one couple heterosexually and one homosexually—breast milk and semen gracefully exploding into the Milky Way, in each of the two drawings, and triggering visual pleasure that defies verbalization.

Ofili has seamlessly fused a truly disparate range of influences, ranging from William Blake to Francis Picabia to Philip Guston to Sigmar Polke to the Bible to African tribal art to Alice Coltrane to Dead Prez to countless others in his quest for a personal art and personal spirituality that might invert into more universal presence. *Devil's Pie*, he has titled this exhibition after a song by D'Angelo—a hip-hop singer and one-man band, the son and grandson of preachers and seeker and creator of a kind of hip-hop Christianity. Ofili himself might be thought of as a seeker and creator of a visual hip-hop spirituality as he explores the roles of sex, violence, desire, betrayal, and more, while infusing the figure with vivid beauty.

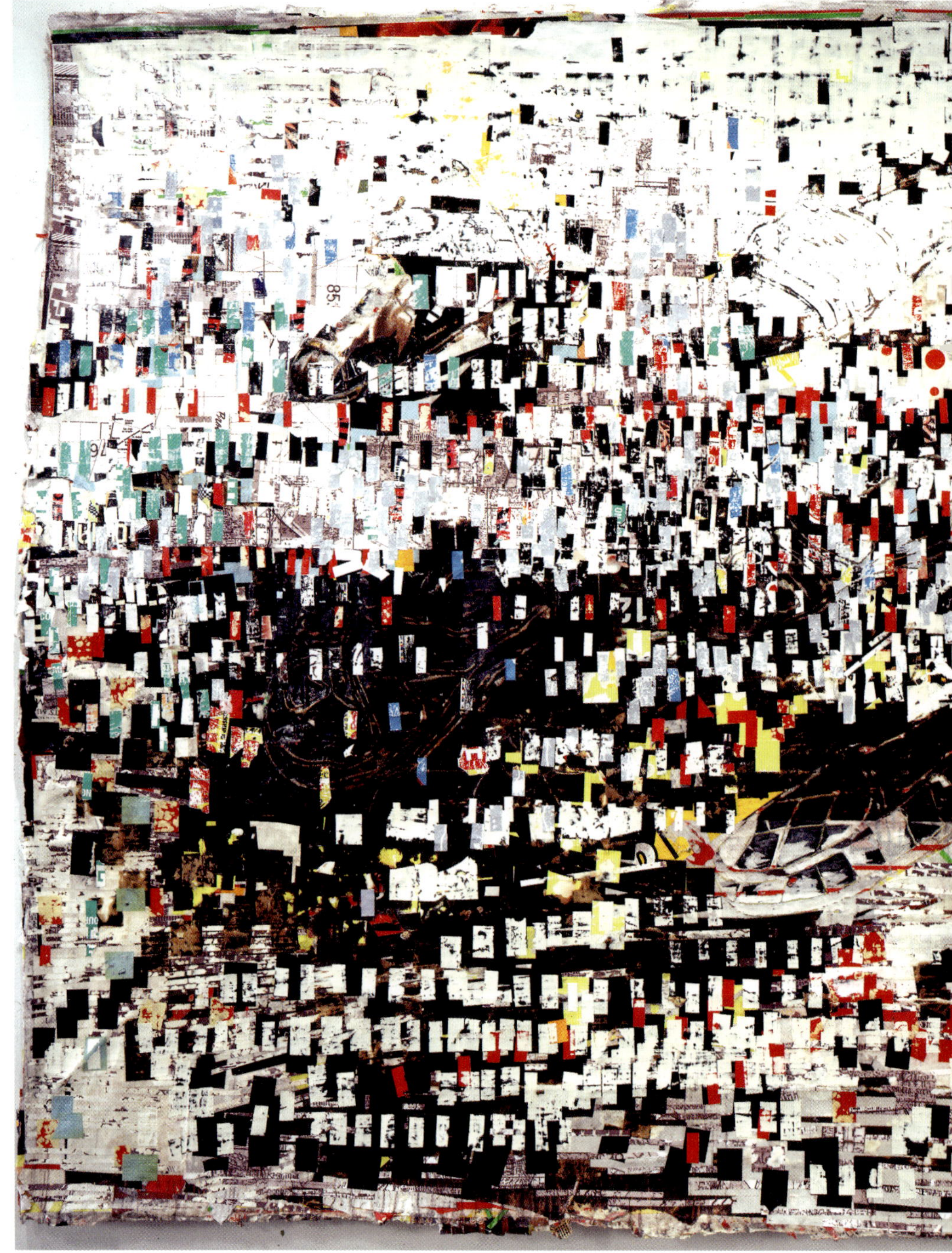

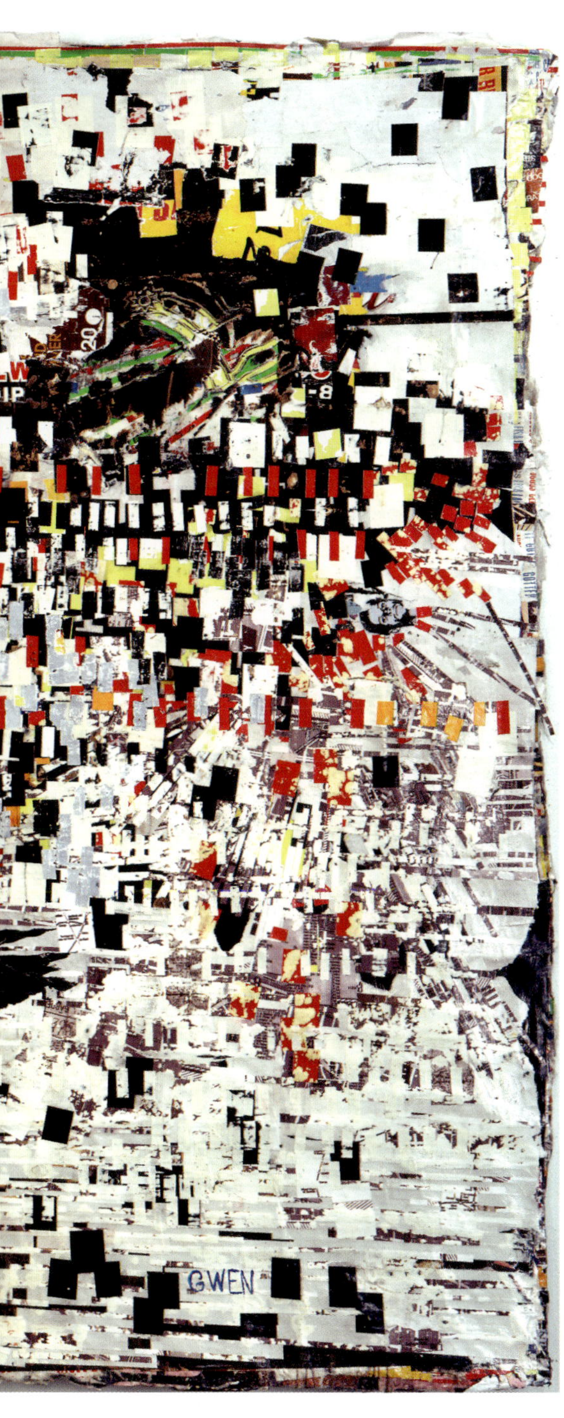

IV. MEDITATIONS IN AN EMERGENCY

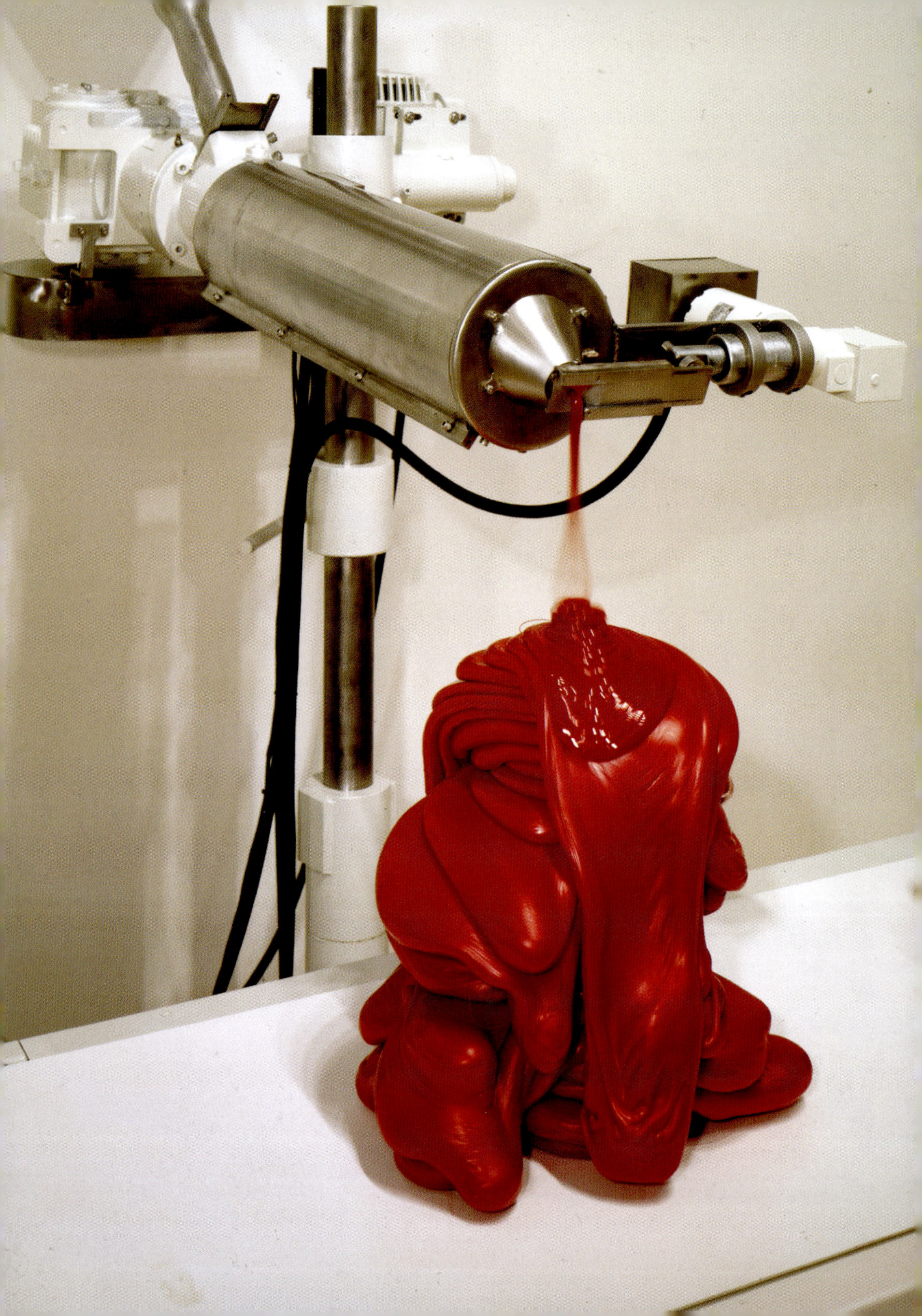

A Velvet Glove Can Hold a Burning Issue

The title of this exhibition, *Meditations in an Emergency*, has been appropriated from a poem written by Frank O'Hara in 1957—when the post-atomic era and the growing power of the mass media had not yet anaesthetized more tender emotions. "All I want is boundless love," O'Hara could write, as he wrapped his narcissism in just enough irony and lyric improvisation to make it necessary to many a reader's life. The emergency that this exhibition's title alludes to bristles with more public turbulence. The globalization so avidly pursued by nations right and left has literally and figuratively enflamed the globe it ostensibly means to ameliorate. The threat of terrorism rides next to each of us in whatever mode of transportation she or he chooses, and our privacy is evermore sucked up by surveillance. In the United States, whether with the torture of prisoners of war at Abu Ghraib or with the flagrant lies that led us into war, our executive branch has mocked the very democratic principles with which it seeks to evangelize the world.

The nine artists included in this exhibition provide no roadmap out of the quagmire. Their art is less prone to the didacticism, sometimes shaded into invective, that marked much of the art dealing with issues of race, gender, and identity in the 1980s. While these issues continue to roil our culture, the work created for this exhibition is more questioning than accusatory and is quite likely to seduce us into meditations via visual ambiguities, detours, humor, and surprises. Perhaps, as James Joyce surmised in *Ulysses*, "the longest way round is the shortest way home."

The building hosting this exhibition has been battered, first by several alterations and then by abandonment. Its open and generous proportions mandated by its original function as an automobile showroom of some twenty thousand square feet remain largely intact. At the same time, its vagrant state is a stark reminder of the decline of Detroit's auto industry. While the nine participating artists in this venture could hardly revive that industry, they enthusiastically took up the challenge of infusing new life into the space. The banality of the exterior façade, remodeled when the avenue it faced was broadened, proved to be an open invitation to a facelift—an invitation gleefully taken up by Barry McGee.

In 1984, at the age of eighteen, McGee, a.k.a. Twist, started tagging on the streets of San Francisco, just as the hip-hop–inspired graffiti art that festivalized New York's subway system was being erased and banned by the law. Today, McGee maintains a precarious balance between his renowned tagging on the streets of San Francisco (and wherever else he might be) and his work for more institutional venues that might undermine his street credibility. Japanese anime and Mexican muralists, especially Diego Rivera, have influenced his work.

For this exhibition, McGee emblazoned the aesthetically challenged rectangular façade with slowly rolling, overlapping, pneumatic volumes spelling out the word "amaze." Amaze is one of the street names of a fellow San Francisco artist invited by McGee to join him and work with him in Detroit. And amaze is literally and figuratively what those letters do, as they turn the façade into a buoyant vessel of wonder.

And yet more amazement as McGee claimed the still larger side wall of the building. A small group of us stood mesmerized in fall's chill, as McGee and Amaze transferred a preparatory study of some three feet in length to the wall well over one hundred feet in length—purely by eyeballing and talk. Neither drip nor false move disrupted the aerosol spray can's heroic trajectory arcing into Amaze's other name, Josh. Stunned by the acuteness of the eye-to-hand coordination, I began to think about Willem de Kooning drawing figures with his eyes closed, which are indistinguishable from those he drew with his eyes open, and then the crowd of equally firm and full curves silhouetting Diego Rivera's figures in his mural two blocks away, at the Detroit Institute of Arts, rumbled in my memory.

Artist surrogates are often to be found in McGee's murals; in Detroit, San Francisco artist/surfer Kevin Ancell fashioned a dummy whose head was cast with Amaze's face. The figure, with its mechanized right arm moving up and down with a spray can in hand, hangs precariously from the roof to surprise and/or alarm many a passerby. However, the fullest surprise radiates from the letters that claim territory not only for their maker, but also for the ordinary building they so rhythmically and joyously enfold. Their cartoony revel, so brilliant and so accessible, brings the street to the museum and vice versa—at once art-smart and street-wise. The bleary homeless faces, shaped by dissolution and lyrically incisive line so often found in McGee's murals, pop up serendipidously here and there inside the building to bring the street further inside. In addition, with the very thin brush employed for the faces, McGee's steady hand wrote "stay rude" on the console of Christopher Fachini's *The Rock Box Sound System Plays the Mental Machine.* Like McGee, Fachini draws rhythm from the street, albeit from another time and in another medium; McGee's "stay rude" acknowledged a kindred spirit.

For me, Christopher Fachini was an answered prayer. Music may well rival automobiles as Detroit's major contribution to American and international culture, and I had, in some way, wanted to include music in the exhibition—not party music for the opening, as most people I queried assumed, but a full participant in the dialogue. Just as I was ready to give up this idea, Fachini was suggested. In Detroit's music club scene, Fachini is known as a virtuoso player of some six or seven instruments, but not so much as a composer. He is a composer, a rhythm-obsessed composer. In a largely abandoned building, early in the day, he played a tape of his music, in which he had played all the parts and then spliced them together. Lush, throbbing rhythms as beautiful and provocative, it seemed, as the early reggae that had so strongly influenced them, filled the air. Impossible to resist: but how could it be presented? I asked. He knew exactly how, but didn't have the means to implement it.

Towers of speakers gave voice to Jamaica's independence in the early 1960s—speakers blasting the energetic and rebellious rhythms of early reggae onto the street, a kind of cornucopia of Africanism including Calypso, soul, and rock 'n' roll. For the towers Fachini wanted to substitute the boom boxes that became so much a part of the breakdancing and other street performances of the early 1980s, which spread out from America's urban ghettoes. He needed to encase his sound in a stack of vintage boom boxes with a microphone and console permitting him to deejay his own music. Fachini is the only artist included in the exhibition whose work was wholly new to me, and, as perfect as his piece sounded, I needed to feel how it resonated in my head the next morning. I woke up smiling. With some assistance from the museum, and with a sign-painter's proper adornment to his boom boxes and their container, Fachini's piece came to fruition.

As I write this, I read for the first time Fachini's title, *The Mental Machine*. Having come of age in the 1960s when, if at all, paintings were often titled *Untitled* (with a capital or lower case U), *No Title*, or simply a number, I still have a tendency to ignore titles. However, titles often do have meaning. Fachini's title seems to tell me he intends his music to do more than infect my body with spontaneous undulations and a big smile, although that is already quite an achievement. Music, more than most other art forms, dissolves the artificial barriers we have created between reason, emotion, and sensuality, as it seamlessly molds time. Like much of the reggae that inspired it, *Mental Machine* urges us to take pleasure and pride in ourselves.

Not until I had visited Detroit several times did it dawn on me that Roxy Paine's computerized assembly line might, in the context of the high technology that eliminated many an autoworker's job in this city, acquire a fraught resonance at a far remove not only from Fachini's machine but also from Paine's own intentions. His *Scumak No. 2 (Auto Sculpture Maker)* (2001) shares the vast first gallery of this museum with Fachini's *Mental Machine*. Since the mid-1990s, Paine has continuously challenged the parameters of sculpture on two fronts: creating by hand a variety of plants (especially mushrooms) indistinguishable from nature but for their sprouting on an art gallery's or museum's floor, and creating machines that make art. In full control, Paine meticulously designs the exquisitely detailed, computer-driven machine that is built by hand and that every two days creates one sculpture. The sculptures are made from molten layers of polyethylene extruded through a funnel and oozing onto a conveyor belt, always consisting of forty layers (forty dispensing cycles, forty cooling cycles, and forty cycles of agitation created by a machine under the conveyor belt). The three cycles are programmed into the computer that drives the machine and vary for each sculpture. The computer, with the program for the piece being made at any given time, is mounted on the wall and visible for all to see. Beyond the computer's control are the polyethylene's interaction with gravity, surface tension, and atmospheric conditions. The overlapping layers that configure each Scumak relate to the interaction of malleable material, gravity, and the artist's bodily movements (tearing, throwing, pouring, etc.) that frequently configured the sculptures of so-called Process artists in the late 1960s. They most closely resemble the poured polyurethane pieces created by Lynda Benglis in the early 1970s.

A handmade machine creating machine-made art. Possibly, Paine's obsessive manufacturing makes mordant commentary on our rabid consumerism, which can transform art into an object that is a barometer of material achievement. Or a Duchamp-oriented irony. Precursors exist, like the rattletrap drawing machines Jean Tinguely created in the 1950s, but nothing as surgically precise and elegantly self-sufficient as Paine's contrivance is known to me. And I was hardly alone in being mesmerized by the seemingly mysterious making of the machine as, again and again, I returned to ogle the end of the funnel and watch the lavalike liquid drool out and slowly lather into another layer of lush physicality. In the course of the installation of this exhibition, three totally different, unique, and visually dynamic works were sent out on the conveyor belt, each one challenging me to deny it as art. When I happily took up Paine's offer to create the program for a future (number 278) piece, I realized I had no idea what form it would take, since I did not sufficiently comprehend the effects of the three programmable variables on the polyethylene. However, Paine's cumulative experience with the polyethylene dispenser's proclivities under the computer's direction, which he programmed, was likely to give him considerable control over the outcome.

Press a weight through life, and I will watch this crush you (2007) were the words handed to me by Jon Pylypchuk when I asked him for the title of his work—a work as visually out of control as Paine's is resolutely precise. Might the title be suggesting that the vagrant mutants publicly urinating, swilling beer, and wallowing in their unproductivity refused to let the choice or causes of their dereliction crush them? How positively could I relate to their belligerent nonconformity—Pylypchuk's conflation of Disney and late Goya?

Pylypchuk's subjects might find themselves vividly entangled in sculptural, painterly, or drawn form. In Detroit they have taken sculptural form, their exacerbated state a teddy bear's nightmare. They come in various sizes and states of dissolution, cobbled together from stuffed socks and bits of old clothing; their mismatched legs made from scraps of wood, their agog eyes from segments of ping-pong balls. They manage to be outrageously funny, bursting with pathos, and endearing all at the same time. Their toy-size and rag-doll fabrication, in spite of their behavior, almost immediately plug into the willingness, still lingering from childhood, to invest dolls and teddy bears with a love that will not be spurned. While their condition is hardly enviable, something about their apparent defiance appeals. My mind wanders from their insubordination to the stuffed dummy of the outlaw artist hanging from the roof of the museum's building.

Pylypchuk's figures were created in his Los Angeles studio. The shacks and tenements they loiter in and around, as well as the miniature cans of Budweiser strewn about, were meticulously constructed from materials scavenged amongst Detroit's various ruins. For several days Pylypchuk and his assistant constructed a rural slum to suit its soon-to-be-inhabitants, and then moved those inhabitants about until they and their neighborhood completely belonged to each other and to the environment they became a part of.

Two other artists who scavenge join this exhibition. Mark Bradford creates very large collage paintings often made up of scraps of maps, posters, and a variety of other paper products. In *Double Stretch* (2003), he employed the yellow-netted fabric many a basketball player's jersey is made from and spread rectangles of white paper across this ground. Bradford comes from a family of hairdressers, and he himself started out as one; the paper rectangles are commonly used in black beauty parlors, in the course of giving a permanent. By my serendipitous choice, one of the short videos Bradford creates adjoins this piece and features the very tall Bradford as a basketball player wearing a yellow-netted fabric shirt—which he was quick to point out to me was made of the same fabric as the collage. It tops an outrageously large-hooped skirt, as he awkwardly bounds around and shoots baskets. Bradford at once mocked the cliché of the male African American's athletic prowess and that of homosexuals as effeminate.

In a still larger piece created in 2006, the shreds of a map with Spanish street names and various posters, including those advertising sneakers, have been dispersed in a vast, shimmering collage of urban detritus. Several sneakers and a flip-flop rise in low relief. Bradford has vastly expanded the collage technique so much a part of the rise of white-male-dominated modernism in the previous century and turned it into an African American metaphor with humor and formal panache.

Out of refuse, Nari Ward invents narratives more elaborate than those embedded in Bradford's rich collages. When I first accompanied him to see the Museum of Contemporary Art Detroit (MOCAD) space, he kept staring at the floor where leak-soaked acoustic tiles had fallen from the ceiling and crumbled. The soft beige accumulation reminded him of looking down at sand through shallow water at a beach. He spoke of creating an oasis with a boat. Homeward-bound on the plane, I couldn't resist sneaking looks at the rudimentary sketches of boats he made in his notebook. But the narrative took a different turn after he flew out to Detroit again and sought out a seldom-noticed public sculpture by Jack Ward (no relation) commemorating the start of the black rebellion in 1967. Nari Ward had the sculpture re-created out of whole acoustical tiles from the ceiling; added to it are long, arcing metal rods with broken tiles meant to resemble a fountain. Surrounding it are ten low tables and forty still lower wooden "cushions" all topped with acoustical tile. Pitchers of green tea and styrofoam cups sit on the table, encouraging viewers to sit, sip, and talk. *White Flight Tea Bar* is the title of the piece.

The sculpture Ward had copied is hard to place in the context of racial upheaval; its generic late-modernist look seems more suitable to a corporate lobby. Indeed, the breakdown of modernism's promise was well underway when the park sculpture was commissioned; Ward's turning his replica into a decorative fountain acknowledges this collapse. As his piece was worked on during the exhibition's installation, I felt ambivalence toward its tacky look; however, when it was completed it more than claimed its space and place—at once a provocation and an invitation. In the *White Flight Tea Bar*, as visitors come and go, I wonder what the talk will be. I do know my aesthetic squirming gave me pause—and that was likely to be one of Ward's goals.

Ward has never pursued a signature style or set of forms, but has sought instead to draw a narrative out of, and expressive of, his largely found materials. *Airplane Tears* (2005) is made from countless backs of television sets mounted in uneven rows on the wall, most of them with white tissues attached—a kind of black wailing wall. The tissues might have caught the tears induced by a soap, *Oprah, The Biggest Loser, CSI: Miami,* or any number of programs and/or advertisements that manipulate the viewer, hopefully loosening him or her up to buy a product. The televisions' loss of face, like that of a delinquent child banned to the corner of a room, is Ward's chastisement of the manipulative media that we have invited to invade our homes. This looming, lugubrious piece commanding so much space had been exhibited to good effect in a previous exhibition; Ward confided that it was a kind of insurance, in the event the tea bar failed and had to be withdrawn.

Paul Pfeiffer, more regularly than Ward, has addressed the overwhelming power of the media in our lives. The celebrity worship that seems to replace or replicate religion in our voyeuristic culture has led him to, among much else, conflate football chants with William Blake's visionary poetry. In *Live From Neverland* (2006), we see Michael Jackson's face on a television monitor as he appeared for a live press conference to claim his innocence of the accusations of pedophilia swirling around him. On the wall behind the monitor, Pfeiffer has projected an image of a young, white-robed choir on a set of stairs. Jackson has been digitally robbed of his voice, while the choir chants his words in sync with his lips. The choir sacralizes the space. The wall upon which the choir is projected cuts across a corner and isolates the viewer in the artificial intimacy so often radiated by the famous—or that of a church confessional. In the corner I'm left to wonder whose words were those once emanating from Jackson's lips. Is fame the lipsyncer? Then I remember the night, now long ago, when Jackson's magic streamed from another television monitor, as he danced his joyous innocence into my partner's loft and spread a trance more than sang: Billie Jean. Neither Pfeiffer nor Jackson can take that memory away. Pfeiffer has not judged Jackson, but rather held up a mirror to voyeurism—mine and yours—and fame. Neverland is the kingdom of fame. Brilliantly, Pfeiffer places us in a space we can know but never fully experience. He is acutely aware of how neutral space is transformed into subjective space. He cornered me.

Kara Walker grew up in Georgia, where she came to feel a strong sense of black history, and that history has fueled her work in a most unexpected manner. With grace, masterful drawing ability, and rapier wit, she has transformed the antebellum South into a rollicking sideshow, grotesquely politically incorrect in its skewering of issues of race, gender, and identity. She turned to the early, homespun craft of cutting out silhouettes to embody her narratives, and more recently has created two animations. The second of these, *8 Possible Beginnings or: The Creation of Africa-America Parts 1–8, a Moving Picture by Kara E. Walker* (2005), drew me in with its transparency of process. Constantly insisting on the artificiality of creation, it moves back and forth between simulations of a silent movie, animation, the making of that animation, written titles, and spoken narration. Like a good magician who reveals the secret of her illusion only to make it more forceful, Walker never loses sight of her goal. In the beauty and clarity of her procedures, I find myself drawn into her equal-opportunity satirization, in which everything is mocked, including our voyeuristic fascination with racism. There are those who find the silliness of the slaves' behavior and the wildly improbable, gender-bending, miscegenated sex act depicted in this work demeaning; some have questioned the value of harping on the era of enslavement. For me, Walker's Blackness becomes a metaphorical blackness not unrelated to the intense grotesquerie found in Goya's late paintings, so often referred to as his Black paintings. In Walker's mirror, I see and review the blackness inside me.

A beauty more immediately ingratiating than Walker's, but one immensely full, radiates from Tabaimo's animation *hanabi-ra* (2002). The alteration—or even the obliteration—of the human body has been a recurrent theme in her work. In this animation, Tabaimo draws from Japanese culture's visual repertoire. A headless figure of chunky, doll-like proportion and indeterminate gender stands with her back to us; upon this back Tabaimo has exquisitely tattooed a still life of chrysanthemums, leaves, and a koi—all related to the linear clarity and grace of many a nineteenth-century woodblock print. Two blackbirds fly by, then the koi slithers away, the leaves begin to fall at the figure's feet, and then the chrysanthemum blooms; the blackbirds fly by once more. When the back is completely bare, the limbs drop off into the pile of leaves and flowers. Taking place in a totally darkened and silent room, this slow-motion animation becomes an exquisite panoply of expiration. However, alternately or even concurrently Tabaimo might have intended this as a deconstruction of her own culture's past. (Again and again we learn that strong art cannot breathe without ambiguity in its air.)

I have often been drawn to the kind of highly refined grace so apparent in Tabaimo's animation, only to find it empty when I recall it to my memory. However, countless times I have watched this piece unfold like an ode to mortality that can never fully be told—deeply mysterious and, in the end, almost brutally blunt.

While Tabaimo rightly insists upon bestilled isolation for *hanabi-ra*, the remaining work in the exhibition seems to thrive in the roughness of MOCAD's space—looking more open and receptive than it might in the tightly tailored whiteness of a standard museum space. More light and street should enter our museums. In the beginning I was nervous about the possibility that no one would want to show in such a space; but almost immediately Barry McGee emailed back that he couldn't resist the "banality" of the façade. Nari Ward and Paul Pfeiffer quickly joined after flying to Detroit with me and touring the city with the relentless and inventive local artist/scavenger Scott Hocking—and so, too, Jon Pylypchuk. Jon would say to anyone who'd listen, during installation week, "Detroit, it's the new Berlin." Indeed, as devastated as much of the city of Detroit still is, there is a palpable energy in the air—and potential, in spite of continued economic decline. Much new domestic construction will hopefully lure some of the more intrepid out of the suburbs. "Emergency" might not have come to mind were I curating an exhibition in another city, but the emergencies I had in mind are nonetheless global and not strictly Detroit-centric.

Video still from Tabaimo, *hanabi-ra*, 2002

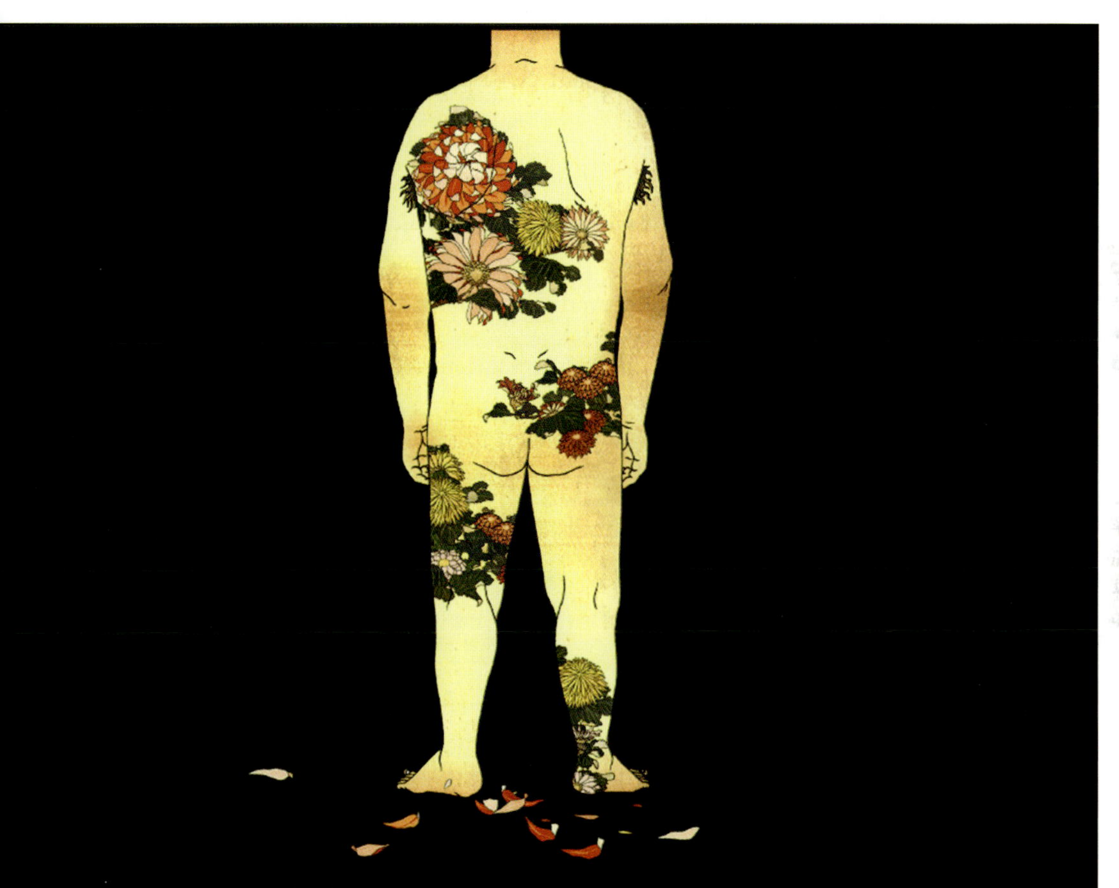

List of Illustrations

JOHN CHAMBERLAIN: SQUEEZE PLAY

John Chamberlain
Stuffed Dog 8, 1970
Urethane foam, cord, and paint
12 ¹⁄₂₄ x 18 ⅛ x 16 ⅛ inches
Photograph by Florian Holzherr
© 2010 John Chamberlain / Artists Rights Society (ARS),
New York
Collection Dia Art Foundation

PETER HUJAR: LENS LOVE

Peter Hujar
Self-Portrait at the Baths, 1979
Vintage gelatin silver print
20 x 16 inches
© 1987 The Peter Hujar Archive LLC
Courtesy Matthew Marks Gallery, New York

Peter Hujar
Duck, Germantown, 1982
Vintage gelatin silver print
20 x 16 inches
© 1987 The Peter Hujar Archive LLC
Courtesy Matthew Marks Gallery, New York

II. SEA CHANGE

Raymond Pettibon
No Title (Well you needn't), 1997
Wall painting (installation view, David Zwirner,
New York, 1997)
© Raymond Pettibon
Courtesy Regen Projects, Los Angeles

OCEANICITY

John Marin
The Written Sea, 1952
Oil on canvas
22 x 28 inches
Photograph by John Bigelow Taylor
© Estate of John Marin / Artists Rights Society (ARS), New York
Courtesy Adelson Galleries, New York

Frank Moore
Birth of Venus, 1993
Oil on linen on panel with gilt antique frame
51 ¼ x 73 ¼ inches
Private Collection
Courtesy Sperone Westwater and The Gesso Foundation, New York

JOHN MARIN: MARIN IN OIL

John Marin
Wave on Rock, 1937
Oil on canvas
22 ¾ x 30 inches
Whitney Museum of American Art, New York
Purchased with funds from Charles Simon and the Painting and
Sculpture Committee
Photograph by Roy Elkind
© Estate of John Marin / Artists Rights Society (ARS), New York

WILLEM DE KOONING: DRAWING NO CONCLUSIONS

Willem de Kooning
Folded Shirt on Laundry Paper, 1958
Ink on paper
17 x 13 ⅞ inches
Private collection
© 2010 The Willem de Kooning Foundation / Artists Rights
Society (ARS), New York

Willem de Kooning
Untitled, 1966
Charcoal on paper
10 x 8 inches
Museum Overholland
© 2010 The Willem de Kooning Foundation / Artists Rights
Society (ARS), New York

ALFONSO OSSORIO: EYEWITNESSES

Alfonso Ossorio
Self-Portrait Balanced Head, 1968
Congregation of mixed media
17 x 13 x 5 inches
Collection of Michael Rosenfeld and
halley k harrisburg, New York
Courtesy of Michael Rosenfeld Gallery, LLC, New York

JOAN MITCHELL: STORMS OF PAINT

Joan Mitchell
Ladybug, 1957
Oil on canvas
6 feet 5 ⅞ inches x 9 feet
© Estate of Joan Mitchell
The Museum of Modern Art / Licensed by Scala / Art Resource,
New York

Joan Mitchell
Sunflowers, 1990–91
Oil on canvas, diptych
9 feet 2 ¼ inches x 13 feet 1 ½ inches
© Estate of Joan Mitchell
Collection of John Cheim

MALCOLM MORLEY: SEEING IS IMAGINING

Malcolm Morley
Windsurfer in Antigua, 1987
Watercolor on paper
20 x 28 ½ inches
Collection of Virginia and Bagley Wright
Courtesy Sperone Westwater, New York

Malcolm Morley
Landscape, 1983
Watercolor on paper
18 ⅞ x 24 inches
The Museum of Modern Art / Licensed by Scala / Art Resource,
New York

Vija Celmins
Untitled (Ocean), 1969
Graphite on acrylic ground on paper
14 x 18 ¾ inches
Philadelphia Museum of Art
Courtesy the artist and McKee Gallery, New York

Vija Celmins
Galaxy (Cassiopeia), 1973
Graphite on acrylic ground on paper
12 x 15 inches
Baltimore Museum of Art
Courtesy the artist and McKee Gallery, New York

III. FABULISM

Carroll Dunham
Two Things (Mound D), 1992
Mixed media on linen
65 x 110 inches
Courtesy Gladstone Gallery, New York

BRUSHES WITH GODS, DEVILS, DEMONS, MONSTERS,
THE MILKY WAY, AND PLANCK'S CONSTANT

Neo Rauch
Schöpfer, 2002
Oil on canvas
82 ⅝ x 98 ½ inches
Courtesy David Zwirner, New York

Neo Rauch
Neid, 1999
Oil on canvas
78 ¾ x 118 ⅜ inches
Courtesy David Zwirner, New York

CARROLL DUNHAM: DRAWN INTO CONSCIOUSNESS

Carroll Dunham
Fourth Birch, 1983
Mixed media on birch
70 ⅛ x 48 inches
Sonnabend Gallery, New York
Courtesy Gladstone Gallery, New York

MATHEW RITCHIE: PAINTING AS INFORMATION JAZZ

Matthew Ritchie
We Will Not Be the Last, 2006
Oil and marker on linen
100 ½ x 136 ½ inches
Image: Ellen Page Wilson
Courtesy Andrea Rosen Gallery, New York

Matthew Ritchie
Installation views of a work created for *The Shapes of Space*,
a group exhibition at the Solomon R. Guggenheim Museum,
New York, 2007
Image: Tom Powel Imaging
Courtesy Andrea Rosen Gallery, New York

CHRIS OFILI: JUST DESSERTS

Chris Ofili
The Holy Virgin Mary, 1996
Acrylic, oil, polyester resin, paper collage, glitter, map pins, and
elephant dung on linen
96 x 72 inches
Courtesy Chris Ofili/Afroco and David Zwirner,
New York
Chris Ofili

Confession (Lady Chancellor), 2007
Oil on linen
110 ⅝ x 76 ⅞ inches
Courtesy Chris Ofili/Afroco and David Zwirner,
New York

IV. MEDITATIONS IN AN EMERGENCY

Mark Bradford
(Untitled) a.k.a. Gwen, 2005–06
Mixed media collage
108 x 144 inches
Collection of The Broad Art Foundation
Courtesy Sikkema Jenkins & Co.

A VELVET GLOVE CAN HOLD A BURNING ISSUE

Roxy Paine
Scumak No. 2 (Auto Sculpture Maker), 2001
Aluminum, computer, conveyor, electronics, extruder, stainless
steel, polyethylene, teflon
90 x 276 x 73 inches
Courtesy James Cohan Gallery, New York

Tabaimo
hanabi-ra, 2002
Single-channel video animation
4:25 minutes
Courtesy James Cohan Gallery, New York

Publication Credits

The essays in this book previously appeared in slightly different form (and in some cases with different titles) in the publications set forth below. The essays are reprinted here with the permission of the author and the original publishers.

"On the Edge: The Paintings of Ralph Humphrey," in *Ralph Humphrey* (New York: Mary Boone Gallery, 1990).

"Brice Marden: Drawing," in *Brice Marden: Paintings and Drawings* (New York: Harry N. Abrams, 1992).

"Agnes Martin: Geometry of Joy," in *Elle Decor*, December 1992/January 1993.

"Barry Le Va's Sculpture: Ellipsis and Ellipse," in *Artforum*, January 1983.

"Alan Saret: Engineer of the Ethereal," in *Alan Saret: Matter Into Aether* (Newport Beach, CA: Newport Harbor Art Museum [now Orange County Museum of Art], 1982).

"Keith Sonnier: Illuminations," in *Keith Sonnier* (New York: PaceWildenstein, 2005).

"John Chamberlain: Squeeze Play," in *John Chamberlain: The Foam Sculptures* (Marfa, TX: The Chinati Foundation, 2008).

"Peter Hujar: Lens Love," in *Peter Hujar: Animals and Nudes* (Santa Fe, NM: Twin Palms Publishers, 2002).

"Oceanicity," in *Sea Change* (Southampton, NY: Parrish Art Museum, 1998).

"John Marin: Marin in Oil," in *Marin in Oil* (Southampton, NY: Parrish Art Museum, 1987).

"Willem de Kooning: Drawing No Conclusions," in *Willem de Kooning: Drawing Seeing/Seeing Drawing* (New York: The Drawing Center, 1998).

"Alfonso Ossorio: Eyewitnesses," in *Alfonso Ossorio: Congregations* (Southampton, NY: Parrish Art Museum, 1997).

"Joan Mitchell: Storms of Paint," in *Joan Mitchell* (New York: Harry N. Abrams, 1997).

"Malcolm Morley: Seeing Is Imagining," in *Malcolm Morley: Watercolours* (London: Tate Publishing, 1991).

"Vija Celmins: Seeing Stars," in *Elle Decor*, February/March 1994.

"Brushes with Gods, Devils, Demons, Monsters, the Milky Way, and Planck's Constant," in *Fabulism* (Omaha, NE: Joslyn Art Museum, 2004).

"Carroll Dunham: Drawn into Consciousness," in *Carroll Dunham: Paintings* (Ostfildern, Germany: Hatje Cantz; and New York: New Museum of Contemporary Art, 2002).

"Matthew Ritchie: Painting as Information Jazz," in *Matthew Ritchie: More Than the Eye* (New York: Rizzoli, 2008).

"Chris Ofili: Just Desserts," in *Chris Ofili: Devil's Pie* (Göttingen, Germany: Steidl; and New York: David Zwirner Gallery, 2008).

"A Velvet Glove Can Hold a Burning Issue," in *Meditations in an Emergency* (Detroit: Museum of Contemporary Art Detroit, 2007).

KLAUS KERTESS graduated from Phillips Academy, Andover, in 1958. He earned a B.A. in History of Art in 1962 and an M.A. in History of Art in 1964 from Yale University. He has lived in New York since 1964 and founded (together with J. F. Byers III) the Bykert Gallery in 1966. Under Kertess's direction, the Bykert Gallery represented Chuck Close, Ralph Humphrey, Barry Le Va, Brice Marden, David Novros, Dorothea Rockburne, Alan Saret, Paul Sharits, Michael Snow, and Joe Zucker, among other artists. Kertess left the gallery in 1975 to pursue interests in writing and curating.

Since 1975, Kertess has published his writings in numerous art and other magazines, including *Artforum*, *Art in America*, *Arts*, *Parkett*, *House & Garden*, *Vogue*, and *Out*. He has written museum catalogue essays on Jean-Michel Basquiat, John Chamberlain, Willem de Kooning, Carroll Dunham, Roni Horn, Robert Irwin, Barry Le Va, Morris Louis, Brice Marden, and Terry Winters. He has published monographs on Brice Marden (1992), Joan Mitchell (1997), Peter Hujar (2002), and Jane Freilicher (2004).

Kertess served as Robert Lehman Curator at the Parrish Art Museum in Southampton, New York, from 1983 to 1989. In 1989, he was appointed adjunct curator of drawing at the Whitney Museum of American Art. He began working fulltime at the Whitney in 1993 as curator of the 1995 Whitney Biennial. Since 1996, Kertess has curated many exhibitions independently, including *Willem de Kooning: Drawing Seeing/Seeing Drawing* (1998) for the Drawing Center in New York and *Willem de Kooning: In Process* (2000), which opened at the Menil Collection in Houston and traveled to the Museum of Art Fort Lauderdale and the Corcoran Gallery of Art in Washington, D.C. In 2002, he curated *John O'Reilly: Assemblies of Magic* for the Addison Gallery of American Art in Andover, Massachusetts. In 2004, he organized *Fabulism* (a group exhibition including Carroll Dunham, Ellen Gallagher, Chris Ofili, Neo Rauch, and Matthew Ritchie) for the Joslyn Art Museum in Omaha, Nebraska. In 2007, he curated *Meditations in an Emergency* (a group exhibtion including Mark Bradford, Christopher Fachini, Barry McGee, Roxy Paine, Paul Pfeiffer, Jonathan Pylypchuk, Tabaimo, Kara Walker, and Nari Ward) for the inaugural exhibition at the Museum of Contemporary Art Detroit.

Kertess received the Lawrence A. Fleischman Award for Scholarly Excellence in the Field of American Art History from the Smithsonian's Archives for American Art in 2009.

Kertess lives in New York City.